3rd edition

A Practical Guide to Working with Babies

Angela
Dare

Margaret
O'Donovan

Published in 2003 by:
Nelson Thornes Ltd
Delta Place
27 Bath Road
CHELTENHAM
GL53 7TH
United Kingdom

03 04 05 06 07 / 10 9 8 7 6 5 4 3 2 1

A catalogue record for this book is available from the British Library

ISBN 0 7487 7349 5

Page make-up by Northern Phototypesetting

Printed and bound in Spain by GraphyCems

CONTENTS

ACKNOWLEDGEMENTS

We would like to thank our colleagues in the Child and Social Care programme area of the City and Islington College for their support, help and encouragement in the development of this book.

We would also like to give special thanks to all the babies whose photographs we have used.

Angela Dare
Margaret O'Donovan

The authors and publishers would also like to thank:

- Bubbles/Loisjoy Thurston for the cover photograph

- The Child Growth Foundation for permission to reproduce the UK growth standards (percentile charts) on pages 151 and 152

- National Standards (DfES) © Crown copyright for permission to use the table on page 210

- NSPCC for permission to reproduce the illustration 'Handle with Care' on page 232

INTRODUCTION

This is a fully revised and updated text, written primarily for students studying Level 2 and Level 3 child-care courses. It covers pregnancy and birth, and offers readers a detailed and practical guide to the needs, care and development of the baby from birth to one year. The book would be valuable in all Early Years settings, serving as an aide memoire for both new and experienced staff.

The theory and practice of child care, threaded throughout the text, is designed to enable students and practitioners to offer babies a high standard of care in a variety of settings. To gain the most from this *Practical Guide*, you will need to cross-reference within the text – relevant chapters and page numbers are indicated throughout. This is particularly applicable for Chapter 9, where principles and practices of care in day care settings are reinforced throughout the whole book.

Within each chapter there are a number of Activities. The aim of the Activities, although practically based, is to help you to link the theory of child care to your practice. Each Activity should always be followed by a written account or summary of your findings.

At the end of each chapter there are Quick Checks, they aim to ensure that you have understood the main points in each chapter.

Throughout the book the baby is referred to as 'she'. We have, of necessity, identified the baby's parents, often the mother, as the prime carer. However, we should stress that consistent, loving care in a stable environment can be provided by other carers, irrespective of sexual orientation or gender.

ABOUT THE AUTHORS

Both authors come from backgrounds of Health Visiting, Midwifery and Teaching. They worked together for many years teaching students on child-care courses at City and Islington College, London, and were examiners for the NNEB/CACHE. Angela Dare was an external moderator for CACHE. Margaret O'Donovan also taught for several years at The Chiltern College, Caversham.

Their previous books, all for Nelson Thornes, include:
Good Practice in Child Safety, 2000
A Practical Guide to Child Nutrition (2nd edition), 2002
Good Practice in Caring for Young Children with Special Needs (2nd edition), 2002.

1 THE FAMILY, PREGNANCY AND BIRTH

> **This chapter covers:**
> - **The family**
> - **Preconceptual care**
> - **Conception and pregnancy**
> - **Antenatal care**
> - **Labour and birth**
> - **The postnatal period**
> - **Useful terms**

The family

Throughout the world there is great diversity and variation in family life and this is increasingly so in the UK. The 'nuclear family' (mother and father, married to each other, plus the children of the marriage), previously seen in the UK as the ideal family unit, is now in decline.

Children today are born into a social environment significantly changed over the last few decades and 'the family' has evolved to embrace many different sets of relationships and alternative family groups, some of which are identified in Table 1.1 on page 2. In particular, parenting situations have had to adapt to meet the needs of children born to single mothers.

KEY POINTS

- A family unit in which same sex men are bringing up children is less common than a same-sex women family unit.

- Government legislation to allow unmarried couples and same-sex couples to adopt children is currently being considered.

Whatever the family grouping or structure, children born into that family, or brought into it through various circumstances, have a right to be cared for in a secure and stable environment, where they are offered unconditional love and care, which meets their physical, learning and emotional needs. They need to feel wanted and valued.

Table 1.1 Family groups

Type of family	Description	Comments
Nuclear family (in decline)	Mother, father (married to each other) and the children born of the marriage	Traditionally seen in the UK as the ideal family unit. Mother's role: Primarily that of homemaker, nurturing and caring for the children Father's role: Breadwinner. Protecting and financially providing for his family
Extended family	Parents, children, grandparents and other close relatives living together or close by. Family members are in close contact with each other	■ Provides opportunities for children to experience a wide variety of caring relationships ■ Families settled in the UK from different cultures for example, those of Asian, Mediterranean, African and Caribbean backgrounds also maintain the tradition of close-knit extended families
One-parent (or lone) families	One parent with dependent child. Most one-parent families are headed by a woman	One-parent families exist because of ■ separation ■ divorce ■ death of spouse/partner ■ personal choice Children often have a close relationship with the absent parent
Re-constituted families	Adults and children who have previously been part of a different family. Step-parents and stepchildren. Children born within the newpartnership are half-siblings to the stepchildren	■ Increasingly common due to divorce and re-marriage ■ Can be a positive experience for children because they see their parents are happier OR ■ The children may have difficulty relating to a step-parent, stepbrothers and sisters and half-siblings

Adoptive families	Adoption provides children with a new family when living with their own families is not possible	■ The Adoption and Children Act 2002 is the first major adoption legislation for over 25 years and will shape all future adoption issues and procedures ■ Only a court can make an adoption order ■ An adoption order severs all ties with the birth family and gives all parental rights and responsibilities to the new adoptive family ■ The local authority or an approved voluntary adoption agency assess and approve people to become an adoptive parent
Foster families	Provision of a temporary home for children who are looked after by the local authority, for a short or longer period of time, because they are unable to live with their own families	■ Foster care is generally accepted to be the most appropriate form of care for children unable to live with their own families ■ Foster parents may choose to care for babies and young children with special needs ■ The local authority makes a payment to foster parents for every child they care for
Same-sex partners	A small number of same-sex women are bringing up children within a family unit	The children may be brought into the family from previous heterosexual relationships or may have been born through artificial insemination by donor (AID)

A nuclear family: father, mother and their children

Families across all social groups currently face pressures such as divorce, alcohol and drug abuse, poverty, unemployment and debt – all of which can affect family stability and the well-being of the children. As child-care workers it is probable you will care for babies from a wide range of family environments, including those experiencing some of these pressures.

Preconceptual care

Healthy parents tend to have healthy babies. The first 12 weeks of a pregnancy are very important. During that time rapid development takes place as the baby's organs (heart, liver, lungs, kidneys and brain) and body systems are forming. Many babies are conceived with no thought or planning and a woman may be unaware she is pregnant in these early weeks. Any necessary adjustment to her lifestyle will not have been made. Even if a woman suspects or knows she is pregnant, she may delay seeing her family doctor or attending an antenatal clinic until 12 weeks or later. By this time the developing baby may have been exposed to, perhaps harmed by, infections, drugs, tobacco or alcohol. Preconceptual care reduces these risks.

WHAT IS PRECONCEPTUAL CARE?

Preconceptual care is medical care and positive health advice offered to a couple before they start a pregnancy, and should begin with the decision to have a baby. It aims to prepare both partners for a healthy pregnancy and ensure they are in the best possible state of health at the time of conception. Preconceptual care also includes self-help by continuing to follow, or changing to, a healthy lifestyle.

Family doctors, midwives and health visitors can offer specific care and advice. Family planning clinics, well woman clinics and hospital pre-pregnancy clinics as well as voluntary organisations, such as Foresight, also provide preconceptual care. Care is free within the National Health Service (NHS). Other agencies may charge a fee.

TEN STEPS TOWARDS A HEALTHY PREGNANCY

Most babies are born healthy. However, planning and preparing for a pregnancy through these ten steps (see diagram below) reduces many of

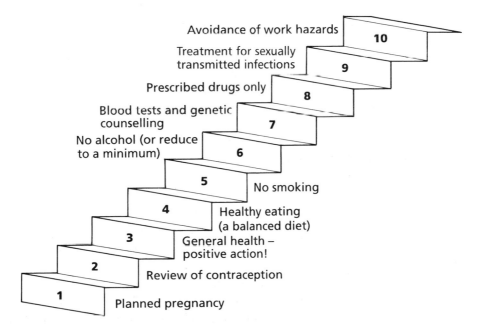

Ten steps towards a healthy pregnancy

the risks to the unborn child and makes the womb a healthy environment in which a baby can safely grow. The whole experience of pregnancy, childbirth and looking after a baby can be a time of uncertainty and upheaval, and it is important for couples to be open to accepting help and assistance from the professionals, as well as seeking to help themselves.

Step 1: A planned pregnancy
Allowing three to six months to plan and prepare for a pregnancy gives a couple time to improve their health, assess their 'readiness to start a pregnancy', and consider the changes that having a baby will bring to their relationship and lifestyle.

Ideally, both partners should want to have a baby and be sufficiently mature to care for a child. While children bring enormous pleasure and satisfaction to their parents and wider family, parenting is a demanding and full-time job that brings many responsibilities. Babies grow rapidly – often into demanding toddlers and, possibly, difficult teenagers – and young people, still perhaps teenagers themselves, may lack the maturity and self-confidence to cope with the demands of parenthood and the changes it inevitably brings to their lives.

Parents, today, tend to be more informed about pregnancy and childbirth and both partners often wish to be involved in all decisions relating to the care of the mother and baby. However, pregnancy and childbirth remain unique female experiences and partners may feel alienated at this time, especially as the mother becomes increasingly involved in the baby. Adjusting to a new life together as a family may take time, but a stable relationship will help to overcome any temporary problems. A baby may not cement an uncertain relationship.

KEY POINT

When babies are born to young, lone parents, those parents particularly need the support of the extended family (see Teenage mothers, page 13).

REMEMBER!

There are many different, equally valid, family units across the whole cultural spectrum.

Step 2: Review of contraception
The contraceptive pill should be discontinued at least three months, and preferably six, before trying for a baby. This allows the natural menstrual

cycle to return to normal. Barrier methods of contraception (such as use of a condom or diaphragm) or the natural method (use of the infertile periods during the menstrual cycle) can be used during this time to prevent a pregnancy. If a woman has an intra-uterine contraceptive device fitted, her doctor or family planning clinic adviser will remove it.

Step 3: General health

Moderate daily exercise, fresh air, rest and sleep will promote a feeling of well-being for both partners. A medical check-up, including blood pressure and weight measurement, is important for a woman. She may gain as much as 12.5 kg (28 lb) or more during pregnancy. Starting her pregnancy as near to ideal weight as possible will reduce the risk of high blood pressure, heart strain, backache and varicose veins. Dental care is essential. A growing baby takes calcium from its mother for bone and tooth growth. Having healthy teeth at the beginning of pregnancy reduces the risk of dental problems for the mother later on. Women with long-term illnesses should discuss the advisability of a pregnancy with their family doctor. It is sensible to have a cervical smear test preconceptually as abnormal cells present before conception can increase during a pregnancy.

KEY POINT

A raised blood pressure in pregnancy may cause problems for a mother and her baby.

Step 4: A balanced diet

A balanced diet is one that contains a wide variety of the essential nutrients (proteins, fats, carbohydrates, vitamins, minerals, fibre and water). It is an important link with good health for everyone. The proportions of nutrients required varies according to age, sex, occupation and state of health (for example, pregnancy). Food intake must balance the amount of energy (calories) taken in against the energy used up by the body. Excess calories are stored in the body as fat. An 'unbalanced' diet can lead to overweight or underweight.

KEY POINT

A balanced diet, preconceptually, allows a woman to store vital nutrients in her body in readiness for her planned baby.

Dieting to lose weight is inadvisable as important nutrients may be missed out. Dietary and exercise advice can be offered to a woman who is overweight. Especially important is folic acid (folate), a B-group vitamin needed to make foetal cells, and for development of the brain and spinal cord. These last two structures form early in foetal life. Inadequate intake of folic acid may be linked to the congenital neural tube conditions spina bifida (a defect of the spinal column with varying degrees of damage to the spinal cord) and anencephaly (a malformation of the skull and brain). Women should be advised of the foods rich in folic acid and take a folic acid supplement daily, both preconceptually and during the first 12 weeks of pregnancy.

KEY POINT

A woman who has previously given birth to a baby with a neural tube condition will be advised by her doctor to take folic acid supplements daily, for the same length of time as above, as a preventive measure.

The 'food groups' diagram on page 9 identifies the five groups described in most nutrition texts.

The basic principles of healthy eating are as follows.

1   Eat daily from the following **four** main food groups (and see the diagram on page 9).
    - *Group one* Starchy carbohydrates – breads, cereals, rice, pasta, potatoes.
    - *Group two* Fruit and vegetables.
    - *Group three* Milk and dairy foods – milk, butter, cream, yoghurt, fromage frais.
    - *Group four* Meat, poultry, eggs, fish and vegetarian alternatives, such as pulses, quorn, tofu and textured vegetable protein (TVP).
2   Cut down on the fatty, sugary and salty foods in group **five**, especially sugar and sugary drinks; biscuits, sweets and chocolate; ice cream and powdered desserts; and crisps, bought pies and chips. Too much saturated (animal) fat may be linked to heart disease. Polyunsaturates (vegetable and plant sources) are a healthier option. Sugar encourages obesity and dental disease and intake should be reduced to a minimum. A high salt intake is linked to raised blood pressure and should be avoided if possible – herbs and spices are tasty and interesting alternative flavourings.
3   Eat fresh food whenever possible.

Vegetarian and vegan diets
Vegetarian diets that include protein foods such as fish, eggs, cheese and milk provide all the essential amino acids – the important small units from which proteins are made – necessary for good health and growth. These, together with carbohydrate foods and a wide selection of fruit and vegetables (excellent sources of vitamins, minerals and fibre), will ensure a balanced, nutritious diet both preconceptually and antenatally.

The five food groups

Vegetarian diets that exclude some of the above protein foods, and vegan diets, which exclude all animal products, can also be adequate, but a rich variety of cereals, pulses, nuts and seeds in the diet is essential to ensure all the amino acids are available. Soya milk, and other soya products, are good sources of vegetable protein and vitamin B12 (necessary for growth and a healthy nervous system), and should form part of the daily nutritional intake. Again, fruit and vegetables are also important.

Dietary advice is always available from the family doctor, midwife, health visitor or dietician.

Step 5: Smoking

Smoking can affect the working of the placenta (afterbirth) causing miscarriage, pre-term birth, low birth weight and perinatal death (stillbirth or death in the first week of life, see pages 36 and 37). Men who smoke may have a low sperm count, which may affect their fertility.

KEY POINT

Both partners should give up smoking for the sake of their own and their baby's health. Babies continually exposed to tobacco smoke after birth are at greater risk of Sudden Infant Death Syndrome (SIDS) (see chapter 7, Table 7.3 on page 184) and are more likely to suffer from respiratory problems such as asthma in infancy and childhood.

Step 6: Alcohol

Moderate drinking (one or two drinks per day) puts a baby at risk of miscarriage and low birth weight. 'Binge' drinking and consistently high levels of alcohol consumption, especially in the early weeks, can cause foetal alcohol syndrome (facial, heart and kidney abnormalities, also learning delay). Heavy drinking may cause male infertility.

Step 7: Blood tests and genetic counselling

Blood tests

A simple blood test will indicate whether either partner is anaemic. Dietary advice and prescribed iron tablets should correct anaemia. Blood is tested to check the woman's immunity to the rubella virus. If not immune, she will be offered vaccination and advised against becoming pregnant for at least three months.

KEY POINT

While the rubella virus may produce only a fleeting rash and a mild feeling of being unwell in an expectant mother, it can seriously affect her unborn baby, causing vision, hearing, heart and kidney damage, as well as learning delay.

Human immunodeficiency virus (HIV)

A woman who thinks she may be infected with HIV may wish to seek professional counselling about being tested for the condition. HIV can be passed to the baby during pregnancy and birth, and through breast milk. Testing and treating HIV positive women with anti-viral drugs preconceptually or during pregnancy reduces the risk of transmission of the virus to the baby. Currently there is no national routine HIV screening programme. Selective screening does take place in high-risk areas, particularly in London, where the majority of HIV positive births in the UK occur. All babies born to mothers who are HIV positive will have HIV antibodies in their blood. These *maternal* antibodies remain in the child's blood for up to 12 to 15 months. However, this does not necessarily mean that the baby is infected. A diagnosis can usually be made by the time a baby is three to four months old, using a special test to detect the presence of the actual virus in the baby's blood.

Genetic counselling

Genetic counselling (usually a hospital-based service) advises on the risk of passing on hereditary disorders, such as cystic fibrosis, haemophilia and sickle cell condition, to a future baby. This service is of particular help to a couple who already have a child with a genetic condition.

Step 8: Drugs and medicines

Only prescribed medication should be taken preconceptually. Women taking prescribed drugs to control conditions such as epilepsy and diabetes must, of course, continue with their medication preconceptually and during pregnancy. Many drugs, including illegal and addictive ones, can pass across the placenta, causing damage to the unborn baby. Babies born to drug addicts suffer from withdrawal symptoms at birth and can be seriously ill, requiring particular medical and nursing care.

Step 9: Sexually transmitted infections

Sexually transmitted infections (STIs), such as chlamydia, syphilis, gonorrhoea and genital herpes, may adversely affect the unborn baby, causing miscarriage, stillbirth or birth abnormalities. If either partner thinks they have been at risk of contracting such an infection, or know they have one, they should seek advice from their doctor or hospital 'special clinic'. Both partners should be seen.

Step 10: Work hazards

Miscarriages and birth defects may result from working with radiation and some chemicals and gases. Either partner worried about their work environment should seek advice from the family doctor, their environmental health officer, or works personnel or safety officer. Unless urgent, X-rays are usually avoided during the first 12 weeks of pregnancy.

Conception and pregnancy

CONCEPTION

Conception occurs when the female egg is fertilised by the male sperm. It takes place in a fallopian (uterine) tube. From the moment of fertilisation all inherited characteristics such as gender, hair and eye colouring are determined. The fertilised egg splits into two then four, eight and so on as it travels towards the uterus (womb) – a journey of about five days. By now it is a ball of cells called a blastocyst that becomes firmly embedded in the wall of the uterus. Then follows the complex process of development and growth. In medical terms an unborn baby is described as an 'embryo' in the first eight weeks of life and a 'foetus' from then until birth.

PREGNANCY

The normal length of a pregnancy is 280 days or 40 weeks. The expected date of delivery is usually calculated by counting forward nine months and seven days from the first day of the last normal menstrual period. If there is uncertainty about dates, ultrasound scanning can accurately determine the unborn baby's age. Pregnancy is not an illness, but it makes demands on a woman's body that need sensitive understanding by the professionals looking after her. In particular, women who have had no preconceptual care need to be seen as early as possible to alert them to the dangers of poor diet, smoking, drinking, taking medication and illegal drugs, and infections.

Expectant mothers are now faced with many different circumstances and challenges. Not all of them have partners – the number of one-parent families is rising. There are many more older mothers who, perhaps for career reasons, have delayed having a baby until well into their thirties or early forties, when the risk of having a baby with Down's syndrome is increased. Other women who have difficulty in conceiving may go through the emotionally draining procedure of infertility treatment and in vitro fertilisation (IVF). Some mothers with same-sex partners have conceived through artificial insemination by donor (AID). Over the last decade, many babies have been born as a result of treatment using donated sperm, eggs or embryos.

Teenage mothers
Currently, the UK has the highest rate of teenage pregnancies in Europe with 56,000 babies born to teenage mothers every year. While many pregnant teenagers live at home and are supported by their family, caring for a baby brings enormous responsibility, which may be difficult for someone, still only a child herself, to handle. Teenagers need a great deal of support from professionals, such as the family doctor and health visitor, particularly if they receive little or no help from their own family. It is important for them to understand their baby's needs and to develop the confidence and ability to meet those needs. Young girls who are pregnant need medical care and support from the earliest weeks of their pregnancy. If a girl is unaware she is pregnant, or wishes to keep her pregnancy private, her attendance at antenatal clinic may be infrequent or not at all and the opportunity for important antenatal care is lost.

Education and employment prospects may be seriously affected. Teenage mothers feel particularly trapped if they lack family support and have no access to flexible and affordable child care. A Government and European Social Fund project, piloted by the National Childminding Association (NCMA), is currently in place to provide high quality childcare facilities for teenage parents. It offers free child care to parents aged 19 or under, provided they are in education, training or employment, and gives them the opportunity and encouragement to achieve.

Activity
1 In a group, think about and discuss the different situations described above.
2 How different might the experiences of motherhood be for:
   (a) a 19 year-old single mother with a young baby;
   (b) a 41-year-old career-minded single mother with a young baby.
3 Research in vitro fertilisation. What do you consider to be the 'pros' and 'cons' of this procedure?
4 Why do you think it is beneficial for babies born from donor sperm, eggs and embryos to one day know the identity of the donor?

A father's role

The idea that pregnancy, childbirth and child rearing are solely 'women's business' has gone. Increasingly, research tells us that fathers are playing a greater role in the whole process of pregnancy, birth and child care. They take a keen interest in their partner's pregnancy and many are with them during ultrasound scan tests, parentcraft and relaxation classes and labour and birth. Often the father cuts the baby's umbilical cord. A father's feelings of pride and elation at the birth of his baby are similar to those of the mother's. After the birth, fathers are generally as sensitive and communicative as mothers with their infants, responding to their cues and behaviour. Such positive involvement helps the early father–baby bonding process. Many fathers are involved in care-giving routines such as feeding, bathing and settling to sleep; they push the buggy or pram and take their baby to and from the child-care setting. Some take on the role of prime child carer with the mother the main income earner.

KEY POINT

In April 2003, under the Employment Act 2002, biological fathers, and husbands/partners (of birth mothers) responsible for the child's upbringing, became entitled to two weeks' statutory paid paternity leave. Certain conditions of entitlement apply. The leave may be taken as a single period of either one full week or two full weeks. The pay is called 'paternity pay (birth)' to distinguish it from the pay available to adoptive fathers.

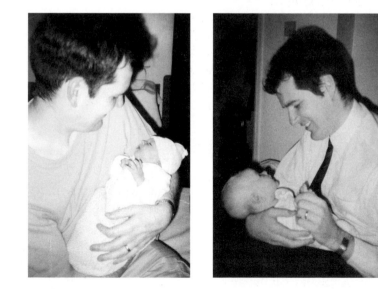

Early father–baby bonding

FOETAL GROWTH AND DEVELOPMENT

The placenta

The placenta (afterbirth) is a spongy, red, disc-like structure attached to the wall of the uterus during pregnancy. It is a complex organ able to select from the mother's blood all the substances needed by her developing baby. It provides oxygen and food for the foetus, produces special hormones to keep the pregnancy healthy and transfers antibodies from the mother to the foetus, giving the baby a certain immunity to infection during the first few months of life.

The placenta is rich with both maternal and foetal blood vessels. These vessels lie very close to each other but the actual bloods do not mix.

KEY POINT

The exchange of substances from mother to foetus and of waste products from foetus back to mother takes place through the thin walls of the blood vessels. This exchange facility of the placenta acts as a barrier to certain micro-organisms (germs), but some are able to cross this barrier and harm the foetus.

The umbilical cord

The umbilical cord is called the 'baby's lifeline'. It links the foetus to the placenta and grows to about 50 cm (20 in) in length. It carries the oxygen and food from the placenta to the foetus, and returns waste products and carbon dioxide from the foetus to the mother. The cutting of the cord at birth separates the baby from her mother.

The amniotic sac

The amniotic sac is a bubble-like structure in which the foetus grows and develops. The sac produces amniotic fluid that gives protection from infection and injury and allows the foetus to move freely. Some time before or during labour this membraneous sac ruptures, a process commonly known as 'the waters breaking'.

During foetal life:

■ Oxygen, food and antibodies pass from the mother to the foetus. If the nutritional needs of the foetus are not adequately met its growth and development will be affected.

■ The risk to the foetus from harmful germs and substances crossing the

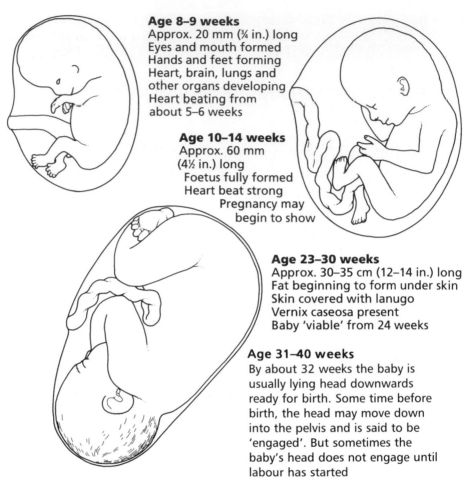

Age 8–9 weeks
Approx. 20 mm (¾ in.) long
Eyes and mouth formed
Hands and feet forming
Heart, brain, lungs and
other organs developing
Heart beating from
about 5–6 weeks

Age 10–14 weeks
Approx. 60 mm
(4½ in.) long
Foetus fully formed
Heart beat strong
Pregnancy may
begin to show

Age 23–30 weeks
Approx. 30–35 cm (12–14 in.) long
Fat beginning to form under skin
Skin covered with lanugo
Vernix caseosa present
Baby 'viable' from 24 weeks

Age 31–40 weeks
By about 32 weeks the baby is
usually lying head downwards
ready for birth. Some time before
birth, the head may move down
into the pelvis and is said to be
'engaged'. But sometimes the
baby's head does not engage until
labour has started

A summary of the stages of foetal growth and development

placental barrier is greatest during the first 12 weeks of pregnancy. Examples include the rubella virus and HIV infection, various drugs, alcohol and nicotine.

■ A large reserve of iron is stored in the foetal liver during the last 12 weeks of pregnancy. Breast milk is low in iron, although it has a relatively high absorption rate. While present day infant formula milks are fortified with iron, the amount of iron available for absorption by the baby may be below her daily needs. The foetal reserve of iron tides the baby over the first four to six months of life when dietary sources, other than milk, will then provide adequate iron intake.

■ Fat is laid down under the skin in the later weeks of pregnancy. This gives the baby a smooth, round appearance at birth and helps to keep her warm.

- Vernix caseosa, a white greasy substance, protects the baby's skin from its watery environment. At birth, vernix is found on the baby's body, especially in the skin folds. It may be more noticeable in pre-term babies.
- Lanugo (fine hair) covers the face and body. Much of it is lost before birth, the remainder being lost during the first month of life.

SIGNS AND SYMPTOMS OF PREGNANCY

- Periods stop (amenhorroea).
- Nausea and sickness, usually in the mornings (but sometimes throughout the day) and most frequently in the first three to four months.
- Tingling and fullness of breasts with darkening of the area around the nipples (the areola).
- Tiredness, particularly in early pregnancy.
- Passing urine more frequently, including having to get up in the night.
- A white, mucusy, inoffensive vaginal discharge – due to increased hormone levels.

Pregnancy test

A special test can detect the pregnancy hormone in a woman's urine. If the test result is positive a woman is almost certainly pregnant. Testing can be done by the family doctor, hospital, family planning clinic or at home using a pregnancy testing kit. Some pharmacies also offer this service.

MINOR AILMENTS OF PREGNANCY

Minor ailments in pregnancy include heartburn, constipation, piles and backache. The doctor or midwife will offer advice and any necessary treatment.

COMPLICATIONS OF PREGNANCY

Two potentially serious complications of pregnancy are:
- pre-eclampsia (pregnancy-induced hypertension)
- vaginal bleeding.

Pre-eclampsia

Pre-eclampsia occurs in the second half of pregnancy and is more common with first babies. It affects the placental circulation, reducing oxygen flow to the baby, with a risk of poor foetal growth and low birth-weight. The three physical signs of the condition are:

- raised blood pressure;
- proteinuria – a serious sign (see chart on page 21);
- oedema (swelling) of hands, feet, ankles and face.

KEY POINT

Sometimes, pre-eclampsia develops into eclampsia – a rare but life-threatening condition for both a mother and her baby. It is characterised by epileptic-type seizures and a severely high blood pressure. If pre-eclampsia cannot be controlled by bed rest and medication to lower the blood pressure, then intervention to deliver the baby, by induction of labour or a Caesarean section, is necessary .

Vaginal bleeding

Slight vaginal bleeding may occur very early on in a pregnancy, close to the time of the first missed period, when the fertilised egg embeds itself in the wall of the uterus. A check with the midwife or family doctor is advisable to reassure the mother that all is well.

Vaginal bleeding before the 24th week of pregnancy may be due to a miscarriage (threatened or inevitable) or an ectopic pregnancy. A threatened miscarriage is characterised by slight vaginal bleeding and abdominal pain. If the cervix is not dilated the pregnancy often settles down and progresses to term. When there is a combination of bleeding, abdominal pain and a dilated cervix the miscarriage becomes inevitable and the pregnancy ends. Statistics suggest that one in three pregnancies ends in a miscarriage.

An ectopic pregnancy means the fertilised ovum has started to develop in a fallopian tube. The pregnancy ends at around four to ten weeks. A woman experiences abdominal pain and vaginal bleeding. An operation, usually with removal of the affected tube, is necessary. A future pregnancy is still possible provided the other fallopian tube is healthy. Sometimes the tube in which the pregnancy is developing ruptures, causing severe abdominal pain and shock, and immediate medical care and surgery is needed.

The most likely cause of vaginal bleeding after the 24th week of pregnancy is premature separation of the placenta from the wall of the uterus. Medical care is essential and, depending on the severity of the bleeding, the baby may need to be delivered quickly.

KEY POINT

- While in medical terms a miscarriage means the loss of a foetus, to a mother it is the loss of her baby. Feelings of sadness, emptiness and failure to 'carry a baby' are very common, and mothers may need a great deal of support from close family, friends and professionals at this time.

■ Women who have had a termination of pregnancy often hold painful memories of their loss for short or longer periods of time. Some may need considerable support at the time of termination; others may cope well initially but require counselling many years later.

Antenatal care

The term antenatal care describes the professional care given to a mother and her unborn baby during pregnancy. In the UK it is free as part of the NHS provision. Good antenatal care, together with better standards of living and the improved health of the population, continues to play an important part in the reduction in maternal and infant mortality rates (see page 36).

THE AIMS OF ANTENATAL CARE

The aims of antenatal care are to:
■ monitor the progress of the pregnancy and promote the safety and good health of the mother and her baby
■ prevent, as far as possible, any problems with the pregnancy and provide early treatment and care for any that do occur
■ prepare parents for labour and birth
■ ensure, as far as is possible, the safe delivery of a live, mature, healthy baby
■ prepare the mother for successful breast-feeding and the integration of the baby into the family.

The professionals who care for the mother and her partner during pregnancy are:
■ obstetricians (doctors experienced in all aspects of caring for women during pregnancy and childbirth)
■ family doctors (general practitioners) who have expertise in obstetrics
■ hospital and community midwives.

Health visitors, social workers, physiotherapists, radiographers and dieticians are also frequently involved in caring for expectant mothers.

WHERE TO HAVE THE BABY?

Different arrangements for managing pregnancy and childbirth are described here. Where a baby is born depends on the mother's previous childbirth history, the type of care available locally, the mother's age, general health and the likely progress and outcome of the present pregnancy. Most babies are born in hospital where immediate access to medical care is available if something should go wrong with the birth. Care of the mother during pregnancy is shared between the family doctor, community midwives and the hospital maternity team. The stay in hospital can be anything from a few hours up to a week or more, depending on the health of the mother and baby. General practitioner units, with a small number of beds, are available in many areas with care shared between the GP and the community midwife.

Women are entitled to ask for a home birth and receive care from the community midwife and family doctor (or from an independent midwife). However, concerns about the lack of immediate medical facilities in an emergency has reduced the incidence of home births.

The Domino (Domiciliary In and Out) system may be an option in some areas. This scheme combines the advantages of community care with the facilities of a maternity unit.

Activity
1   Think about and list the advantages and disadvantages of:
    (a) a home birth;
    (b) a hospital birth.
2   Find out about the Domino system of antenatal care.
    (a) What does it involve?
    (b) For which mothers would it be appropriate?
The community midwife at your local health centre will be able to help you with this activity.

PROVISION OF ANTENATAL CARE

Professional care during pregnancy is set out in the chart on page 21. The first antenatal appointment, the booking visit, should take place as soon as possible after a pregnancy has been confirmed. This is an important hospital appointment with the obstetrician and midwife, and will determine whether all antenatal care is with the hospital or shared between hospital, family doctor and community midwife.

Mothers having their babies at home attend for their booking visit at the surgery or health centre and subsequent care will be provided there or in the mother's home. All mothers are offered an ultrasound scan at around 18 to 20 weeks. Should complications arise during the pregnancy they are referred to hospital to see the obstetrician. It is important that help and support following a home birth (or Domino delivery) is available

PROFESSIONAL CARE DURING PREGNANCY

BOOKING VISIT (hospital or surgery/health centre)

History taking – details of:
- Past pregnancies, births, miscarriages
- Present pregnancy (date of last period, expected delivery date)
- Medical history (heart disease, high blood pressure, diabetes can all affect the pregnancy)
- Family history (twins, serious illness)
- Social history (housing, help and support at home)

Physical examination
- Heart and lungs
- Blood pressure and weight (give baseline for future comparison)
- Breasts (inverted nipples make feeding difficult)
- Teeth (mother will be reminded of dental care)
- Legs (varicose veins can get worse in pregnancy)
- Internal examination and cervical smear may be offered (women must feel free to say no to these)

Investigations
1. Urine test for:
   - proteinuria (protein in urine), a sign of pre-eclampsia and that kidneys not working properly
   - glycosuria (sugar in urine), may be a sign of diabetes
2. Blood sample taken and tested for:
   - blood group and Rhesus factor
   - anaemia (iron and folic acid may be prescribed)
   - rubella immunity (if not immune, mother should avoid contact with virus during pregnancy and be offered immunisation after birth)
   - sickle cell anaemia and thalassaemia where appropriate
   - syphilis (an STI which can affect the unborn baby) **NB** No routine blood testing for HIV or AIDS

FOLLOW-UP VISITS
1. Mother seen at regular intervals up to birth. Examination includes:
   - blood pressure, weight, urine test to detect any sign of pre-eclampsia or diabetes
   - checking position of baby in uterus
   - listening to baby's heart
   - checking if baby is moving
   - checking for swelling of hands, feet or face
2. Possible blood re-test for anaemia
3. Opportunity for discussion

SPECIAL TESTS
- Ultrasound scan
- Nuchal translucency scan
- Alphafetoprotein (AFP)
- Amniocentesis
- Chorionic villus sampling (CVS)
- (Bart's) Triple blood test – if available

HEALTH EDUCATION
- Antenatal classes
- Breathing and relaxation techniques
- These are offered in later weeks of pregnancy

Discussion
- Opportunity for mother to ask questions
- Advice on diet, smoking, drinking and general health
- Appointment with dietician or social worker, if appropriate

UW
CN

and arrangements for partners and other family members to help out are usually made.

There may be regional differences in the care patterns described here.

In partnership with the professionals, mothers can help themselves during pregnancy by following the advice in the chart 'Self-care in pregnancy' on page 23.

Respect for cultures and customs

Recognising and respecting different cultures and customs is an important aspect of antenatal care. A sensitive approach is needed to help women who neither understand nor speak English and who may find a busy, unfamiliar antenatal clinic both uncomfortable and threatening. They may be reluctant to ask questions, so that queries and anxieties they have about their pregnancies are never resolved. Relatives and friends can act as interpreters and information leaflets in different languages should be readily available. In some inner city areas, interpreters are provided by the local health authority. If an expectant mother wishes to be seen and examined by a female doctor everything possible is done to facilitate this.

Activity

Parentcraft classes organised by the midwife or health visitor are usually offered to couples during the later weeks of pregnancy. Discussions and advice on a variety of topics take place, for example, childbirth and pain relief in labour, care of a newborn baby, breast and formula feeding and the inevitable emotional changes couples experience following their baby's birth. Relaxation and breathing techniques to help mothers during labour and birth are taught.

1 Try and obtain information (possibly a leaflet or incorporated into a booklet on pregnancy and childbirth) about the parentcraft classes offered by your local health centre or hospital.
2 For which mothers, in particular, might parentcraft classes be especially valuable?

SPECIAL TESTS OF PREGNANCY

Special tests of pregnancy include: ultrasound scanning, amniocentesis, chorionic villus sampling and particular blood tests. They may identify certain conditions but cannot alter them.

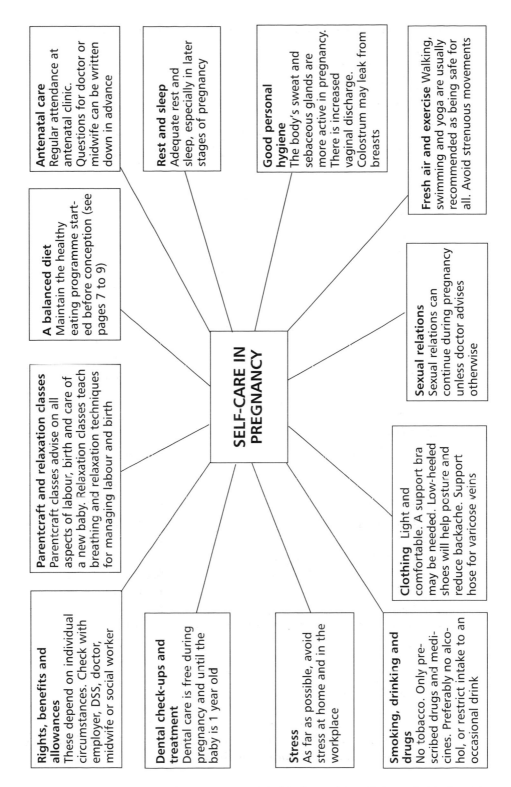

SELF-CARE IN PREGNANCY

Antenatal care
Regular attendance at antenatal clinic.
Questions for doctor or midwife can be written down in advance

Rest and sleep
Adequate rest and sleep, especially in later stages of pregnancy

Good personal hygiene
The body's sweat and sebaceous glands are more active in pregnancy. There is increased vaginal discharge. Colostrum may leak from breasts

Fresh air and exercise Walking, swimming and yoga are usually recommended as being safe for all. Avoid strenuous movements

A balanced diet
Maintain the healthy eating programme started before conception (see pages 7 to 9)

Sexual relations
Sexual relations can continue during pregnancy unless doctor advises otherwise

Parentcraft and relaxation classes
Parentcraft classes advise on all aspects of labour, birth and care of a new baby. Relaxation classes teach breathing and relaxation techniques for managing labour and birth

Clothing Light and comfortable. A support bra may be needed. Low-heeled shoes will help posture and reduce backache. Support hose for varicose veins

Rights, benefits and allowances
These depend on individual circumstances. Check with employer, DSS, doctor, midwife or social worker

Dental check-ups and treatment
Dental care is free during pregnancy and until the baby is 1 year old

Stress
As far as possible, avoid stress at home and in the workplace

Smoking, drinking and drugs
No tobacco. Only prescribed drugs and medicines. Preferably no alcohol, or restrict intake to an occasional drink

Parents and society naturally expect perfect babies. The emphasis on special tests, with the expectation that a mother will seek a termination if there is something wrong with her baby that cannot be 'cured', puts great pressure on women. Sophisticated testing and screening can cause confusion and on-going anxiety for parents as questions and queries cannot always be answered. Waiting for the results of invasive tests or deciding whether or not to have the test at all is stressful for them. Mothers especially have to consider the following:

- what they would do if the results do not give peace of mind, but rather point to a high risk of abnormality
- how they would feel if a test diagnosed Down's syndrome or other chromosome disorder
- the possibility (one in one hundred) of a miscarriage following amniocentesis or chorionic villus sampling
- how accurate the tests are and the possibility of terminating a healthy pregnancy or giving birth to a baby with special needs.

KEY POINT

Parents may seek information about an inherited condition and the risk of passing it on to children or grandchildren. Genetic counselling, a sensitive area of medicine, advises on the probability or degree of risk and the choices parents need to think about. Professionals should support parents in the decision they make.

The following tests may be carried out to check that all is well with the pregnancy or to confirm or discount any concerns the doctor may have about the baby. Expectant mothers have the right to decline the tests.

Ultrasound scanning

Ultrasound scanning is widely used in obstetrics. It is an easy and painless procedure. The ultrasound machine uses high frequency sound waves, bounced back from the uterus, to give television images of the unborn baby. From the images it is possible to determine:

- the size, age and position of the foetus
- the position of the placenta
- the gender of the baby, although this is not usually disclosed to the mother unless she specifically wishes to know
- multiple pregnancies
- Down's syndrome, spina bifida, hydrocephalus, heart and kidney defects and other conditions.

A scan may be carried out at any time in the pregnancy if there are concerns about the baby's health or to confirm the size of the baby. Expectant mothers are routinely offered a scan at around 18 to 20 weeks' gestation (see 'Useful terms', page 36), when the foetal organs are developing well and can be clearly seen. The scan checks that all is well with the pregnancy or whether any further investigation is needed. More sophisticated scanning technology is being developed to provide clearer, more defined images of the foetus.

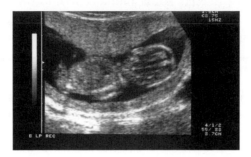

An ultrasound scan taken at 12 weeks' gestation

Nuchal translucency scan

A foetal nuchal translucency scan is the most accurate screening test to assess the risk of a baby having Down's syndrome (Trisomy 21). It is offered selectively (and for a fee) at 11 to 13 weeks, to mothers over 30 years old (the age may vary slightly in different areas), those with insulin-dependent diabetes, if there is a history of a previous baby being affected by a chromosomal disorder, or if the mother is expecting two or more babies. The scan measures the amount of fluid between two layers of skin (the nuchal fold) at the back of the baby's neck. Babies with Down's syndrome have a greater measurement of fluid than babies without the condition. This measurement, together with the mother's age and the level of two particular hormones in the mother's blood, enables the doctor to calculate the likelihood of the baby having Down's syndrome. The incidence of a baby being born with Down's syndrome increases with the age of the mother.

KEY POINT

A further ultrasound scan test, which may become a routine part of screening for Down's syndrome, involves checking the profile of the baby's nose. Research has found that the nasal bone is missing or underdeveloped in a high percentage of babies with Down's syndrome.

Amniocentesis

Amniocentesis is the withdrawal of amniotic fluid from the uterus by inserting a needle through the abdomen into the amniotic sac. The test is carried out at or around 16 weeks' gestation, following an ultrasound scan. It is offered to expectant mothers over the age of 35 years, to those whose AFP test (see below) is raised or low and to mothers whose nuchal scan indicates the likelihood of the baby having Down's syndrome. Amniocentesis detects spina bifida, chromosomal abnormalities such as Down's syndrome and gene-carrying conditions such as Duchenne muscular dystrophy, sickle-cell condition and thalassaemia.

KEY POINT

Amniocentesis is a stressful procedure and mothers are under no obligation to undergo the test. There is a slight risk of infection and miscarriage following amniocentesis.

Chorionic villus sampling

Chorionic villus sampling involves the removal of a small piece of placental tissue via the cervix or abdomen under the guidance of ultrasound. It can be carried out at around eight weeks of pregnancy, making it more acceptable to parents than the later test of amniocentesis. The test is used to detect Down's syndrome, sickle cell and thalassaemia conditions and Tay-Sachs disease. It can also be used to determine the sex of a baby if there is a family history of sex-linked disorders such as haemophilia and muscular dystrophy.

Particular blood tests

Alphafetoprotein (AFP) test

The AFP blood test is offered to expectant mothers between 16 and 18 weeks' gestation. A raised level of AFP (a protein normally present in the mother's blood and in the amniotic fluid during pregnancy) may indicate that the baby has a neural tube defect, or there is a multiple pregnancy or the pregnancy is further advanced than was thought. A low AFP can be associated with Down's syndrome or a wrong gestational age. When AFP levels are found to be higher or lower than normal an amniocentesis is usually offered. The AFP test may be carried out on its own or as part of the triple blood test (see below) where available.

(Bart's) triple blood test

The full name for this test (first used at St Bartholemew's hospital) is 'the maternal serum screening test'. It measures the levels of three substances in the mother's blood (including the alphafetoprotein level) and is designed to identify women whose babies may be at greater risk of having Down's syndrome or neural tube defects. It is offered at about 16 weeks' gestation.

(See also Chapter 10, page 236, for further reference to these special tests.)

(See also Chapter 10, page 236, for further reference to these special tests.)

> ### Activity
> Why do you think some expectant mothers fail to attend the antenatal clinic? What could be done to encourage these mothers to attend?

DIET IN PREGNANCY

The healthy eating pattern started prior to conception will meet a mother's health needs during pregnancy, prepare her for labour and breastfeeding, and also nourish the developing baby. The extra calories needed for the growing baby are provided partly by the diet and partly from naturally conserved energy as mother rests during pregnancy.

Expectant mothers should try and make sure their diet contains:

- an extra pint of milk daily, or cheese or yoghurt to provide calcium for baby's bones and teeth;
- iron-rich foods such as red meat and fortified cereals to prevent anaemia during pregnancy, or resulting from a heavy blood loss during delivery;
- foods containing folic acid (see Activity, page 12) as a precaution against neural tube defects;
- sources of fibre, such as fresh fruit and vegetables, whole grain bread, pasta and rice to guard against constipation – a common ailment during pregnancy. Bran-enriched cereals and drinks of water will also help.

REMEMBER!

Women eating vegetarian and vegan diets should include vegetable protein foods (see page 8) in their diet.

Expectant mothers on low incomes need sensible dietary advice. Milk, eggs, cheaper cuts of meat, as well as a wide variety of pulses can be included in the diet. Baked beans, wholemeal bread, hard cheeses and fresh fruit and vegetables are nutritious and no more expensive than many bought convenience foods.

Vitamins, iron and folic acid supplements are usually prescribed by the family doctor for women on low incomes and income support as well as those on a restricted diet.

- Iron intake must meet the foetal need to store iron in the liver.

- Soft cheese, paté, raw or lightly cooked eggs and meats carry the risk of infections that are harmful to the unborn baby and should be avoided. Liver is not recommended because of its high vitamin A content, which may be linked to foetal abnormality.

Activity

1 Explain the basic principles of balanced diet.
2 Make up a three-day menu of three meals a day for the following expectant mothers:
   (a) a mother on a low income;
   (b) an Asian mother;
   (c) a mother who eats a vegan diet.

POVERTY IN PREGNANCY AND INFANCY

Antenatal care and support is particularly important for mothers on a low income, or who live below the 'poverty line'. Poor housing, unemployment and a low standard of living have implications for both the mother and her baby. Maternal anaemia is a common result of a poor diet. Attendance at an antenatal clinic may be irregular or non-existent – perhaps because the mother cannot afford transport, does not know or understand the system, or is unaware of the importance of health checks. Some mothers may also lack the confidence to express their needs and concerns to the medical staff and so do not attend the antenatal clinic. As a result, problems may arise later which otherwise might have been prevented.

Some families may suffer discrimination in selection for housing, employment and promotion. This can lead to a lower standard of living with adverse consequences for the health and development of the children.

Babies born into poverty or a poor environment tend to be of low birthweight (see page 36). They are more likely to be bottle fed. Respiratory infections and gastro-enteritis are more common and statistics show a higher incidence of infant mortality. A poor diet in infancy can result in anaemia and faltering growth. All these factors put a baby at a disadvantage right from the start of her life. Health care professionals, and those involved in Sure Start programmes, are aware of the risks to these babies and make health promotion, surveillance and immunisation (see pages 113–18 and 169–71) a top priority in their work with these families.

Labour and birth

Towards the end of pregnancy the baby moves into position ready for birth. A mother will know labour has started by one or more of the following:
- 'a show' – a blood-stained vaginal discharge;
- rupture of membranes, usually called 'the waters breaking';
- regular contractions – movements of the muscles of the uterus that slowly dilate (open up) the cervix at the neck of the womb. They usually start slowly and irregularly with long gaps in between each one. Then they become much stronger and more frequent as labour progresses.

THE THREE STAGES OF LABOUR

- **Stage 1.** Dilatation of the cervix to allow baby's head to pass through. Most babies are born head first but in a breech birth the baby is born bottom or feet first. The length of time for this stage varies from a few hours up to 24 hours. Throughout the first stage the midwife monitors the contractions, supporting and encouraging the mother, and listens to the baby's heartbeat.
- **Stage 2**. The birth of the baby. Once the cervix is fully open the midwife encourages the mother to push with each contraction until the baby's head is ready to be born. It is the time when mothers work very hard to push their baby out. The head is 'panted' out and, shortly after, the baby's body slips out easily (see the diagram on page 30).
- **Stage 3**. The delivery of the placenta and membranes. These are always checked to make sure they are complete. If a piece of placenta is left behind in the womb it can cause a serious blood loss. Once the placenta and membranes have been delivered and checked the birth process is complete.

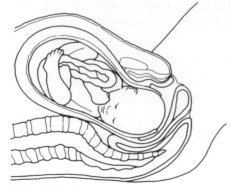

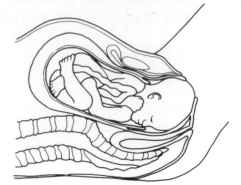

1 The baby is curled up in the foetal position. The cervix gradually dilates.

2 When the cervix is fully dilated, the contractions push the baby out along the birth canal.

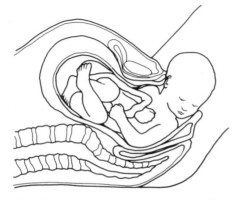

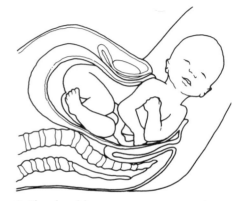

3 As the head emerges, it twists half round.

4 The shoulders emerge one at a time.

The birth process

MANAGING LABOUR

In the early stage of labour a mother is usually at home. The hospital advises her when to come in to the labour ward. If it is a home birth the community midwife and family doctor provide all care and support until the baby is safely born. Women may move around freely in labour for as long as they wish, providing there are no complications and they have not had any pain-relieving drugs. As the contractions become stronger some pain relief may be needed (see Table 1.2 on page 31), although many mothers prefer to manage their labour using only the breathing and relaxation techniques learned at relaxation classes.

A birth partner (husband, partner, a close relative or friend) may stay with the mother during labour and birth, providing reassurance, encouragement and emotional support, particularly towards the end of the first stage when contractions can be very strong and painful.

Table 1.2 Pain relief available during labour

Pain relief	How it is given	Comments
Pethidine (most commonly used drug for pain relief)	By injection	If given late in labour, baby can have breathing problems and may be sleepy at birth
Gas and air (oxygen and nitrous oxide)	Breathed in by face mask, particularly used near end of first stage of labour	Takes effect quickly. Can cause nausea and light-headedness but baby unaffected
Epidural anaesthesia	Injection of a local anaesthetic into space around spinal cord. Numbs from waist down	May deaden the urge to push, so forceps delivery may be needed. Mother cannot move around freely. Caesarean sections often performed under this form of anaesthetic – mother remains awake and able to hold baby immediately
TENS (transcutaneous nerve stimulation)	Electronic blocking of pain. Electrodes are placed on lower back and connected to a 'pulsar' control box. Mother adjusts strength of pulses	Easy to use by mother. No side-effects for mother or baby. Mother can move around freely.
Acupuncture	Special needles are inserted into different parts of the body to block pain messages	Not available within the NHS. Used with breathing exercises. Comments generally favourable

KEY POINT

A mother may choose to squat, kneel on a mattress on the floor, or sit in a 'birthing chair' to give birth, rather than lie on a bed. 'Water births' are popular but controversial.

HELPING THE BIRTH PROCESS

Sometimes a baby needs help to be born. Table 1.3 on page 33 lists the medical procedures that are commonly carried out in all maternity units.

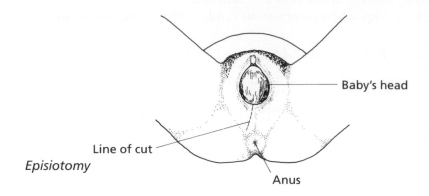

Episiotomy

Baby's head

Line of cut

Anus

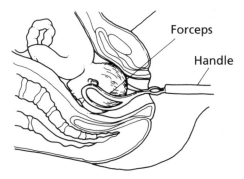

Forceps delivery

Forceps

Handle

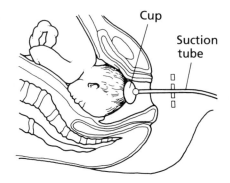

Assisted births

Cup

Suction tube

Table 1.3 Medical procedures to help the birth process

Procedure	Description	Reason for procedure
Episiotomy	Small cut in the perineum (the tissue between the vagina and anus) to enlarge vaginal opening. Stitched up under local anaesthetic following birth	To prevent serious tearing during birth. To speed up delivery. To help the effort of pushing if mother has a medical condition. To aid ventouse extraction or forceps delivery To ease pressure on head of premature baby
Induction of labour	Starting labour by artificial means, such as: ■ rupturing membranes ■ hormonal intravenous drip ■ hormonal vaginal pessaries	Pregnancy beyond expected date. Maternal conditions, such as: ■ pre-eclampsia ■ heart conditions ■ kidney disease ■ high blood pressure ■ diabetes
Forceps	Special instruments with curved blades, which fit and lock around the baby's head. Used only when cervix is fully dilated. Local anaesthetic given. Episiotomy necessary. Gentle traction used	Long second stage of labour. Either mother or baby showing signs of distress. Medical conditions in mother (as in induction above). To prevent too much pressure on head of a premature baby
Ventouse/vacuum extraction	Alternative to forceps. Metal or rubber cap placed on baby's head and attached to suction pump. Gentle traction used. Local anaesthetic and episiotomy necessary	Same as for forceps delivery. Can be used if cervix not quite fully dilated
Caesarean section	Operation under general or epidural anaesthesia. Baby delivered through cut in abdominal wall. Can be elective (planned) or emergency	Baby too big for vaginal delivery. Serious vaginal bleeding. Prolapsed cord. Baby in a difficult position. Failed induction of labour. Baby distressed. Serious distress or medical condition in mother

IMMEDIATE CARE OF THE MOTHER FOLLOWING BIRTH

If an episiotomy was necessary, it is repaired under local anaesthetic. The mother's temperature, pulse and blood pressure are recorded, she is made clean and comfortable and encouraged to rest. Labour is hard work and rest and sleep are important after birth to enable a mother to care for her baby's needs, as well as possibly looking after other children and the home. The length of time spent in hospital depends on the health of both the mother and her baby and the help available at home. If all is well, the hospital stay can be as little as six hours.

The postnatal period

This is the period of six to eight weeks following birth. A midwife visits the mother and baby at home for the first 10 days following delivery (or for longer if necessary), after which the health visitor takes over care of the mother and baby. During the postnatal period:

■ the mother recovers from any pregnancy problems and from the birth

■ mother and baby bonding takes root and the baby becomes part of the family

■ the baby's feeding pattern is established

■ postnatal exercises are encouraged to strengthen and tighten all the pelvic muscles, which were stretched and slackened during pregnancy and labour.

After having a baby there should be an opportunity for a mother to talk with her doctor or midwife about her birth experience. Many mothers are elated and excited following delivery, but some, even those who have attended antenatal classes, may feel they were unprepared for the powerful feelings and experiences of childbirth – although they may not initially express these feelings to anyone. Women can find labour and birth frightening and painful. In recent years emphasis has been placed on the ideal birth experience and occasionally mothers can have feelings of disappointment or failure if everything did not go according to plan, for example, if they had more pain relief than expected or needed a Caesarean section. Birth partners, too, can find the birth experience overwhelming and may feel inadequate that they were unable to fully meet the mother's needs during a demanding time.

Any unresolved negative thoughts and feelings of inadequacy can interfere with the emotional relationship between the mother and her baby, so it is important to encourage mothers (and birth partners if they wish) to talk about their feelings and experiences. Labour and birth are not an exam to be passed, so there is no right or wrong way to get through them. Each woman and each labour is unique.

Birth is part of the process of becoming a parent and not an end in itself.

POSTNATAL EXAMINATION

A postnatal check-up is offered to a mother around six weeks after the birth to make sure she has recovered from pregnancy and childbirth and her uterus has returned to its normal size. Her blood pressure is checked and, if she shows signs of anaemia, her blood haemoglobin level is tested. A cervical smear may be taken and family planning is usually discussed.

'BABY BLUES' AND POSTNATAL ILLNESS

'Baby blues'
A period of weepiness and sadness is extremely common around the fifth day following birth. Giving birth is a time of heightened emotions but, for many mothers, feelings of achievement and joy often give way to a sense of anti-climax linked to tiredness, perhaps painful stitches, sore breasts as the milk comes in and alterations in hormone levels. In addition, the baby may have a mild health problem such as jaundice or feeding difficulties. The 'baby blues' rarely lasts more than two or three days, but a mother needs plenty of reassurance that it will quickly pass. She also requires as much rest as possible, together with support and understanding from her partner and family. Tact and kindness from professionals such as the midwife, family doctor and health visitor are essential at this time.

Postnatal illness
Postnatal illness encompasses postnatal depression and puerperal psychosis.

Postnatal depression is not uncommon. It is different from the 'baby blues', usually occurring between a few weeks and three months after the birth and possibly lasting many months. The mother appears chronically tired and exhausted, although she may be sleeping quite well. Anxiety, panic attacks, unhappiness, weepiness and poor appetite are all common symptoms. She may feel inadequate and unable to respond to her baby, although the baby is usually well cared for. Lack of social support or a major life event around this time may be a contributory factor in postnatal depression.

Mothers with postnatal depression can remain at home as long as they receive adequate support and reassurance from the family doctor and health visitor, as well as family and friends (if they live close by). Anti-depressant medication is often prescribed. Early Years workers in a day nursery can support mothers with postnatal depression through listening, being patient and non-judgemental and helping them to interact with their babies. Parent–infant psychotherapy is available in some areas. Support groups (see below) also offer help and advice and encourage mothers to talk about their feelings.

Puerperal psychosis is a serious illness. It starts abruptly around 3 to 14 days following the birth. The mother looks unwell and is in a state of fear, distress and confusion. She is restless and unable to sleep and may have hallucinations. Both the mother and baby are admitted to hospital – this is to avoid separation at such a crucial time. Treatment is through special medication and therapy. Both the short-term and long-term out-look are good.

The Association for Postnatal Illness, the Meet-a-Mum Association (MAMA) and the Anna Freud Centre (see page 264) offer help, support and advice to mothers with the 'baby blues' and postnatal illness.

Activity
In what ways can family and friends offer help and support when a mother comes home with her new baby?

Useful terms

Gestation The length of time an individual pregnancy lasts

Infant mortality rate The number of deaths of infants in the first year of life (including those occurring in the first four weeks) per 1000 regis-tered live births

Infancy The first year of life

Low birth-weight baby A baby weighing 2.5 kg (5½ lb) or less at birth

Maternal mortality rate The number of maternal deaths directly attrib-utable to pregnancy and childbirth per 1000 registered total births

Miscarriage The loss of a baby before 24 weeks of pregnancy

Neonatal mortality rate The number of deaths of babies within the first four weeks of birth per 1000 registered live births

Neonate A baby during the first four weeks of life

Newborn or neonatal period The first month of life

Perinatal mortality rate All stillbirths and deaths of babies in the first week of life per 1000 total registered births

Post-term (postmature) baby A baby born after 41 completed weeks' gestation

Pre-term (premature) baby A baby born before 37 weeks' gestation

Stillborn baby A baby born dead after 24 weeks of pregnancy

Term baby A baby born between 37 and 41 completed weeks of pregnancy

Viable Capable of surviving outside the womb – applied to a foetus from the 24th week of gestation

QUICK CHECK

1 Describe several different family groupings.
2 Name the **10** steps of preconceptual care.
3 At what stage of pregnancy is the unborn baby most at risk from the rubella virus?
4 Name **three** genetic disorders.
5 Name **three** functions of the placenta.
6 Which mineral is stored in the foetal liver and why?
7 Name the greasy white substance that protects the skin of the unborn baby.
8 Describe lanugo.
9 Which B-group vitamin is linked to the prevention of spina bifida?
10 Identify the nutrients important for growth of the unborn baby's bones and teeth.
11 Describe:
   (a) the signs of labour;
   (b) the stages of labour.
12 What is the postnatal period?
13 (a) How would you recognise the 'baby blues'?
   (b) Why is it important to encourage a mother to talk about her experience of labour and birth?
14 What is the neonatal period?
15 A baby weighs 3 kg at birth. Is she a low birth-weight baby?

2 CARE OF THE NEWBORN BABY

> **This chapter covers:**
> - **Immediate care of the newborn**
> - **Early mother–baby bonding**
> - **Examination of the newborn**
> - **Neonatal screening tests**
> - **Keeping the newborn baby warm**
> - **Neonatal jaundice**
> - **Twins**
> - **Low birth-weight and postmaturity**
> - **Bereavement**

Immediate care of the newborn

ESTABLISHING BREATHING

As soon as the baby's head is delivered the midwife or doctor wipes away any mucus from around the baby's mouth and nose, and checks that the umbilical cord is not around the neck. Before birth, the baby's oxygen came from the mother but now the baby's lungs must take in oxygen. Most babies breathe spontaneously within a few seconds of birth. Sometimes mucus and amniotic fluid, which can obstruct breathing and cause lung damage and infection if inhaled by the baby, have to be gently sucked away from the air passages with a soft tube called a mucus extractor. When breathing begins, the baby's colour changes as oxygen is drawn in.

The Apgar score
The Apgar score is the international standard method used to assess the condition of a baby immediately after birth and to identify those who are poorly and need rescusitation.
    Five vital signs are observed:
- heart rate
- breathing
- muscle tone
- reflex response to stimulation
- colour.

Table 2.1 The Apgar score table

Sign	0	1	2
Heart rate	Absent	Slow (below 100 beats per minute)	Fast (above 100 beats per minute)
Breathing	Absent	Slow, irregular	Good, crying
Muscle tone	Limp	Some movement of hands and feet	Active
Reflex response (stimulation of foot or nostril)	No response	Grimace	Cry, cough, sneeze
Colour	Blue, pale	Body oxygenated, hands and feet blue	Well-oxygenated

The heart rate and breathing pattern are the most important signs.

For each sign the baby is given 0, 1 or 2 points (see Table 2.1 above). The points are added up giving a maximum score of 10.

The baby is assessed at 1 minute and 5 minutes after birth, and the test repeated every 5 minutes until the maximum score of 10 is achieved.

KEY POINT

The Apgar scoring system was first devised by Doctor Virginia Apgar for white babies. The word 'oxygenated' instead of the original 'pink' embraces all skin colours.

Interpreting the score
- A score of 10   The baby is in the best possible condition.
- A score of 8–9 The baby is in good condition.
- A score of 5–7 The baby has moderate asphyxia (breathing problems) and may need further clearing of the airways and some oxygen by face mask.
- A score of 4 or less The baby is poorly, has severe asphyxia and needs urgent resuscitation. A tube is inserted into the windpipe to allow oxygen to flow directly into the baby's lungs. If she still has a low score at 5 minutes there is the possibility of brain damage occurring.

KEY POINTS

- Most healthy babies have an Apgar score of 9, losing one point for the colour of the hands and feet, which are not fully oxygenated and remain blue for some hours after birth.

- Pre-term babies, low birth-weight and breech birth babies, and those born by Caesarean section are more likely to need resuscitation.

The table below sets out the essential procedures following a baby's birth.

Table 2.2 Important procedures following birth

Procedure	
Labelling the baby with name and hospital number of mother, date and time of birth and sex of baby	This should be done before the umbilical cord is cut. Bracelets should be securely fastened around one wrist and ankle. A 'cot card' also records identification details
Electronic security tagging	An electronic security tag may be attached round the baby's ankle. The tag activates an alarm if the baby is taken, unauthorised, from the ward, unit or hospital (see Safe Practice, opposite)
Cord care	The umbilical cord is clamped and cut after birth. The cord stump, about 2.5 cm (1 in), shrivels and falls off after 5-7 days. Cord hygiene is important (see page 77)
Weight	The baby is weighed after birth. The average weight of a term baby is 3.5 kg (7½ lb). Weight is influenced by gestation and the mother's health in pregnancy. Poor diet, smoking, alcohol, drugs and illness can all cause delayed foetal growth, resulting in low birth-weight. A record of birth-weight is kept as a guide for future growth patterns. On average, birth-weight doubles by 6 months and trebles by 1 year
Length	The measurement is taken from the top of the head to the heels with the baby in the supine (on her back). The average length of a term baby is 51 cm (20 in). The average length at 1 year is 76 cm (30 in)
Head circumference	This should relate to body size. The average head size at term is 35 cm (13¼ in). A very small head in relation to weight and length can indicate that the baby will have some degree of learning delay. An unusually large head can be due to hydrocephalus (fluid on the brain). The average head circumference measurement at 1 year is 46 cm (18 in)
Immunisation (injections) (a) BCG (Bacille Calmette Guerin)	Given to babies: (a) likely to be in contact with someone who has tuberculosis, e.g. close family member (b) routinely in areas where there is a large population from countries with a high incidence of tuberculosis
(b) Hepatitis B (1st dose)	Given to babies whose mothers were hepatitis B positive during pregnancy

Parents need to feel confident that their baby is safe at all times in a maternity hospital or unit. To reduce the possibility of a baby being taken away by an unauthorised person, stringent safety precautions are essential. Doors to all wards and nurseries are usually secured by use of combination locks. Electronic tagging of babies is widely used and further reduces the risk of abduction. Footprinting all babies is an identity control used in some hospitals in case the identity bracelets are lost or removed.

KEY POINT

Obviously, babies born at home do not need identification bracelets, 'cot cards' or electronic tagging.

THE APPEARANCE OF A NEWBORN BABY

- A newborn baby is wet from the amniotic fluid and may be bloodied from her passage through the birth canal.
- Her head is large in proportion to her body and may be misshapen and lopsided from moulding, a caput or cephalhaematoma (see below). Babies born by Caesarean section usually have nicely rounded heads.
- She may look wrinkled and skinny or smooth and plump.
- Vernix is usually present, especially in the skin folds. It gradually diminishes and disappears within a few days. Rubbing it off will damage the baby's skin. In some cultures the vernix is used as a moisturiser and massaged into the baby's skin.
- Lanugo may be seen, especially on the back and shoulders of dark-haired and pre-term babies, but it soon disappears.
- She may have a full head of hair or be quite bald.
- Skin colour varies and depends on her ethnic origin and health. In the first 48 hours blueness of the hands and feet is common due to poor circulation. Black babies appear lighter than their eventual colour because the brown pigment, melanin, has not yet reached its full concentration. A 'mongolian blue spot' – a bluish black area of discolouration, not to be confused with bruising – is commonly found over the base of the spine or the buttocks of babies of African-Caribbean, Mediterranean and Asian origin. 'Blue spots' gradually disappear but are always recorded to prevent any future allegations of child abuse.

Moulding
This is the altered shape of the baby's head as it makes its way through the birth canal. Overlapping of the skull bones makes the head longer and a bit smaller. The head returns to normal shape within a short time.

Caput succedaneum

A swelling on the part of the head that was pressing on the dilating cervix during labour. Parents need reassuring it is not harmful to their baby and will disappear within a few days.

Cephalhaematoma

A blood-filled swelling on the head, caused by rupture of small blood vessels during labour, appears a little while after birth and may take several weeks to subside. Parents should be reassured that there is no danger to the baby's brain.

Early mother–baby bonding

A baby is usually delivered on to her mother's tummy, or into her arms, which allows immediate contact and stroking at the time of birth. (Many mothers like to touch their baby's head as soon as it is delivered and actively take part in delivering the baby into their arms). Either the mother or the baby's father may wish to cut the umbilical cord – a symbolic gesture indicating the start of a new, independent life. Once the cord has been cut, and providing the baby is well, the mother can continue to hold and cuddle her baby. The importance of 'touch' for the development of the baby and the on-going mother–baby relationship is very important. A newborn baby's skin is highly sensitive to the pleasure of touching and the first moments of holding a new baby are emotional and special, even more so if the baby's father is present as well.

Many women are overwhelmed by the experience of giving birth. Some mothers fall in love with their baby immediately, while for others it is a more gradual process. There is no right or wrong way, and the mother must be allowed to proceed at her own pace. What is important, though, is that she has the opportunity to be with her baby as soon as possible after birth. This is the start of getting to know each other in what will be a gradually evolving relationship. A mother is particularly sensitive and alert to her baby in the immediate newborn period and will spend time looking into her baby's eyes, which are open in the first hour after birth. This eye-to-eye contact is a crucial part of the bonding process. The mother will talk and make soothing noises to her baby before moving on to explore the infant's hands and feet, counting fingers and toes before gathering her to the breast.

Mothers are encouraged to put their babies to the breast. The rooting and sucking reflexes (see page 48) are strong in the newborn and although the baby may spend some time just exploring round the nipple she will gradually start sucking. This not only helps the mother–baby relationship but also stimulates the breasts to produce milk.

Midwives and doctors are sensitive to the need for a mother and her baby to be together and avoid separating them other than for medical reasons. Once the routine procedures of weighing, measuring and cord care have been completed (see Table 2.2 on page 40), the baby should be dressed and placed in a cot beside her mother. With her baby beside her, a mother can quickly respond to the infants' needs and be close to her through the intimacy of breast-feeding and cuddling. Each time she responds to these needs a mother feels increasingly necessary for her infant's survival.

Early bonding may be inhibited if a mother and her baby are separated either because one of them is ill or the baby is pre-term and in the special care unit, but everything possible will be done to keep a mother in contact with her baby (see also, The pre-term baby, Mother–baby bonding, page 64 and Attachments, Chapter 6, page 158).

KEY POINT

A mother who has had a long and difficult labour and birth may need to rest before enjoying a prolonged period with her baby.

Activity
You are a nanny caring for a new baby. How could you help mother–baby bonding in the early weeks after birth? What factors might influence the bonding process?

Examination of the newborn baby

Soon after birth a brief examination is carried out by the doctor or midwife to make sure there is nothing obviously wrong with the baby. A detailed examination is carried out 24 to 48 hours after birth.

DETAILED EXAMINATION

The paediatrician (a doctor caring for children from birth to 16 years) makes a full examination of the baby with the mother present. Fathers are encouraged to be present. Babies born at home are examined by the family doctor. The examiner's hands must be clean and warm. The baby is examined from 'top to toe'.

Heart and lungs
The heart and lungs are examined first, while baby is still and quiet. Any heart murmurs or worrying lung sounds are investigated further.

Head
The size and shape are noted and the head circumference measured. Mothers are always reassured that any marks from a forceps or ventouse delivery will disappear within a few days. The anterior and posterior fontanelles (soft spots, see illustration below) are observed and felt.

Anterior fontanelle
The anterior fontanelle is at the front of the head above the brow. It is a diamond-shaped area covered by a tough membrane and its size varies from 1 cm to 5 cm (½ in to 2 in) across. It is slightly depressed and may be seen pulsating. The fontanelle closes between 12 to 18 months of age. A tense, bulging anterior fontanelle may indicate increased pressure around the brain or an infection. A sunken fontanelle may be a sign that the baby is dehydrated.

KEY POINT

Mother and other carers may worry about touching the fontanelle, but normal washing, drying and handling procedures are perfectly safe and the baby's brain will not come to any harm.

Posterior fontanelle
The posterior fontanelle is a smaller, triangular shaped area near the crown of the head. It is sometimes closed at birth or closes within the first few months of life.

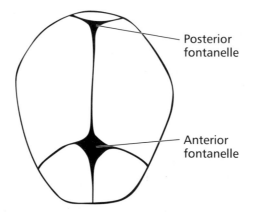

The anterior and posterior fontanelles

Eyes

Sticky eyes are common in the first 48 hours after birth (see Table 3.1, page 88). The eyes are examined for any signs of malformation and for congenital cataract (a cloudiness of the lens), which can be due to rubella or toxoplasmosis infection before birth, or could be a symptom of Down's syndrome.

Wandering eye movements and squinting are normal in the newborn. The baby is unable to use both eyes together until she is a few months old. Tears are rare until the third or fourth week of life.

The baby's permanent eye colour is established by six weeks.

Vision See Chapter 4, page 116, and Chapter 6, pages 153 and 162–5 (Developmental Tables).

Ears

Differences in position, shape and size can occur, and may be seen in babies with foetal alcohol syndrome and chromosome disorders. Any discharge from the ear is abnormal.

Hearing see page 153, also Chapter 4, page 116, and Chapter 6, pages 153–4 and 162–6 (Developmental Tables).

Mouth

With a clean finger the doctor checks the roof of the mouth (hard and soft palate) for any evidence of cleft palate. A baby with cleft lip or palate is referred promptly to a plastic surgeon. Sometimes a baby is born with one or more teeth. If the baby has a loose tooth it should be removed to prevent her inhaling it.

Chest and abdomen

The doctor palpates (feels) the baby's abdomen and checks the internal organs. It is normal for the abdomen to appear rather large. The umbilical cord is checked for any sign of infection. It will have already started to shrivel up (see Chapter 3, page 77, Step 5: Umbilical cord).

Breast engorgement can occur in both girls and boys with sometimes a little leakage of milk. This is due to the mother's hormones crossing the placenta during pregnancy and subsides in a week or so. There is no treatment other than to gently wipe away any leakage, but it is important to reassure the mother.

Genitalia

The genitalia of both girls and boys appear rather large at birth.

A whitish or blood-stained vaginal discharge may occur in baby girls soon after birth. Again, this is hormonal. If unexpected, it can cause anxiety for mothers and carers. The discharge will clear within a few days.

In male babies the testes are normally in the scrotum at birth – if not, they usually descend (come down) in the first month or so. A further examination is made at eight weeks – and at successive health checks if necessary. Undescended testes can be brought down into the scrotum by surgical operation some time in the pre-school years.

Back
With the baby lying prone (face down) the back is checked for any evidence of spina bifida, which in its mildest form may only be a dimple or small growth of hair at the base of the spine, rarely causing problems. In its most serious form, the bones of the spine have failed to form properly in foetal life, leaving a gap or split in the vertebral column through which the covering of the spinal cord and the cord itself may protrude. Wherever this abnormality occurs on the back, the cord and nerves below it will be affected causing paralysis and loss of sensation.

Anus
The anus (back passage) is checked to make sure it is normal and that the baby has passed meconium – the greenish-black sticky stool the baby passes in the first day or two of life. As the baby begins to take milk feeds the colour of the stools becomes greenish brown and then yellowish brown – these are known as changing stools.

Hips
All babies' hips are routinely tested for congenital dislocation (see this Chapter 2, page 52).

Limbs
Fingers and toes are counted – accessory (extra) digits are sometimes present. Any webbing of fingers or toes is noted. Foot disorders are common in the newborn baby. Talipes (club foot) is a congential deformity in which the foot is at an abnormal angle to the leg. It is partly genetic and partly due to the baby being in a cramped position in the womb. There are different types of talipes. 'Mild positional talipes' is temporary and can be corrected with prompt physiotherapy. The more severe types of talipes need early treatments such as physiotherapy, manipulation, splinting and possibly an operation, to prevent permanent disability.

Skin
Vernix and lanugo may still be present. Very small white spots called milia (which are tiny sebaceous glands) are frequently seen around the nose. They soon disappear.

Birthmarks (naevi)

Small, reddish-purple 'stork marks' on the skin are often found on the eyelids, above the nose and at the back of the neck. They will fade and disappear.

Other birthmarks, such as moles and 'blue spots', are checked and noted by the medical staff. Not all birthmarks are present at birth. Some (such as strawberry marks) may appear later and grow rapidly in infancy – parents need reassuring they are harmless and should be left alone.

KEY POINT

It is important to know that a newborn baby's bladder and bowels are working normally. Midwives check nappies until they know the baby has passed urine and a meconium stool. Baby boys should pass a good stream of urine. A poor stream or difficulty in passing urine should always be investigated.

EXAMINATION OF THE NERVOUS SYSTEM

Examination of the nervous system includes testing a number of primitive or automatic reflexes and observing and evaluating the baby's posture, movements and muscle tone.

Automatic or primitive reflexes

An automatic reflex action is one that happens without thinking – a prompt and certain movement or response to a specific stimulus. 'Protective' reflexes (which most people have) include sneezing, swallowing, blinking, coughing or the rapid removal of the hand from something too hot. During the first few months of life babies have a number of automatic or primitive reflexes, several of which are tested as part of the examination of the nervous system. The reflex responses disappear at different times, but by three months of age they have mostly been replaced by voluntary, learned responses – for example, the grasp reflex has to disappear before a baby learns to hold objects placed in her hand. Some primitive reflexes are explained below and illustrated on page 48.

KEY POINTS

- A baby's reflex responses depend on her state of alertness at the time of testing.

- Reflex responses that last beyond the time they should have disappeared may be a sign of some disorder of the nervous system, which may lead to developmental delay.

■ While reflex-testing is important in any neonatal examination, their responses must be judged in relation to the more important evaluation of posture, movement and muscle tone.

Rooting reflex

If one side of a baby's cheek or mouth is touched gently, she turns her head in the direction of the touch. This ensures that she will seek the nipple when her cheek is brushed by her mother's breast. The rooting reflex is essential for the baby's successful feeding, as are the sucking reflex (placing the nipple or teat into the baby's mouth, causing her to suck) and swallowing reflex.

Asymmetric tonic neck reflex

If a baby's face is turned to one side, she extends (straightens) her arm and leg on that side and flexes (bends) her arm and leg on the opposite side.

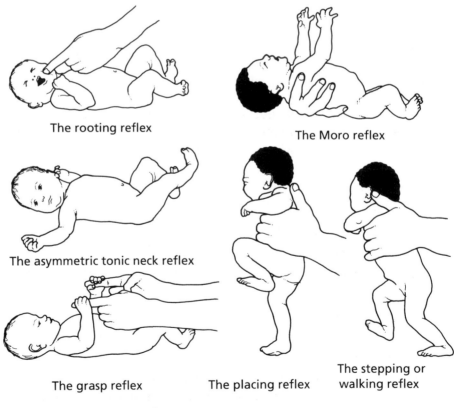

The rooting reflex

The Moro reflex

The asymmetric tonic neck reflex

The grasp reflex

The placing reflex

The stepping or walking reflex

Primitive or automatic reflexes

Grasp reflex
A baby automatically grasps an object placed in the palm of her hand. If a finger is slipped into each of her palms, she will grasp them so tightly that she can support her own weight. This can also be done with the toes.

Moro reflex
The baby's head is held in the doctor's hand and raised a little way off the examination surface before being released quickly. The baby stretches out her arms with fingers curved before bringing them back over the chest as if in an embrace.

Startle reflex
This should not be confused with the Moro reflex. At a sudden, loud noise, or tap on the breastbone, the baby moves her arms outwards with her elbows bent and her hands closed. It is a less exaggerated response than the Moro with a different stimulus.

Placing reflex
If the front of the baby's leg is gently brought into contact with the edge of a table, the baby raises her leg and places her foot on the hard surface.

Stepping or walking reflex
If a baby is held upright with the soles of her feet on a flat surface and is then moved forward slowly, she will respond with 'walking' steps.

KEY POINT

Testing a baby's automatic reflexes and interpreting the responses should only be carried out by those trained in the correct examination technique, such as doctors, midwives and health visitors.

Posture
The typical postures adopted by a newborn baby when placed in certain positions (see page 50) are outlined below.

Prone (face downwards)
The baby's legs are flexed (bent) and drawn up under the abdomen, her pelvis is high, her head turned to the side and her arms are flexed.

Supine (face upwards)
Usually the baby's head turns to one side. Her legs are flexed, her knees are apart and the soles of her feet turned inwards.

Ventral suspension (held horizontally, face downwards)
The baby's head is held momentarily in line with her body. Her limbs hang down, partly flexed.

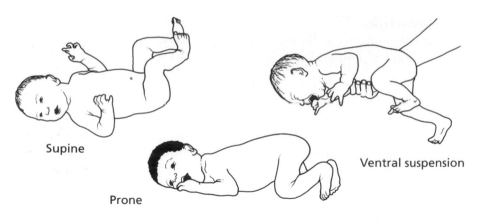

Supine

Prone

Ventral suspension

Posture

Movements

The movements of the newborn baby's four limbs are jerky and uncoordinated. Her hands are closed with the thumbs tucked under the fingers, but she opens and closes her hands when feeding or when you stroke the back of her hand. If pulled to sit, her head will lag (fall back).

Muscle tone

Muscle tone is the firmness or tension in muscles that allows the body to have normal posture and enables the joints to go through their full range of movements.

KEY POINT

A baby with very floppy or stiff limbs and body may have some problem of the nervous system.

Activity

If possible, observe a new baby. Watch her movements and posture. Look at her skin and gently feel the anterior fontanelle. Describe what you observe, having regard to the information given so far in this chapter.

Neonatal screening tests

Screening tests aim to identify babies who have, or who are at risk of developing, specific conditions that can be treated in early life.

GUTHRIE TEST

The Guthrie test is a blood test used to detect the rare inherited metabolic disorder phenylketonuria (PKU), which occurs in 1 in 10,000 births. It is caused by an excess of phenylalanine, an amino acid that, due to a missing enzyme, cannot be broken down and used in the body. Phenylalanine builds up as a poison and leads to brain damage and learning delay. A small blood sample, dripped directly on to special absorbent paper, is taken from the baby's heel 6 to 14 days after birth by which time the baby has had several days of milk feeds. The test is carried out on the dried blood spots.

KEY POINT

A baby with phenylketonuria appears normal at birth but becomes ill within a few weeks. There is no cure for the condition, but treatment is successful. Early diagnosis is essential.

Treatment for phenylketonuria

It is important to remember that treatment is dietary and for life.

- A baby requires special phenylalanine-free formula milk. A small feed of breast milk can be given after the formula feed.
- Special substitute protein foods, available on prescription, form the basis of the diet from the start of weaning.
- Prescribed vitamins and minerals are taken with the protein substitute or as medicine.
- Regular blood tests are necessary to determine the level of phenylalanine.
- Normal growth and learning can be achieved by keeping to the diet. It may be possible to relax some dietary rules once brain growth is complete.
- A woman with phenylketonuria must maintain a strict low phenylalanine diet preconceptually and during pregnancy to reduce the risk of brain damage to her baby.

REMEMBER!

The diet for PKU is restrictive. Family support and encouragement from the doctors, dietician, health visitor and child-care workers is important and very necessary, especially when the child is young.

The National Society for Phenylketonuria (NSPKU, see page 266) provides support for families and dietary information.

THYROID STIMULATING HORMONE (TSH) TEST

This is a test for hypothyroidism, an endocrine disorder, in which the thyroid gland produces insufficient thyroxine for normal growth and development. The test is carried out on dried blood spots from a heel prick as for PKU on page 51.

Treatment for hypothyroidism
The missing hormone is given in medicine form and the baby's progress assessed after one year. Medication may need to be continued for life, adjusting the dose as necessary to ensure normal growth and development. The earlier the treatment starts the better. Support for the parents is crucial.

CONGENITAL DISLOCATION OF THE HIP

Congenital dislocation of the hip is more common where there is a family history of the condition. Girls are more often affected than boys. Very large babies and breech birth babies are more at risk.

A dislocated hip means that the head of the thigh bone (femur) does not sit correctly in its socket in the pelvis. Consequently, the hip joint cannot move properly. If left untreated, one leg will be shorter than the other and the child will walk with a limp. There are varying degrees of this disorder and treatment will depend on the medical diagnosis.

A special test (the modified Ortolani/Barlow manoeuvre) is used to detect hip instability or established dislocation at the examination of the newborn and the eight-week check-up. The hips are further checked for signs of dislocation at developmental reviews from 6 to 12 months.

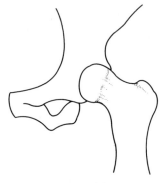

Normal hip

Dislocated hip

Congenital dislocation of the hip

Treatment for congenital dislocation of the hip

Treatment is to splint the baby's legs in a frog-like position to keep the head of the thigh bone in place. The diagram below shows a Malmo splint, one of several types that may be used.

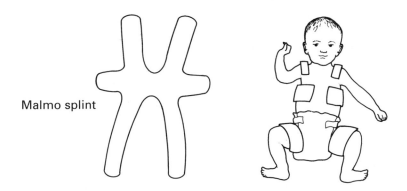

Malmo splint

Treatment for congenital dislocation of the hip

Early treatment is very successful. Sometimes an operation is needed followed by several months in plaster. Less serious conditions may be treated by folding an extra nappy between the thighs to keep them apart. X-rays are taken regularly to check progress.

'Clicky hip' describes the clicking or grating noise of the ligaments around the hip joints sometimes heard when the doctor is examining them.

KEY POINT

Although the splint may be clumsy and present some problems, it is padded and does not cause a baby pain. Always keep the baby's skin in good condition to prevent soreness and rashes. The doctor or health visitor will advise about bathing. Cuddle and care for the baby in the normal way and encourage parents to do the same. The mother may need extra help with breast-feeding.

OTHER SCREENING TESTS

Screening for sickle cell condition, thalassaemia and cystic fibrosis may be carried out if there is a family history of these disorders. Screening for hearing impairment (around the third day after birth) is routine in some hospitals.

Keeping the newborn baby warm

Keeping a baby warm, but not overheated, is essential. The amount of heat a newborn baby is able to produce depends mainly on her metabolism (how the body uses food) and a store of special brown fat around the back and neck, which can be converted into body warmth. Movement and activity also generate heat but the newborn baby does not move a lot and in some cultures remains tightly swaddled.

A newborn baby is unable to regulate her body temperature properly because:

■ the heat regulating centre in her brain is immature
■ she is unable to shiver efficiently
■ she has a large surface skin area in relation to her weight, which means she can lose heat quickly, especially when exposed to cold air or if her skin is wet, as it is at birth.

The temperature of the outside world is considerably lower than the temperature inside the womb so there is always the danger of a baby becoming cold. The baby's temperature should be checked in the first hour after birth.

To prevent chilling:

■ a baby should be gently patted dry at birth and wrapped loosely in a warm towel or blanket
■ the cot can be warmed by an overhead radiant heater prior to the baby being placed in it. (If the baby is born at home a covered hot water bottle can be used to warm the cot but **must** be removed before the baby is placed in the cot)
■ if necessary, the baby can be warmed up in an incubator for a while
■ bathing can be delayed to prevent the baby becoming cold.

KEY POINT

A large amount of heat can be lost from the baby's head.

SAFE PRACTICE

■ Always keep the baby in a constantly warm environment of 20–21°C (68–70°F) for the first few weeks. She should not be moved around between rooms with different temperatures.
■ Room temperature at night should not fall below 18°C (65°F).

- Physical contact such as cuddling provides warmth.
- All baby care routines such as bathing, topping and tailing, dressing and undressing, which involve the baby being naked, must be carried out in a warm environment.
- Bath towel and clothes should be warmed before use.
- Layers of loose light clothing will keep the heat in by providing good insulation. Cellular-type blankets are ideal coverings and can be taken off or an extra one put on according to baby's needs.
- The baby should not be taken out in cold or foggy weather.
- In cooler weather, the baby may be taken outside providing she is warm before leaving home and wearing a bonnet to prevent heat loss from her head.
- If the baby sleeps outside in her pram, she must be checked regularly.
- Heat sources such as radiators, gas, electric and open coal fires must be properly guarded, contolled and well maintained.

REMEMBER!

A baby's ability to maintain her body temperature is dependent on:

1 her own individual heat generating capacity
2 food intake
3 physical contact
4 appropriate warm clothing and bedding
5 temperature of surroundings (indoors and outdoors), especially in the early weeks.

KEY POINT

Hypothermia (see Chapter 7, Table 7.3 on page 185) and overheating are potentially dangerous conditions for a baby. To keep a baby safe and comfortable keep a wall thermometer at a constant temperature of around 20°C (68°F) day and night.

Neonatal jaundice

Jaundice in itself is not a disease, but a sign that something is wrong. The baby's skin and whites of the eyes are stained yellow due to an excess of bilirubin in the blood. Bilirubin is formed when red blood cells are broken down. It is normally removed from the bloodstream by the liver and excreted from the body in the stools. Other signs and symptoms of jaundice include: dark orange or brown urine, pale stools, vomiting, poor feeding and excessive sleepiness.

A baby with jaundice should always be seen promptly by a doctor. A high level of bilirubin in the blood can be serious and jaundice should never be ignored.

CAUSES OF JAUNDICE

There are many reasons why jaundice occurs, just three are mentioned here:

■ physiological jaundice
■ breast milk jaundice
■ rhesus blood incompatability.

Physiological jaundice

Physiological jaundice affects one in three babies in the first few days after birth until the immature liver begins to break down the bilirubin effectively. Most babies do not require any treatment. However, a baby with a high level of bilirubin in the blood is usually given phototherapy treatment. The baby is nursed naked in warm surroundings (often in an incubator) and fluorescent light with a high output of blue light is shone directly on to the baby's skin. This reduces the amount of bilirubin in the skin and superficial blood vessels. The baby is turned over at intervals so that the light can reach both the front and back. Special pads protect the baby's eyes from too much light, and the baby wears a nappy to protect the ovaries and testes. Extra fluids are offered to counteract the increased loss of body fluid. Phototherapy is continuous for two or three days. The baby's blood is tested daily for levels of bilirubin.

A mother may become anxious and tearful when her baby is receiving phototherapy. She must be reassured, and encouraged to feed, cuddle and care for her baby as normal.

Breast milk jaundice

Prolonged jaundice can be associated with breast-feeding. Temporary cessation of breast-feeding (and substituting formula milk feeds) results in the level of bilirubin falling, only to rise again when breast-feeding is continued. Jaundice may last up to three months but should not cause any ill effects and breast-feeding can continue.

Rhesus blood incompatability

This is a serious cause of jaundice but much less common today. A mother who is rhesus-negative forms antibodies in her blood, which can cause anaemia in a rhesus-positive baby. First babies are rarely affected, but to prevent problems for future babies all mothers who are rhesus-negative are given a special injection after the birth.

Infections such as hepatitis can also cause jaundice in the neonate and treatment will depend on the results of investigations.

Twins

The incidence of multiple births (twins, triplets and more) has risen dramatically since the growth in popularity of in vitro fertilisation (IVF) – 'test tube babies'. A multiple pregnancy is considered high-risk as it brings with it complications such as gestational diabetes (diabetes of pregnancy), pre-eclampsia, premature birth, low birth-weight, a high infant mortality rate and babies born with special needs.

Twinning occurs in about 1 in 90 pregnancies.

- Identical (uniovular, monozygotic) twins develop when one fertilised egg divides into two and each half becomes a separate baby. They have the same genetic make-up and blood group and are the same sex. Hair and eye colouring are also similar.
- Non-identical (binovular, dizygotic) twins develop when a woman produces two eggs at ovulation and both are fertilised. The babies may or may not be the same sex and can be as similar or unalike as any two children in a family. Non-identical twins are sometimes called fraternal twins.

A woman's chance of producing twins increases if she herself is a fraternal twin or has blood relatives who are fraternal twins. The more children she already has also increases her chances. A woman's race affects the incidence of twinning with Nigerian women having the highest rates and women from the Far East having the lowest.

KEY POINT

The use of infertility treatments, such as drugs to stimulate ovulation, and specialist techniques such as in vitro fertilisation (IVF) greatly influence a woman's chance of producing twins or more.

DIAGNOSING TWINS

Routine ultrasound scanning can diagnose twins (also triplets, quads and more) early in pregnancy, although occasionally one baby 'hides' behind another. A mother expecting twins is likely to be bigger than her dates would suggest with a larger than normal weight gain. A raised alphafeto-protein (AFP) level can indicate the presence of twins but it can also be a sign that there is something wrong with a baby, such as spina bifida, so a correct diagnosis is important in cases of a raised AFP.

Antenatal care

Antenatal care for twins is the same as for singletons (single babies). The mother is advised about diet. Vitamin, iron and folic acid tablets are usually prescribed. Anaemia is common. Minor ailments of pregnancy may be more of a problem and breathlessness, tiredness and a large, cumbersome abdomen are usual towards the end of the pregnancy. Rest is important and a stay in hospital may be advised.

Labour and birth

The babies will be born in hospital. Twins are more likely to be born pre-term (around 36 weeks). Triplets, and the rarer quadruplets and quintuplets, are likely to be very pre-term and small. Breech births and Caesarean section births are more common, although the majority of twins are born normally. Identity labels may be kept on twins a little longer than normal, especially in the case of identical twins.

KEY POINT

One twin may be much smaller and weaker than the other, because of poor nutrition in the uterus. The closer twins are to a weight of 2.5 kg (5½ lb), the less likelihood there is of complications.

CARING FOR TWINS

The problems and special needs of low birth-weight twins are the same as for single babies (see pages 62–7).

Feeding

Twins can be breast-fed successfully, so providing close physical contact between a mother and both her babies. Whether breast-fed or formula-fed, the midwife helps the mother to establish a feeding routine, which makes sure both babies get sufficient milk and are thriving. Much depends on their size, ability to suck and general health. One twin may

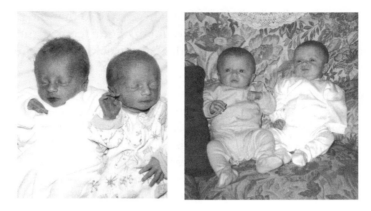

Non-identical twin boys at 3 days old and 2½ months old. At birth the babies weighed 4lb 8oz (2.04kg) and 4lb 7oz (2.01kg)

have a much stronger suck than the other. The protection against infection given by breast milk is particularly important as the probability of the babies being pre-term makes them more vulnerable to infection.

KEY POINT

Breast-feeding both babies at the same time is possible and mothers should be helped to experiment with different positions (see diagram).

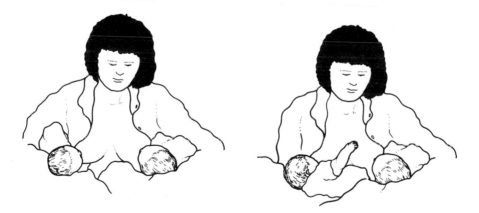

Comfortable positions for feeding twins

Formula-feeding needs much organisation. There is a lot of work involved in preparing feeds, cleaning and sterilising equipment. The cost of buying milk is high, but formula feeding has the advantage of the babies' father or another carer being able to help with the feeding.

A night-time feeding routine is necessary so that the parents do not get overtired. Twins need more frequent night feeds if they are small. It is advisable to keep a record in the early weeks of how much formula milk each baby takes.

REMEMBER!

- Twins are two separate, individual babies, not a pair, but they have the advantage of feeling close to another person from birth.
- Using terms such as 'twinnies' or 'the twins' is not appropriate. Always remember that twins have their own names, personalities and identities. Professional help and advice on caring for them should reflect this.
- Although twins will spend much of their early years sharing (parents, room, pram or buggy), being a twin should not be the most important part of their lives.
- Dressing twins alike should not be done just to draw attention to them.
- Recognising and meeting the individual needs of each twin is an important part of your role in caring for them.

DEVELOPMENTAL MILESTONES

Twins develop at a different rate, and should not be expected to reach their developmental milestones at the same time as each other. Some areas of development, such as sharing, may be in advance of their peers. Other areas may be delayed due to lack of opportunity or stimulation.

Language is commonly an area of developmental delay. For singletons, their role models for speech are usually parents and perhaps older siblings, but for a twin the strongest role model is often the other twin whose language is probably at the same level as their own. It is a mistake to think they are able to help each other with language. Twins often have a 'secret language' (cryptophasia), which only they may understand. Normal language development must take place alongside this special language. Individual time alone with the mother, carer, family members and friends helps language development, as does reading to each twin separately.

KEY POINT

Although twins may learn early about sharing and have 'common' toys, they also need toys and possessions of their own.

SIBLING RIVALRY

Older children in the family may be jealous of the attention given to the twins. They may feel left out and displaced by the new arrivals. Friends, relatives and people in the street may be quick to admire 'the twins' while ignoring an older child.

KEY POINT

If you are caring for a sibling of twins in a day care or education setting she may need extra attention and the opportunity to talk about her twin siblings with you.

SUPPORT FOR PARENTS AND CARERS OF TWINS

The community midwife, and later the health visitor, visits more frequently when the babies come home. Arrangements can be made for weighing and immunisation to be done at home. Extra help for a few weeks, from either family, friends or a home help, enables the mother to concentrate on caring for her babies. Difficulties can arise in the daily routine: which baby to feed first, to pick up first if they are both crying, how to manage the sleep routine, how to cope with shopping and using public transport. Talking to others who have been through the same experience is always helpful. TAMBA (Twins and Multiple Birth Association) listed on page 266 offers information and help. Local twins clubs networks are also a valuable source of support.

Activities

1 Talk to parents of twins and ask them:
   (a) what were the areas of greatest difficulty in the twins' first year?
   (b) what kind of help would have been appreciated most?
   (c) how did other children in the family react to the arrival of the twins?
2 You are employed as a nanny caring for newly born, bottle-fed twins. Think about how you might:
   (a) organise the preparation of feeds;
   (b) decide which baby to feed first;
   (c) manage night feeding?
3 Approximately how much per week would babies' formula feeds cost?
4 If you are caring for twins aged under one year in a day care setting, how could you help them to develop their own identities?
5 Contact the local twins club and ask about its activities.

Low birth-weight and postmaturity

LOW BIRTH-WEIGHT

A baby weighing 2.5 kg (5½ lb) or less at birth, regardless of the period of gestation, is said to be of low birth-weight (World Health Organisation 1961).

Babies may be of low birth-weight because they are:
■ pre-term – born before 37 weeks of pregnancy
■ small for gestational age (light-for-dates).

KEY POINTS

■ Some babies are both pre-term and small for gestational age.
■ Congenital abnormalities are more common in low birth-weight babies.

PRE-TERM BABIES

Reasons why babies are born pre-term include: multiple pregnancies, pre-eclampsia and medical conditions in the mother such as high blood pressure, heart disease or diabetes.

Appearance
Any of the following charateristics may be present – they will be more marked in very small babies and less marked in those born nearer to term: less than 51 cm (20 in) long; shiny, red skin; lack of fat beneath the skin; thin limbs and soft and short nails; few skin creases on soles of feet; plenty of lanugo; little or no vernix; undescended testes in males; head unusually large in proportion to body; soft skull bones; widely spaced sutures and fontanelles.

Behaviour of the pre-term baby
■ Pre-term babies tend to sleep most of the time.
■ They have weak cries.
■ Generally inactive, movements tend to be jerky. They lie in a frog-like position.
■ Cough and sucking reflexes, as well as other neonatal reflexes, are poorly developed.

Problems for pre-term babies
For babies born at 32 weeks or more the outlook is generally good. The main problems for the pre-term baby (especially those that are very small) are set out on page 63.

Breathing

Breathing problems occur because of immaturity both of the lungs and the breathing centre in the brain. Oxygen can be given by face mask or piped directly into the incubator. A baby may also be 'ventilated' (breathing is done for her through a machine). The smaller the baby the greater the risk of serious breathing problems.

Feeding

A pre-term baby needs frequent, small feeds. The sucking and swallowing reflexes, which develop around 30 to 34 weeks and are very strong in the term baby, may be weak or absent in a pre-term baby and tube feeding (via the nose to the stomach) with expressed breast milk or special formula milk may be necessary. Babies born very early may have a problem digesting and absorbing milk, as well as being unable to suck and swallow, and require special intravenous (through a vein) fluids.

KEY POINT

If a baby is able to suck and swallow, she can be offered the breast or bottle. Small babies tire easily, so alternate sucking and tube feeds (expressed breast milk if possible) may be preferable. Breast-feeding should always be encouraged as it is best for the baby and contains antibodies to help against infection.

Pre-term babies lack the store of iron that full-term babies have and are often anaemic. Multi-vitamin supplements are given daily and iron supplement is started at about four weeks.

Temperature control

The heat regulating centre in the brain is immature in the term baby, but much more so in the pre-term baby. Lack of body fat, especially brown fat, and a large skin surface area in relation to body weight, puts a pre-term baby at risk of hypothermia.

An incubator or an 'infant care centre', in which the baby is nursed under a radiant heater, provides a constantly warm environment.

KEY POINTS

- A pre-term baby of adequate weight and well enough to be cared for at home, should stay close to her mother at all times in a constantly warm, draught-free environment. The room temperature should not drop below 20°C (68°F).
- Clothing must be light, warm and non-irritating to the skin, allowing her freedom to move and breathe easily.

Infection

The risk of infection in the pre-term baby is very great. Her immune system is immature and her ability to make antibodies is poor.

KEY POINT

Good personal hygiene practice, particularly hand washing, is essential for hospital staff, carers and visitors. Anyone with a cough, cold or skin or bowel infection must neither care for nor visit a pre-term baby.

Any sign of infection in the baby is treated promptly with antibiotics as she can become seriously ill very quickly. A pre-term baby can be immunised against infectious diseases according to the Immunisation Schedule, but whooping cough immunisation should not be given to a baby who has had seizures.

Jaundice

Any jaundice may be treated with phototherapy (see page 56).

Care of pre-term babies

Some pre-term babies may be healthy and well enough to be kept near their mothers. Others will be nursed in incubators in a Special Care Baby Unit (SCBU) or, in the case of very sick babies and those with serious breathing problems, a Neonatal Intensive Care Unit.

Incubators are special enclosed cots with the temperature and humidity inside them carefully controlled to resemble as closely as possible the conditions of the womb. Special 'portholes' allow babies to be fed and cared for without being taken out. The baby is usually nursed naked, often lying on sheepskin for comfort and warmth, so that any change in her condition can be easily noticed.

As well as the round-the-clock monitoring procedures in these units, gentle cleansing of the skin, especially the nappy area and parts of the body where tubes are attached with sticky tape, is carried out within the incubator. Bathing is delayed until the baby is big enough and well enough to be transferred to a ward nursery or to go home.

As with term babies, a pre-term baby initially loses weight, but providing her ability to digest and absorb nutrients is satisfactory, birth-weight is usually regained in a few weeks.

Mother–baby bonding

Inevitably, some pre-term babies miss much of the close contact with their mother and other family members that term babies have, but everything possible is done to limit separation and help a mother to establish a relationship with her baby. It may be possible for the mother to hold baby for a moment immediately after birth. However, breathing problems and the risk of chilling may mean baby is transferred quickly to the Special or Intensive Care Unit. Photographs of the baby are taken, which the mother can have straight away. As soon as possible, the mother is taken to see her baby and to touch, stroke and talk to her through the incubator. Depending on baby's size and general condition, the mother may be able to feed and care for her baby.

KEY POINTS

- Siblings, as well as parents, are welcome in Special Care Units, and are encouraged to touch and hold their new brother or sister after they have washed their hands.
- Leaving a small baby behind in hospital or the baby being transferred to a neonatal unit some distance from home, can be extremely stressful for the family. Parents particularly need help and support at this time from the medical and nursing staff, also from friends and family.

Going home

Most pre-term babies can go home when they weigh about 2.5 kg (5½ lb) although, if they are feeding well and the mother is confident about caring for the baby, they are often allowed home at a lower weight.

KEY POINT

Preparation of parents and siblings for home-coming will lessen anxiety and possible sibling jealousy.

While it is important to guard against infection and keep the baby warm and adequately fed, over-concern and special treatment should be avoided as it may lead to behavioural problems later on. Once a small baby is thriving, she can be cared for just the same as other babies. The baby's progress is closely followed up by the family doctor and health visitor. Some areas have special Premature Baby Visitors who visit daily for a while to advise and reassure parents on their baby's care and progress. Development is linked to the expected, rather than the actual, date of birth and this is taken into account when plotting growth measurements on the baby's percentile chart and reviewing her progress.

KEY POINT

A pre-term baby will usually 'catch up' by about two years of age. Hospital check-ups and reviews at the child health clinic continue for some time. The smaller the baby the greater the risk of vision and hearing problems, smaller stature and learning delay.

SMALL FOR GESTATIONAL AGE BABIES

A baby whose birth-weight is below the ninth percentile line (see Chapter 6, pages 150–2) for gestational age is said to be 'small for gestational age'. This means growth before birth has been limited. Reasons why babies are born small for gestational age are not always known but can include: maternal smoking and drinking in pregnancy; poor nutrition in the womb; and poor maternal social and economic conditions. Congenital disorders such as Down's syndrome and infections in the womb, such as rubella, may also be causes.

KEY POINT

Often, the babies are small for genetic reasons and are perfectly healthy.

Appearance of small for gestational age babies

At birth the baby may appear obviously undernourished. She is long in proportion to her weight. She lacks body fat and has difficulty in keeping warm. She may look wizened with an anxious expression. Her skin may be cracked, dry and loose, possibly with meconium staining. (A baby that becomes distressed in the womb will open her bowels. The meconium mixes with the amniotic fluid and stains the baby's skin, nails and cord green.)

KEY POINT

Unless the baby is also pre-term she is unlikely to have breathing problems, but she is prone to infection. Most babies who are small for gestational weight spend time in the Special Care Unit where they are observed and cared for in the warmth of an incubator.

The greatest need for these babies is food in order to put on weight. There is usually no problem with the sucking and swallowing reflexes and breast-feeding should be encouraged. The baby's developmental progress depends on how badly her growth pattern has been affected by the time she is born. Some children may later show signs of clumsiness and learning difficulties and may always be smaller than their peers but most catch up by two to three years of age.

POSTMATURITY

A baby born at or after 42 weeks gestation is said to be post-term or post-mature. A pregnancy continuing beyond the expected date carries some risks. Post-term, the placenta 'ages' and the baby may not receive adequate food and oxygen. Once 42 weeks is reached the placenta can fail rapidly, causing foetal distress. Inhalation of meconium may occur, possibly leading to pneumonia in the early days of life. The incidence of perinatal deaths rises in postmature babies. When a mother has gone 'past her dates' or there is doubt over the accuracy of her dates, a decision is made by the obstetrician whether and when to induce labour. Ultrasound scanning, to accurately date a baby's age, makes the decision easier and reduces the risk of the baby being born postmature.

The appearance of the postmature baby

Her skin is dry, cracked and peeling, possibly with meconium staining of nails, skin and cord. There is usually no vernix present. Her face is thin with a worried expression. The baby often appears alert, restless and hungry for feeds. Her feet may show signs of talipes (club feet).

Care of the postmature baby

The postmature baby may need some time in the Special Care Unit before being well enough to go home. She requires frequent feeding in the early days after birth and should be breast-fed if possible. Antibiotics are given if there is any sign of chest infection.

Bereavement

Inevitably some babies are stillborn, while others die soon after birth or later on in infancy. Whether the death is sudden or expected the loss of a baby is deeply traumatic and almost unbearable for the parents and other family members. It produces a most profound grief and may change the family for ever. Parents feel that part of them has died and that nothing can replace that missing part. Initial emotions felt by parents include shock, pain, numbness, disbelief and perhaps anger. Parents who have lost one of their twins, triplets or more, may feel the loss is worse than losing a single baby, as the other babies are there as a constant reminder. Inappropriate remarks such as 'Well at least you've still got another one' are still encountered by bereaved parents.

Parents inevitably endure further stress when the police and coroner are involved, as routinely occurs in the case of a sudden infant death.

Doctors, midwives, staff in Accident and Emergency departments, in Neonatal Care units and on paediatric wards are sensitive to the needs of bereaved parents, and offer sympathetic support and help, quietly offering them the opportunity to spend private time with their baby, holding her, saying goodbye, taking photographs and hand and foot prints and dressing her in particular clothes. Many parents find it helpful to assist in arranging the baby's funeral according to their particular beliefs or religious customs.

Parents, especially mothers, need constant memories and reminders of their baby. They need to talk about her, look at photographs, fondle a lock of hair or touch and smell clothes she used to wear. Family events such as birthdays, anniversaries and holidays emphasise the loss and absence of their baby.

Relationships within the immediate family may become strained. Parents may find it difficult to express their grief and feelings to each other, siblings may show their sadness through disturbed sleep, bed-wetting, poor appetite, attention seeking behaviour and poor school work. A surviving twin may be over-protected by parents who fear he or she may die as well. Twins and other multiples also suffer from the loss of their brother or sister, and a twin, in particular, may take a long time to come to terms with being a lone twin.

Early Years workers in day care settings and nannies in private homes are in a unique position to help siblings come to terms with the loss of their brother or sister. Extra one-to-one time and support, encouraging them to talk about their loss or express their feelings through drawing and painting activities or through play in the home corner can be beneficial experiences for a bereaved child.

Counselling is available for all the family. Bereavement counsellors are in agreement that mourning and grieving are essential to the healing process and that parents should be helped to mourn and grieve in their own way and in their own time. Support groups can put parents in touch with others who have suffered in a similar way.

The Child Bereavement Trust, which produces helpful videos and books for grieving families, and the Twins and Multiple Births Association are listed on page 265–6.

QUICK CHECK

1 (a) Name the scoring system for assessing a baby's condition at birth.
   (b) Which **five** vital signs are assessed?
2 What do you understand by:
   (a) moulding?
   (b) a caput succedaneum?
   (c) a cephalhaematoma?
3 Describe the anterior fontanelle.
4 Why is the inside of a baby's mouth checked during the examination of the newborn?
5 Describe:
   (a) a mongolian spot
   (b) milia
   (c) stork marks.
6 By what age have the primitive reflexes largely disappeared? Describe the grasp reflex.
7 What do you understand by:
   (a) prone?
   (b) supine?
8 Name **three** screening tests of the newborn baby.
9 What are the signs of neonatal jaundice?
10 Which area of development is often delayed in twins?
11 Give the definition of a low birth-weight baby.
12 Name **three** problems typically associated with low birth-weight.
13 Why is a newborn baby unable to regulate its body temperature?
14 What is the ideal temperature for a baby's room in the early weeks after birth?
15 As a worker in a day care setting, how could you help a child whose baby sibling has recently and suddenly died?

3 PERSONAL CARE ROUTINES

> **This chapter covers:**
> - **Functions of the skin**
> - **Bathing a baby**
> - **Topping and tailing a baby**
> - **Nappy changing and nappy rash**
> - **Skin care in the sun**
> - **Common skin conditions and infections in infancy**
> - **Teeth and dental care**

Functions of the skin

The skin covers and protects the body. It helps to regulate body temperature and gets rid of waste products through sweat. It is sensitive to touch. In the presence of sunlight the skin synthesises (makes) vitamin D. Vitamin D works with the minerals calcium and phosphorus to form strong bones and teeth. The skin also produces the brown pigment melanin, which gives colour to the skin and hair. Large amounts of melanin are produced in naturally dark people.

KEY POINT

Clean, healthy, undamaged skin is one of nature's defences against infection. Because a newborn baby has little immunity against infection skin care is very important.

Adults who care for babies are responsible for keeping them clean and comfortable. Cleaning and refreshing a baby's skin removes germs, as well as sticky milk, urine and faeces, vomit, excess sebum (grease), dust and grime. These are all irritants that make the baby's skin sore.

SKIN CARE ROUTINES

Skin care routines include bathing, 'topping and tailing', hair and nail care. They are carried out according to:
- a baby's needs

- the wishes of the baby's parents
- cultural or religious preferences
- medical advice, for example, if the baby has eczema or another skin condition.

KEY POINTS

- In day care settings a baby's personal care routines should be undertaken by her designated carer or key worker (see Chapter 9, page 216). In most settings disposable gloves are worn when attending to a baby's nappy during bathing, topping and tailing and nappy changing routines.
- At all times handle the baby gently, confidently and securely.

Carers should aim to establish personal care routines for young babies that are fun and encourage cleanliness from an early age. The skin care routines identified in the text below provide opportunities for enjoyable and intimate exchanges between the baby and her carer. Always maintain eye contact with the baby, talk to her, tickle her, laugh and sing. Action rhymes and songs that name parts of the body are fun as well as a learning experience. Older babies enjoy a range of interesting and colourful bath toys. Make sure you allow time for a baby to kick and exercise freely with her nappy off.

Activity
Make a list of action rhymes and songs particularly suitable for babies during skin care routines.

SAFE PRACTICE

Because infection can spread rapidly, especially via the hands, carers must pay particular attention to personal hygiene and hand washing routines. In particular, always wash your hands:

- before handling a baby
- before preparing babies' feeds and meals
- after changing a baby's nappy or attending to her nasal care
- after cleaning up body fluids
- after using the toilet.

KEY POINT

Hand washing means washing your hands and scrubbing your nails with soap and water, not just running them under the tap.

Bathing a baby

BENEFITS OF BATHING

Bathing:
- cleans and refreshes the skin
- provides pleasurable contact time and opportunity for meaningful interaction (talking, smiling, eye contact) between the baby and her carer
- gives the baby opportunity to kick and exercise her limbs
- often calms a restless or fretful baby
- affords the carer the opportunity to observe the condition of the baby's skin and to note any rashes, spots, marks or bruises (see also Child protection, Chapter 9, pages 228–34).

ESSENTIAL PRINCIPLES

- Remember which are:
  - the baby's delicate areas – eyes, nose, umbilical cord, genitalia
  - the baby's vulnerable areas – ears and skin folds.
- Always wash and dry carefully around the neck, behind the ears, under the arms, behind the knees, in the groins and between the fingers and toes.
- A baby's skin should be gently patted dry, not rubbed, using a warm towel. Make sure the above areas are dried properly to prevent the baby becoming sore.
- Use toiletries such as soap, baby-bath preparations, shampoo, oils and moisturisers, and barrier creams that are recommended for a baby's skin.
- If a baby is allergic to perfumes and additives use simple, unperfumed products, or those recommended by the doctor.

KEY POINTS

- Discuss with the baby's parents the toiletries they prefer you to use and how to care for and groom their baby's hair. You may be asked to use a certain kind of shampoo or moisturiser, or a liquid baby bath preparation rather than soap.
- Talcum powder should not be used. A baby can inhale particles of the 'sprinkled' powder, possibly resulting in choking or chest infection. A baby with asthma or other respiratory disorder could become seriously ill. If parents particularly wish you to use talcum powder, place a little on your hands and gently smooth it on to the baby's well-dried skin.

Cultural preferences

Always respect cultural preferences. Black skin tends to be dry, and a moisturiser such as cocoa butter or a petroleum jelly preparation is generally applied after bathing. Excessive skin dryness is common especially in winter and daily massaging with oils (see Baby massage and Safe practice below) can lessen this condition, which is sometimes mistaken for eczema. The African-Caribbean tradition of combing, plaiting and weaving hair can be seen even in very young babies. Muslim babies have their heads shaved within the first 40 days of birth.

SAFE PRACTICE

Safe practice at bathtime includes measures to prevent both accidents and infection.

To prevent accidents

- When carrying or caring for a baby:
  - do not wear bulky, dangling jewellery
  - wear comfortable, supportive, low-heeled shoes
  - keep your nails trimmed
- prepare the room, equipment and clean clothes before attending to the baby. Once you have picked up a baby and started the bathing procedure, you cannot leave her unattended to get something you have forgotten
- always put cold water in the bath before hot water. Test the water temperature with your bare elbow – it should feel pleasantly warm. Alternatively, a special 'baby bath' thermometer can be used. Scalding causes a baby severe pain, damages her skin (with the consequent risk of infection) and may cause death
- the use of cotton buds in any aspect of baby care is dangerous practice. Do not use them to clean a baby's ears, nose or umbilicus. Dry or moistened cotton wool swabs are safer
- never leave a baby alone in the bath. Babies can drown in just 1 cm (½ in) of water
- guard the baby at all times with your body while she is on a changing mat on a raised surface
- keep the baby's head well supported during the bathing procedure.

To prevent infection

- Before attending to the baby wash your hands thoroughly, make sure your nails are unvarnished and your hair is tidy.
- Wet and soiled disposable nappies and used cotton wool swabs from eye, cord and nasal care must be placed in a lidded bucket or bin or secured in a tie-up bag for later disposal. Never flush them down the toilet or

leave them lying around. Place reusable nappies (see Chapter 8, page 198) in a lidded bucket ready for laundering in the washing machine. Soiled nappies should be soaked in a sanitising solution (check manufacturer's instructions on container) before being put in the washing machine. Soiled and wet nappy liners can be flushed down the lavatory. Wash and disinfect changing mats after each use.

■ A carer with diarrhoea or vomiting should not be working with babies until he or she has recovered.

A young baby does not have to be bathed every day. Limiting bathing to two or three times a week and 'topping and tailing' (see page 82) on the other days is an acceptable routine. Find out from the parents the best time to bath the baby and how she reacts to water. Babies can feel insecure when unwrapped and undressed and should be handled gently, with confidence and care. Bathing can be done at any time of the day but immediately after a feed is not a good idea as the baby may be sick.

REMEMBER!

Remember, normal washing and drying over the fontanelle area will not cause any harm.

PREPARATION OF THE ROOM

The room (or bathing area) must be warm, not less than 20°C (68°F) with the windows closed and no draughts. Make sure you have all the equipment to hand. A baby bath placed on its own stand or on a safe, firm surface makes bathing easy. A baby can also be bathed in a basin or sink provided the taps are securely turned off and covered, to prevent her hitting against them or receiving a burn or scald. Operating at ground level by placing the baby bath inside the empty big bath, or putting the baby bath on the floor, are other options.

Equipment needed
Baby bath; thermometer (optional); chair (if sitting to bath baby); waterproof baby-changing mat; waterproof or towelling apron; lidded bins, buckets or tie-bags for used nappy, swabs and clothes; clean clothes and nappy; warmed towel; toiletries; cool boiled water; cotton wool swabs; brush and comb; and nail scissors. If the baby is bottle-fed the feed should be ready for after her bath.

Activity

1 Before you bath a baby what information will you need to know from her parent or carer?

2 What **personal** hygiene and safety precautions would you take **before** you bath a baby?

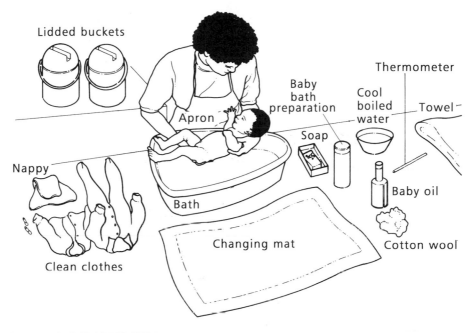

Equipment for bath time

Procedure

■ Having prepared for the baby's bath, put on the apron and wash your hands.

■ Fill the bath, remembering the safety precautions. A liquid baby bath preparation (not bubble bath), or baby soap can be used. Undress the baby down to her nappy, either on your lap or on the changing mat, and wrap her in a warmed towel. Place used clothes in a bin, bucket or tie-bag. Follow the steps for bathing baby as shown in the diagram on pages 76–8.

BATHING BABY: STEP-BY-STEP

STEP 1: FACE
- Wipe each eye gently using separate cotton wool swabs moistened in cooled, boiled water. Dry carefully with a clean swab. Always wipe from inside corner to outer edge of eye in one movement. (If you wipe from the outside to the inside corner there is a risk of infection spreading from one eye to the other.)

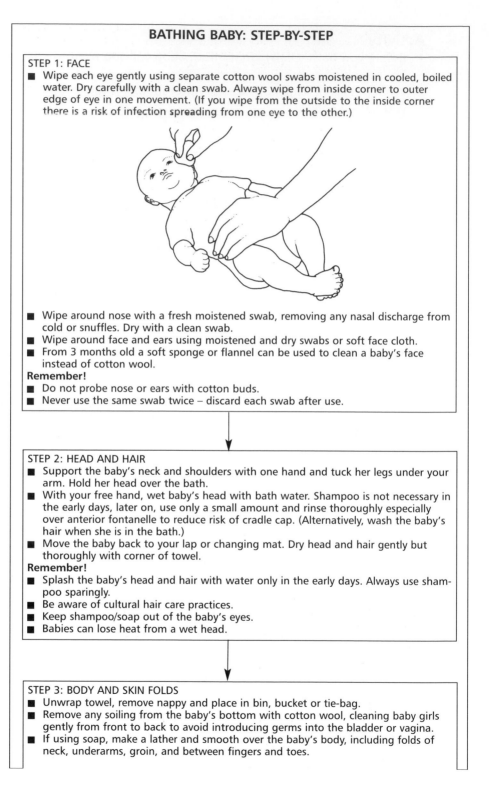

- Wipe around nose with a fresh moistened swab, removing any nasal discharge from cold or snuffles. Dry with a clean swab.
- Wipe around face and ears using moistened and dry swabs or soft face cloth.
- From 3 months old a soft sponge or flannel can be used to clean a baby's face instead of cotton wool.

Remember!
- Do not probe nose or ears with cotton buds.
- Never use the same swab twice – discard each swab after use.

STEP 2: HEAD AND HAIR
- Support the baby's neck and shoulders with one hand and tuck her legs under your arm. Hold her head over the bath.
- With your free hand, wet baby's head with bath water. Shampoo is not necessary in the early days, later on, use only a small amount and rinse thoroughly especially over anterior fontanelle to reduce risk of cradle cap. (Alternatively, wash the baby's hair when she is in the bath.)
- Move the baby back to your lap or changing mat. Dry head and hair gently but thoroughly with corner of towel.

Remember!
- Splash the baby's head and hair with water only in the early days. Always use shampoo sparingly.
- Be aware of cultural hair care practices.
- Keep shampoo/soap out of the baby's eyes.
- Babies can lose heat from a wet head.

STEP 3: BODY AND SKIN FOLDS
- Unwrap towel, remove nappy and place in bin, bucket or tie-bag.
- Remove any soiling from the baby's bottom with cotton wool, cleaning baby girls gently from front to back to avoid introducing germs into the bladder or vagina.
- If using soap, make a lather and smooth over the baby's body, including folds of neck, underarms, groin, and between fingers and toes.

- Support the baby's neck, shoulders and upper arm furthest from you with one hand and forearm. With other hand support bottom and legs. Lift her into bath (see illustration on page 75). Release hand supporting her bottom and legs and rinse soap from her body paying attention to skin folds.

- If using baby bath preparation, wash baby with massage movements, again remembering skin folds.
- Allow a short time for kicking and splashing, but avoid chilling.
- Lift baby out of bath using same manoeuvre as for lifting her in. Wrap her in a warm towel on your lap or changing mat.
- Pat her dry, especially between the fingers and toes and in the skin folds. Remove wet towel.

Remember!
- Safe practice: water temperature, lift baby correctly, avoid chilling.
- If bathing a baby in a day care setting, put on disposable latex gloves before removing the baby's nappy. Gently clean any soiling from the baby's bottom, then remove and dispose of your gloves.

STEP 4: GENITALIA
- Leave a baby boy's foreskin alone other than to gently make sure it is dry. Any attempt to pull it back may cause pain, bleeding and possibly infection.

STEP 5: UMBILICAL CORD
- Gently dry cord area after bath. Sterile 'wipes' may be provided by midwife.
- Cord must be kept dry and free from irritation of clothing or wet nappy.

Remember!
- Cord infection can be serious and requires medical attention.

STEP 6: OIL, MOISTURISER AND CREAM
- Baby oil or moisturiser may be massaged into skin.
- Barrier cream applied to the baby's bottom will guard against nappy rash.

Remember!
- Dangers of talcum powder (see page 72).

STEP 7: DRESSING
- Dress the baby in clean clothes and nappy.
- Groom hair.
- Trim nails when necessary, with parents' permission, using blunt-ended scissors. If baby is scratching face, use cotton scratch mittens.

Remember!
- If fastening a nappy with a safety pin make sure the pin is securely closed. (See nappy changing on page 82.)

BATHING AN OLDER BABY

At this age (six months to one year), a baby will be spending more time on the floor and making progress with her motor development. She will become grubby and sticky. Topping and tailing in the morning and an evening bath are probably the best routines. At around six to seven months she will progress to the big bath, giving her room to kick and splash. Kneel on the floor rather than bend down, to attend to her. Always be gentle and reassuring particularly if a baby does not seem too keen on the water.

Find out from parents:
- if the baby prefers to sit or lie supported in the water;
- whether she enjoys her bath and which are her favourite bath-time toys;
- if she minds having her hair washed and the best procedure for washing her hair. The use of a plastic 'halo', or face mask, keeps water off a baby's face, but if she is still frightened a dampened flannel or sponge can be used to keep her hair clean until she loses her fear.

Maintain the principles and safe practice of skin care mentioned earlier in the chapter and in addition:
- place a rubber safety mat on the bottom of the bath – it will help a baby to feel safe and secure;
- keep the water shallow or the baby will float;
- make sure the hot tap is securely turned off – taps are an attraction and should be covered with a cloth during bathtime, especially the hot one;
- keep soap out of reach – it tastes nasty and will sting her eyes;
- wash the baby's hair with a non-sting shampoo;
- use a soft nail brush to clean a baby's nails;
- if a baby is frightened by the big bath, continue to use a baby bath or sink, or keep to a routine of an all-over wash until she feels more secure.

As a baby gets older she will become increasingly active, kicking, twisting and trying to stand. Always be ready with a steadying hand and supervise her at all times. **Never leave her alone in the bath even for a second.**

Bath time should be fun for both the baby and carer. Water play with floating and pouring toys (they can be made from safe household objects) provides enjoyment and stimulation. A baby may be happy in the big bath with an adult.

By 11 months a baby will have progressed to the 'big bath'

REMEMBER!

- Change a baby's clothes regularly.
- Wash and groom her hair according to parental wishes. Keep her hair brush and comb clean by washing them in hot, soapy water, rinse well and dry.
- Clean and trim her nails as necessary.

- Launder towels and face cloths daily.
- Dispose of nappies, used cotton wool swabs and tissues (and gloves, if used), safely and securely.
- Wash a baby's hands before and after meals.

MASSAGE

Massage is an ancient, tactile form of healing, which uses flowing, stroking movements (not rubbing) over the body and limbs, and light circular movements over the head, to relieve stress and tension and promote relaxation and emotional calm. Infant massage after birth, and throughout infancy, is a well-established routine in many countries, for example, in Africa, Central and South America and across Asia. Touch is an important part of a baby's emotional, social and physical development. Newborn babies enjoy being touched and stroked and to feel their skin being caressed by their parents' or carer's hands. A gentle, 'light touch' massage can be a soothing and pleasurable sensory experience for babies at any time, but may be particularly beneficial and relaxing after a bath, before bedtime for those who have difficulty in settling to sleep, or whenever babies are distressed, irritable, lonely or crying. It also provides the opportunity for meaningful and totally focused interaction between the person giving the massage and the baby.

SAFE PRACTICE

- Make sure the room is warm (the baby will be uncovered), and warmed, soft towels are to hand.
- Remove any bulky jewellery.
- Check nails are trimmed and clean.
- Do not give a baby a massage just after a feed.
- Oil on the baby's skin will make her slippery. Always wrap her up in a towel when lifting her up after a massage.
- Never use aromatherapy massage (see Chapter 4, page 109) on a baby.
- Do not use massage on an unwell or sick baby without seeking medical advice.
- Make sure the oil you use does not contain nut products, as a baby may be allergic to them.

While professional paediatric massage therapists use many different techniques, just the use of simple, light, stroking movements over baby's body and limbs can be both comforting and calming. The use of a little ordinary baby oil, warmed in your hands before you massage the baby, helps to maintain smooth movements over the baby's skin. Lay the baby on a warmed towel on a safe, firm surface. Keep her covered in a warm towel, apart from the part of her body being massaged.

KEY POINTS

- If at any time a baby becomes distressed or appears unhappy discontinue the massage.
- Always make sure you have the parents' permission before you give a baby a massage.

Activity
Find out as much as you can about the benefits and techniques of baby massage through:
1 reading different baby and child-care books;
2 talking to parents who practise the technique;
3 discussing the practice of baby massage with your colleagues from different cultures, both in college and in your work setting.

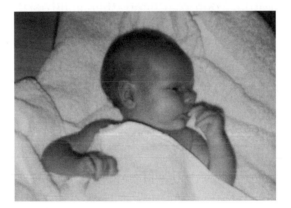

Keep a baby warm and appropriately covered when giving a massage

Activities
1 Watch a baby being bathed, carefully noting the sequence of the procedure. Observe and write down his or her reactions to bathing.
2 Bath a doll following the procedures set out in this chapter.
3 (a) Think about, and write down, the differences between bathing an 8-week-old baby and a 10-month-old baby.
   (b) What learning opportunities does bath time provide for a baby?
4 In how many ways do babies 'experience water' in the course of a typical day?

Topping and tailing

Topping and tailing is the procedure of cleaning a baby's face, hands and bottom only. It is a simple way of keeping a young baby clean and fresh instead of, or between, baths. Always remain calm, gentle and unhurried when changing and dressing the baby.

EQUIPMENT NEEDED

Make sure you have the following equipment to hand before you pick up a baby.
- Waterproof baby-changing mat; cooled boiled water (for eye care in first three months); cotton wool swabs; disposable gloves (if in day care); apron; lidded bins or buckets, or tie-bags for soiled nappy, used swabs and clothes; warmed towel; bowl of warm water; soap; creams (if used); clean clothes; and nappy.

Procedure
- Put on apron. Wash your hands then gently lay the baby down on the changing mat.
- Remove the baby's clothes down to her vest and nappy. Place them in a bucket or bin if they are to be changed.
- Wrap the baby securely in the towel.
- Clean and gently dry her eyes, nose, face and ears as for bathing. Take care to pat dry behind her ears and between the skin folds under her chin.
- Unwrap the towel and wipe and dry the baby's hands, not forgetting in between the fingers.
- (Put on gloves, if necessary). Remove her nappy, carefully wiping faeces away with a clean corner of the nappy, and place it in a bucket or tie-bag. Soiled and wet nappy liners can be flushed down the toilet.
- Clean the baby's bottom, and all the skin folds, with moistened cotton wool swabs or soap and water and a flannel, or baby wipes if parents prefer them. Avoid a baby girl's vaginal area. Clean around a baby boy's foreskin but never attempt to pull it back. Rinse well with cotton wool, or flannel. Pat all skin areas dry, remove gloves and apply cream. Dress the baby in clean nappy and clothes.

Nappy changing and nappy rash

NAPPY CHANGING

Nappy-changing trolleys or units, with in-built changing mat, are widely available and popular. However, a single waterproof changing mat is equally suitable as a nappy changing surface. Most babies wear disposable nappies rather than reusable ones. Some reusable nappies have popper or velcro fastenings, but others fasten with a safety pin, which must always be closed properly. Make sure waterproof pants or ties fit cosily but not tightly.

The nappy changing procedure is as stated in 'Topping and tailing' on page 82. The routine requires the same level of care for the baby's skin, and measures to prevent an accident or infection, as for bathing and topping and tailing, and as far as possible should be in accordance with parental wishes.

A baby's nappy should be changed whenever it is wet or soiled and always checked before and after a feed or mealtime and before a baby is settled to sleep. Make sure the nappy fits snugly – there are variations in the design of disposable nappies depending on the age and weight of the baby. Cream or powder on your hands will prevent the tabs from fastening securely

KEY POINT

- Never show disapproval at a soiled nappy.
- Do not put a baby down to sleep in a wet or soiled nappy.
- Seek further advice if a baby:
  - has consistently dry, or only slightly damp nappies – it could indicate that the baby is dehydrated or unwell
  - passes an abnormal stool (see page 85);
  - has any mark or rash on her body.

Carer interaction during nappy changing

Changing a baby's nappy provides the opportunity for close, intimate interaction and communication between a baby and her carer. Do not rush this routine. Remember to smile, talk and sing to the baby. Allow her the opportunity to exercise her legs. Cuddle her when the routine is completed.

REMEMBER!

- Always wash your hands after completing bathing, topping and tailing or nappy changing routines.
- Clean the changing mat with hot soapy water, or an antiseptic solution, after every use.

SAFE PRACTICE

Never leave a baby alone on the changing mat.

NAPPY RASH

Even the best cared for baby can get nappy rash. It is uncomfortable for her, can cause stinging and pain and, if the skin is broken, there is a risk of infection. Extra absorbent disposable nappies keep the skin drier and may help to prevent nappy rash. The areas typically affected by nappy rash are: bottom, groins, genital area, upper thighs, lower abdomen and lower back.

Causes of nappy rash
- Faulty washing technique of bottom and/or nappies.
- Soiled and wet nappies left on too long.
- Diarrhoea.
- Infections such as thrush or chickenpox.
- Eczema and seborrhoeic dermatitis.
- Reaction to creams, detergents, wet wipes or nappy liners.
- Concentrated urine due to insufficient fluid intake.
- Tightly-fitting plastic pants.

Two particular types of nappy rash are:

- thrush (monilial) dermatitis
- ammonia dermatitis.

Thrush (monilial) dermatitis
Thrush dermatitis is a common cause of nappy rash in small babies, especially those who are breast-fed or who have had (or whose mother has had) antibiotics. It is caused by a yeast fungus that lives naturally in many parts of the body including the vagina, and babies may become infected during birth. Dirty feeding bottles and teats are another source of the infection. A baby may have oral thrush at the same time. The nappy rash is pink/red and pimply and is found in the moist folds of the groin and upper thighs, as well as around the anus and genital area.

Treatment
Prescribed anti-fungal cream should be applied lightly at each nappy change. The thrush organism thrives on zinc and castor oil barrier cream so it should not be used.

If a baby has oral thrush, a gel or medicine will be prescribed. The mother may be treated as well.

Ammonia dermatitis
This is the most usual type of nappy rash once a baby is sleeping for longer periods and her nappy is not changed so frequently. It is more

common in bottle-fed babies as their stools are alkaline. (The stools of breast-fed babies are acid.) Urine contains the waste product urea, while stools contain bacteria: urea + bacteria = ammonia (alkaline) = burning. The rash starts in the genital area and can spread to the whole nappy area. Because ammonia burns, the skin appears inflamed and ulcerated, and the baby is in pain.

Treatment
- Skin care: wash the affected area with warm water and mild soap, gently pat dry and let the baby lie on a nappy with her bottom exposed to warm air. Use a barrier cream or prescribed treatment – make sure the skin is quite dry first. Change the baby's nappy frequently, including at night.
- Nappy care: use a non-biological powder for washing reusable nappies. Add white distilled vinegar (acid) to the final rinsing water to neutralise the alkaline ammonia (30 ml/1 oz vinegar to 4.8 litres/8 pints warm water), then wring lightly and hang out on the line to dry.

PREVENTION OF NAPPY RASH

- Change nappies frequently; preferably use disposable nappies.
- Wash and dry the nappy area gently, and apply barrier cream (or prescribed cream) to well-dried skin.
- Allow a baby time to kick and exercise freely without her nappy on. Make sure the room is warm.
- Use a non-biological (enzyme-free) washing powder when laundering reusable nappies. Rinse thoroughly and dry in the fresh air when possible.
- Identify the cause and treat appropriately.

ABNORMAL STOOLS

The typical, normal stools of breast-fed and bottle-fed babies are described on page 135. Some abnormal stools include diarrhoea, constipation and blood-stained stools.

Diarrhoea
Diarrhoea describes loose, watery, smelly stools. Never ignore it, as a baby can quickly become dehydrated and seriously ill (see also Chapter 7, page 183, Summary of ailments in babies).

Constipation
Constipation describes small, infrequent, hard, greenish brown stools that are difficult and painful to pass. The cause is often incorrect diet and

under-feeding. Health visitors and child-care workers can help and advise parents on the types and variety of food their baby should be eating. Other causes will need specialist medical help.

Blood-stained stool
Sometimes, a normal stool is streaked with a little fresh blood. It may indicate an anal crack (fissure), possibly due to constipation and straining. The baby should be seen by a doctor.

KEY POINT

Some foods and medicines may make the stools a different colour. Reddish stools may be due to rosehip syrup or blackcurrant drinks, or eating beetroot. Medicine for threadworms may cause a bright red stool. Iron medicine can make the stools black. Pale, bulky, fatty, smelly stools usually indicate poor absorption of fat in the diet.

TOILET TRAINING

Control of the bladder and bowels is achieved when:
■ the nervous system is sufficiently mature to allow a child to recognise the need to use the potty;
■ a child has the ability to control the appropriate muscles.

There is wide variation in the age at which a child is clean and dry. Around 18 months to 2 years may be the right time to start introducing the potty. Toilet training is detailed in most child-care text books that cover the second and third years of life.

Skin care in the sun

A baby's skin can very easily burn, especially on a sunny and windy day when sun can be very hot, so remember the following principles.
■ Never expose a baby to direct sunlight.
■ Dress a baby in cool, loose, cotton clothing and a full-brimmed sun hat. Make sure her neck, tops of the arms and thighs are covered.
■ Use a total sun-block cream for babies on all exposed skin areas.
■ Place a baby's pram in the shade (but remember a baby's skin can also burn in the shade), watch as the sun moves around and change the pram position accordingly.
■ Use the pram or pushchair canopy when a baby is outdoors.

- Cars can become like ovens on a hot day – make sure there is a cooling draught through the car.
- Never leave a baby alone to sleep in a car, especially on a hot day.

- The above precautions also apply to babies with darker skin tones as they also need protection from the sun.
- To keep a baby cool: keep her indoors when the sun is hottest; do not over-wrap her; open the windows; use a fan; and offer her extra drinks of cooled boiled water.

REMEMBER!

Heatstroke can be very serious in babies. It can occur without sunburn. A baby with heatstroke looks flushed, with dry, hot skin and a very high temperature. Urgent medical care is essential. In the mean time tepid sponging and use of a fan can help to cool the baby, but avoid very rapid cooling.

Common skin conditions

Some common skin conditions and infections to which babies are susceptible are listed in the following tables (see pages 88–90). If you are at all concerned about the condition of a baby's skin, make sure you talk to the parents or day care supervisor. When caring for a baby with a skin condition always remember to wash your hands thoroughly before and after carrying out any treatment.

REMEMBER!

To maintain good practice when caring for a baby's skin remember:
- your own personal hygiene especially hand washing
- the daily routines for babies of bathing, 'topping and tailing', nappy changing, hair and nail care
- parental, cultural and religious preferences and practices
- how to prevent sunburn and sunstroke

and to:

- use appropriate toiletries;
- observe a baby's skin for any rashes, spots, marks or bruising
- change a baby's clothes and nappy regularly
- note and report abnormal conditions (of skin, stools etc.).

Table 3.1 Some common skin conditions

Condition	Cause	Description	Treatment
Erythema toxicum (Urticaria neonatorum)	Change of environment from womb to outside world	Red, blotchy areas with small central white spots. Appear on face, limbs, trunk. Not infectious. Common in first few weeks	No treatment Clears up in 2–3 days
Sweat rash (Miliaria)	Overheating Sweat glands of newborn are immature	Rash of small red spots in areas where sweat glands are numerous, for example, face, chest, skin folds	Remove some clothes Avoid wool next to skin Keep blankets and shawls away from face Bath to refresh skin Apply calamine lotion after drying Avoid over-wrapping baby
Chafing (Intertrigo)	Inefficient washing and drying of skin folds.	Inflammation and soreness of skin folds. Usually seen around neck, under arms and in groins	Use a baby cream or prescribed ointment. Prevent by good skin care practice, especially washing and careful drying
Cradle cap (May be seen on its own or as part of seborrhoeic dermatitis)	Build up of sebum Excessive use of shampoo Inefficient rinsing after hair wash	Yellowish-brown crusting on scalp. May be patchy or cover large area. Frequently seen over anterior fontanelle	Soften with a little baby oil over night Lift off softened flakes with comb, shampoo and rinse well Special shampoos available Prevent by use of shampoo once or twice a week only, and rinse well
Infantile seborrhoeic dermatitis	Uncertain	Occurs in first three months. Similar to cradle cap, but spreads to neck, behind ears, shoulders, chest and nappy area. Skin is red, scaly and may weep. Rash is not itchy or infectious. Greater risk of infantile eczema	Medicated shampoo for scalp Mild, unperfumed soap when washing or bathing Prescribed cream for nappy area Care of nappy area

Table 3.1 Some common skin conditions continued

Condition	Cause	Description	Treatment
Infantile eczema	An allergic response	Irritating red rash on cheeks and forehead. May spread to whole body, especially skin folds. Scratching causes broken, weeping skin with risk of infection. More common in bottle-fed babies. Usually starts at 2-3 months. Boys affected more than girls. Often family history of eczema, asthma or hay fever. May clear up in first three years. Not infectious. Can cause enormous distress and discomfort	Medical treatment – cortisone or tar preparations applied as directed by doctor. Aqueous soap solutions should be used – avoid ordinary soaps and bath preparations. Emulsifiers added to bath water prevent skin drying out. Use emollient ointments liberally. Sedatives may reduce severe irritation. Keep baby's finger nails short, use cotton scratch mittens. Avoid wool next to skin, dress baby in pure cotton or cotton mix fibres. Antibiotics may be given for infection and antiseptic solution added to bath water. Breast-feeding may delay onset

Table 3.2 Infections in the newborn baby

Condition	Cause	Description	Treatment
Sticky eyes	a) Blood, amniotic fluid or meconium entering during birth	a) Common in first 48 hours. Yellow crusting or discharge on the eyes or eyelids	a) Bathe eye(s) with saline solution or cooled, boilec water using same technique as in bathing baby to prevent infection being carried to other eye. Lie baby on affected side
	b) Blocked tear duct	b) Watery eye. May also be sticky. Tears cannot drain from eye to back of nose	b) Treat as above. Tear duct will normally open without treatment. If condition persists after 6 months, duct may be opened by operation. A sticky eye after 48 hours of birth is probably due to a bacterial infection. Hygiene procedure as above to prevent spread. Antibiotics given
Nail bed infection and skin (Paronychia)	Bacterial infection	Inflammation and infection of tissues and skin folds surrounding nail	Antibiotic ointment to cure infection Cotton mittens Strict hygiene measures
Septic spots (Pyoderma)	Bacterial infection	Small septic spots or pustules. Can occur anywhere on baby	Antibiotic ointment to heal spots Strict hygiene measures Isolate baby

Babies who develop a skin or eye infection while in hospital are isolated from other babies to prevent cross-infection.

Activities
1 Visit your local shops and make notes on the toiletries recommended for babies. Look for:
   – baby bath preparations
   – toilet soaps
   – shampoos
   – baby oils, moisturisers and lotions
   – barrier creams
   – preparations for cradle cap.
   Your research should reflect products for different skin types and different cultural preferences.
2 If you were caring for a baby on holiday in a hot climate, how would you protect her skin from sunburn?

Teeth and dental care

Teeth buds form beneath the gums in the early weeks of pregnancy. They are made of a soft substance called cartilage. Around the fourth or fifth month of pregnancy, calcium, phosphorous and vitamin D are laid down on the cartilage in a process known as calcification. The hard bone that subsequently develops is called dentine. It forms the bulk of a tooth and is sensitive to touch, temperature, sugar and acids. The inner cavity of a tooth is filled with pulp containing blood vessels and nerves. Enamel, the hardest substance in the body, covers the crown of all teeth. (The crown of a tooth is the part seen in the mouth protruding from the gum.) Enamel does not contain nerve endings.

At birth, the first teeth are present in the jaw and the second teeth are starting to develop. Teeth are necessary for biting, grinding and chewing food, as well as for speech. They also affect appearance, and sucking a dummy, a thumb or fingers over many years can push the front teeth forward. A baby's first teeth are called 'deciduous' teeth (also known as milk teeth, baby teeth or primary teeth). They start to appear at around four to six months (see the diagram on page 92). Deciduous dentition is complete by two-and-a-half years. There are 20 teeth in this first set. They are smaller and more widely spaced than the second set of permanent teeth. Although there is a recognised sequence for the appearance of these teeth there is often individual variation. A firmly fixed tooth present at birth can be left alone, although it may cause some problems with breast-feeding. A loose tooth is usually removed to prevent the baby choking or inhaling it should it fall out. From the age of about five years the roots of deciduous teeth loosen and are absorbed by the body causing the teeth to

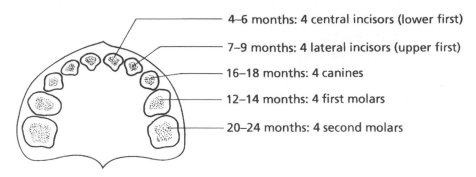

4–6 months: 4 central incisors (lower first)

7–9 months: 4 lateral incisors (upper first)

16–18 months: 4 canines

12–14 months: 4 first molars

20–24 months: 4 second molars

Deciduous teeth

Her first teeth – the two lower central incisors

shed at intervals. Permanent dentition starts at six years. There are 32 teeth in the permanent set.

CARING FOR TEETH

Adequate protein, calcium and vitamin D intake by the mother during pregnancy is important for the development of healthy teeth. After birth, a baby's first diet of milk plus vitamin supplements provide essential nutrients. Later, weaning and family foods should continue to supply calcium, phosphorous and vitamin D and be as sugar-free as possible. Chewing massages the gums, increases the blood supply and flow of saliva and helps to keep the teeth clean. Foods that encourage the baby to chew, for example, crusts of bread and pieces of peeled apple or partially cooked carrot, can be offered in the weaning process from around seven months (see Chapter 5, page 141).

Sugar and dental decay
Sugar is the main cause of tooth decay and the longer the sugar remains in the mouth the greater the chance of decay. Dental decay is a common condition even among very young children and it is estimated that by the age of two years 4 per cent of children already have some decay. Tooth decay is unsightly, causes pain and often the affected teeth have to be extracted. Children are reluctant to eat if they have toothache, making dietary problems likely. Teeth extractions at an early age, rather than natural 'fall out', may lead to crowded, uneven permanent teeth because of gum shrinkage, speech problems and, possibly, emotional problems due to poor self-image or bullying. Dummies dipped in sugar or honey and feeding bottles or soothers of sugar water or sweet fruit drink should not be given as comforters. These practices bathe the teeth with sugary substances for as long as the baby has the dummy or teat in her mouth. Check the labels on fruit drinks. They may say 'no added sweetening' but may be naturally high in sugar. Always dilute well before giving them to a baby. Sugar-free prescriptions and over-the-counter remedies are available.

Fluoride
The mineral fluoride guards against tooth decay by protecting the enamel from acid attack. It is found naturally in the drinking water in some areas; in others it has been added by the local water company. Where no fluoride is present in the water, fluoride drops or tablets may be prescribed. The dose of any fluoride treatment must always be carefully regulated and advised by the dentist or pharmacist. Drops can be given to babies from birth and fluoride treatment can be continued until 16 years of age. Too much can cause softening and discolouration of the teeth.

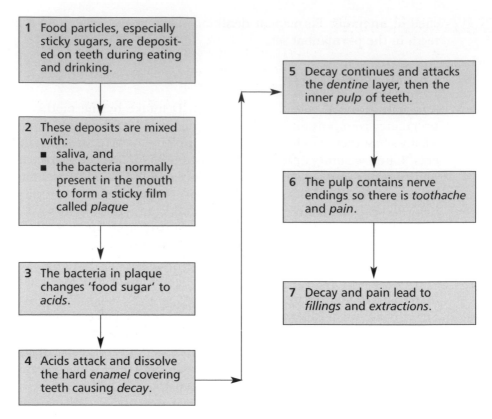

How tooth decay occurs

Preventing dental decay

Dental decay is preventable by: attention to diet; milk and cooled boiled water as regular drinks (occasionally diluted unsweetened fruit juice can be offered); a daily routine of teeth cleaning; the use of fluoride if recommended; and regular check-ups by the dentist.

It is important to establish good dental care routines for babies and young children that, hopefully, will continue throughout life. Start a daily routine as soon as a baby's first tooth appears. Wipe over the tooth and gum with a clean, non-fluffy cloth or the baby's own small toothbrush, smeared with a little toothpaste, then rinse with clean water. Use toothpaste specially formulated for children, as they have lower levels of fluoride than adult toothpastes. Ideally parents should take their baby to the dentist at the start of the second year, or even sooner. The baby can sit on her parent's lap and begin to get to know the dentist and become familiar with the surroundings. The earlier dental problems are identified the better for the health and social and emotional development of the child.

- Keep a baby's toothbrush clean and in good condition. Inevitably, a baby will chew on the bristles, so replace the brush as necessary.
- Child-care workers are health educators. Be ready to help and advise parents on the importance of dental care and encourage them to ask for sugar-free prescriptions and medicines for their babies.

Cleaning teeth at 12 months old

Activity

1 Find out if fluoride has been added to the water in your local area.
2 Collect leaflets and literature from your dentist on caring for children's teeth, including fluoride treatment. In particular, study the diagrams in the leaflets showing the correct technique for brushing teeth. This will enable you to help babies and young children to clean their teeth properly and correctly.

TEETHING

Teething is not an illness. Most babies cut their teeth without any problems other than, perhaps, dribbling and some swelling of the gum and reddening of the cheek where the tooth is erupting (coming through). A baby usually chews on her hand, thumb or a hard teething ring is she feels discomfort. If she is in obvious distress during teething the family doctor may prescribe a mild analgesic. Teething gels and solutions may give some relief, but check the labels for sugar content. Teething is wrongly blamed for many symptoms such as coughs and colds, earache, diarrhoea and nappy rash. It is usually just coincidence that these occur during the teething period. A baby with any of these symptoms should be seen by the family doctor.

REMEMBER!

- Teeth buds form early in foetal life.
- There are 20 deciduous teeth and 32 permanent teeth.
- Dental decay is common in young children. It is unsightly and causes pain.
- Dental extractions at an early age can cause gum shrinkage, speech problems and social and emotional difficulties.
- Professional carers can promote dental care and offer advice to parents and other carers.
- Healthy teeth depend on:
  - a mother's diet in pregnancy
  - a baby's weaning diet
  - avoidance of sugary foods, drinks and medicines
  - an appropriate routine of dental care, including dental check-ups.

QUICK CHECK

1 Name **three** functions of the skin.
2 Name **three** irritants that can make baby's skin sore.
3 Why is a healthy, clean, undamaged skin important for a baby?
4 Identify the delicate and vulnerable areas of a baby's body that need special care.
5 What is the danger of 'sprinkling' talcum powder over a baby's body?
6 Why is diarrhoea potentially very serious in a baby?
7 What are the causes of nappy rash?
8 Describe the principles of preventing nappy rash?
9 What is cradle cap and how would you advise a parent to treat it?
10 How would you treat a baby's sticky eyes?
11 How many deciduous teeth are there?
12 What are the functions of teeth?
13 At what age would you normally expect a baby's first tooth to appear?
14 (a) What is the main cause of tooth decay?
   (b) How does tooth decay occur?
15 At what age should dental care begin?

4 SLEEP; CRYING; PRIMARY HEALTH CARE

> ## This chapter covers:
> - **Sleep and sleep routines**
> - **Why babies cry**
> - **Complementary therapies**
> - **Primary health care**
> - **Sure Start**

Sleep and sleep routines

It takes time for the part of a baby's brain that controls sleep and wakefulness to function properly. Because the newborn baby requires frequent feeds she sleeps in relatively short spells of 3 to 5 hours, waking up when she is hungry. In total she sleeps around 17 hours out of 24. By about 6 months a pattern emerges of a prolonged night-time sleep of possibly 10 hours or so, with a period of sleep in the morning and afternoon making up a further few hours. By the first year the baby usually sleeps a total of 13 hours, including two naps during the day.

REMEMBER!

Each baby is an individual with his or her own sleep pattern and, while sleep patterns vary, most babies sleep well. Some babies require less sleep than the average; others, including pre-term babies, require more. Parents may have high expectations of how much sleep their baby should have, and often need reassuring that their baby is, in fact, having all the sleep she requires.

No one can make a baby sleep and all parents will experience disturbed nights. However, a baby can be made sufficiently comfortable and secure to help her to sleep whenever she wants to. A young baby takes time to settle into a pattern of feeding and sleeping. Hunger will wake her up, as will pain, feeling cold and the jerking and twitching movements common in the newborn. Normal household noises should not disturb a baby unless they are sudden and loud, such as the phone ringing or the vacuum cleaner being switched on immediately beside her. Creeping around trying 'not to wake baby' will lead to unnatural quietness in the home.

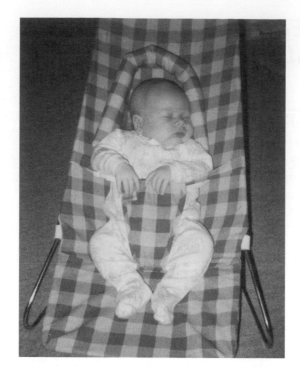

A peaceful daytime sleep

Many babies quickly adjust to sleeping more at night than during the day, and it is important to provide a routine that helps a baby to recognise night as a time for prolonged sleep. A baby may initially whimper or make a variety of little noises when she is first put down to sleep, but unless she is obviously distressed there is no need to pick her up. A soft nightlight and musical box may soothe her. Night feeds should be given without fuss or undue disturbance – the light should be dimmed and interaction and eye contact kept to a mimimum. Once a baby has fed, her nappy should be checked and changed before laying her gently and quietly in her cot to resume sleeping.

A baby benefits from the familiarity and repetition of routines. From about three months of age a bedtime routine can be established:

- 'top and tail' her or give her a warm bath
- change her into night clothes and a clean nappy
- feed her without too much stimulation
- check her nappy and settle her on her back in the cot, in the 'feet to foot' position. (see photograph on page 99)
- a soothing tape or music box may lull her to sleep.

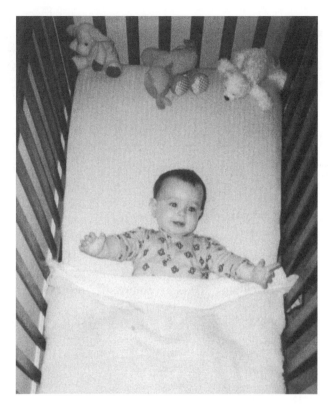

A baby in the 'feet to foot' position

KEY POINT

To place a baby in the 'feet to foot' position:

- lay the baby in the cot on her back (supine) with her feet at the foot of the cot
- cover her securely but not tightly with the bedclothes. Make sure they do not reach above her shoulders so that she cannot slip under the covers during the night.

(See also Sudden infant death syndrome, Chapter 7, page 184.)

REMEMBER!

During the bedtime routine make sure your voice is quiet and calming as you talk, sing and say 'goodnight' to her.

WHERE SHOULD A BABY SLEEP?

A new baby needs the security of being close to her mother rather than isolation in a room on her own. During the day this will probably be in a moses basket, carry cot or pram in whichever room her mother is in. Sleeping in a cradle or cot beside her mother at night in the early months reduces the risk of cot death and also means there can be immediate physical contact between mother and baby when needed. Breast-feeding can be achieved quietly, in a soft light and with minimum effort and the baby placed gently back in her cot to sleep. At about three to four months a baby may be moved into her own room. The room where the baby sleeps at night should be ventilated during the day and kept at a constant temperature of about 20°C (68°F) during the night. A baby should be warm, rather than hot, and chilling must be avoided.

SAFE PRACTICE

- Cots and travel cots, prams and mattresses should meet the British Standards Institution (BSI) safety regulations.
- The Foundation for the Study of Infant Deaths (FSID) recommends the use of firm mattresses. They must be kept in good condition (clean, dry and well aired) to prevent the possibility of bacterial contamination.
- Place a baby down to sleep on her back and in the 'feet to foot' position (see page 99), checking that the bedclothes are no higher than her shoulders.
- Cot duvets, pillows and baby nests are unsuitable for a baby under one year old. She would be unable to lift her head or wriggle free should her face become pressed against or 'buried' in the soft material. There is also the risk of overheating.
- Use cotton rather than nylon sheets – they allow adequate circulation of air around the baby and absorb perspiration.
- Clothes for sleeping in should be warm and comfortable and allow for freedom of movement.
- A baby must never be left with a bottle 'propped' in her mouth ('prop' feeding) in her pram, cot, on a sofa or anywhere else.
- Use a cat and insect net when a baby sleeps outside in her pram. Do not put babies to sleep outside in very cold, foggy or wet weather, nor in direct sunlight.

- Parents or other adults who are smokers, or who have taken alcohol or medication that leave them drowsy, or who are unwell or very tired should not take a baby into their bed to sleep. If a baby is taken into an adult's bed to sleep she should be positioned safely to prevent her falling out, covered with light weight blankets and kept cool. Pillows and duvets should be kept away from the baby's head.
- Adults should not fall asleep with a baby on a settee or sofa.

DIFFICULTIES IN SETTLING TO SLEEP

- Discomfort – feeling too hot or cold, uncomfortable clothes or a wet or soiled nappy.
- Settling into day care.
- Emotionally insecure and unsettled – lacking cuddles and carer interaction.
- Medical conditions – pain, illness, skin irritation such as eczema, breathing problems such as asthma or infestation with threadworms, head lice or fleas.
- Disruption of routine, for example, a period of hospitalisation or a family crisis.
- Limited accommodation where a baby may share a room with her parents or siblings. Bed and breakfast or hostel accommodation is often poor with little opportunity for a bedtime routine leading to settled sleep.
- Loud, persistent noise within the home or from the outside environment.
- Lack of fresh air, exercise and appropriate stimulation during the day, as well as a poor diet and hunger.

All these factors can lead to irritability, discomfort and a poor sleep pattern. In turn, a poor sleep pattern can lead to an unhappy, fractious baby during the day.

KEY POINT

A poor pattern of care, in which a baby's needs are neither understood nor met, will make her miserable and insecure and less likely to sleep. A mother who is tense or anxious, or has a postnatal illness, may adversely affect her baby's sleeping pattern.

SLEEP AND AN OLDER BABY

Bedtime for an older baby should be calm and enjoyable with the constant, familiar routine and rituals of the early months continued. It will help if she has had an interesting and stimulating day, and is neither hungry nor thirsty as bedtime approaches. Before bedtime allow a little time for her to 'wind down', perhaps with a warm bath and a quiet look at a book. Bathing in the evening is probably better at this age (six months to one year), not only because a baby may be grubby and sticky from playing on the floor, but also because a bath at the end of the day can have a calming effect. A gentle massage (see Chapter 3, page 80) after the bath can be beneficial in promoting calm and sleepiness. Continue to put her down to sleep in a comfortable cot and in the recommended position, but remember, at this age she will turn over, wriggle and move around the cot, eventually finding her own sleeping position. Make sure her comfort object (see below) is close to her. The use of an all-in-one sleep suit in colder weather will prevent chilling. Using a double reusable nappy may reduce the chances of her waking up because she is wet. However, if a baby has a nappy rash this is not good practice – the baby should have her nappy changed.

The bedtime routine should be consistent. It helps if there are regular sleeping habits among all family members, although this may be impossible where parents and others in the house are working shift patterns. Make sure a baby does not fall asleep while feeding from the breast or bottle. Babies often dislike being left alone at bedtime and some may have difficulty in settling to sleep or getting themselves back to sleep if they wake up during periods of light sleep. They may cry and become distressed. Subdued lighting, a half open door and household sounds can be reassuring, but this may not be sufficient for some babies. If crying is persistent and excessive, help can be obtained from voluntary groups such as Cry-sis and the National Childbirth Trust (see pages 264–5). They offer advice and support and put parents in touch with others who have had similar problems with a crying baby. Talking to other parents helps them to understand that they are not alone, and encourages them to try and work out some positive solutions. Sleep groups and management programmes, approved by child psychologists, and usually organised by the family doctor and health visitor, can be of great benefit in helping exhausted parents and other adults in the home to 'manage' the baby's bedtime so that good sleep habits are developed. Parents are advised to talk to the health visitor if their baby will not settle to sleep. Once any of the difficulties in settling to sleep (identified above, page 101) have been eliminated, it may be appropriate to try a sleep management programme.

The basic procedures of one sleep management programme are as follows.

- A baby is settled in her cot in the usual way in the evening, making sure she is dry and comfortable and neither hungry nor thirsty. The bedroom should be warm but not hot.

- When the baby cries the parent sits quietly by the cot until the baby goes to sleep – perhaps patting or stroking her but not engaging in eye contact or conversation.
- Whenever the baby cries the parent adopts the same routine of sitting by the cot, quietly patting, stroking and settling the baby back to sleep, but with little or no interaction.
- Gradually, over the following nights, the parent sits further away from the cot until the baby falls asleep with the parent now outside the open bedroom door.

KEY POINT

Managing this type of programme requires effort and commitment from parents and other adults caring for a baby, also support and encouragement from the health visitor. The length of time it may take for a baby to finally settle and sleep through the night can be anything from a few nights to a few weeks. Talking to other parents who have managed a sleep programme successfully is helpful in building confidence for a positive outcome.

COMFORT OBJECTS

A baby will suck what she enjoys and what is available to her from birth. Many babies need more sucking than is derived from feeding. A non-nutritive sucking habit eventually becomes automatic and comforts a baby when she is unhappy, bored or tired. Many babies use a soft toy, or piece of cloth to cling to when they are tired, settling to sleep or separated from their mother as at bedtime or attending day care. These are called comfort objects. They are familiar, important possessions that give babies a sense of security. They are soft and smooth and develop their own special smell. A baby may cling to or suck a comfort object, rub it against her cheek or just keep it close by. They do no harm and the habit may persist well into the early years with the child eventually growing out of it. However, they do need washing from time to time, and they may also wear out and even get lost. If possible, spare ones should be kept both in the home and in the day care setting.

Finger or thumb sucking may develop early or later on. Unlike other comfort objects fingers and thumbs are part of a baby – she can feel and find them at any time and control the sucking – making the habit possibly more difficult to let go of in childhood.

Dummies
A dummy is frequently used to quieten and comfort a baby. It is under the control of the parent or carer and can be removed at any time. Research

suggests a significant relationship between dummy sucking and poor speech development (see Language development, Chapter 6 page 155). By six months, babies take everything to their mouths. Sucking, mouthing and handling toys and objects provides babies with pleasure and essential sensory learning experiences. A baby misses these opportunities if she constantly has a dummy in her mouth. Importantly, there is a link between a baby sucking on a dummy dipped in sugar or honey and dental caries (decay) Chapter 3, see page 93.

SAFE PRACTICE

- Parents should be advised to buy dummies that carry a BSI number.
- A dummy should have a smooth teat and be free from flaws and cracks that could collect germs. Check that it is made of safe, non-toxic material, which will not easily disintegrate, possibly causing the baby to inhale or choke on small particles.
- A baby must have her own individual dummy. Dummies often end up on the floor and need to be kept clean, hygienic and sterilised daily.
- Do not put a baby down to sleep with a dummy in her mouth.
- Adults should not suck a dummy to 'clean' it. Babies have not yet built up their immune system and any bacteria transferred to a dummy from an adult's mouth can lead to infection in the baby.

REMEMBER!

- Periods of rest and sleep are an important part of a baby's daily routine.
- Babies have individual sleep requirements and patterns.
- A baby needs to feel comfortable when settling to sleep:
  - adequately fed
  - dry nappy
  - warm
  - secure.
- Keep a small baby close to her mother or carer.
- Daily fresh air and developmentally appropriate stimulation and interest will help to promote satisfying sleep.
- Establish a bedtime routine.
- A variety of physical and emotional factors can lead to difficulties in settling to sleep.
- Many babies enjoy a comfort object when settling to sleep.
- Apply the principles of safe practice in relation to sleep (see pages 100–1).

(Rest and sleep routines in day care – see Chapter 9, pages 219–20.)

Why babies cry

All babies cry. It is their language, a way of communicating their needs. Some babies are naturally calm and content, while others are wakeful, active and need constant attention. It is important to understand the physical and emotional needs of a baby, and to be aware of the developmental stages in order to interpret and respond to her cries.

■ Physical needs – food, warmth and shelter; rest and sleep, fresh air and exercise; also cleanliness, and protection from infection and injury.

■ Emotional needs – love and security; consistent, predictable care and knowing her needs will be met; sensory experiences and opportunities to explore her environment; encouragement and response to achievement (smiling, clapping); praise and recognition; and exposure to language.

Developmental stages during the first year are discussed throughout Chapter 6 and set out in Table 6.1, pages 162–6.

Crying can mean 'I'm hungry'; 'I'm lonely'; 'I'm bored'; 'I'm in pain'; 'I want to go to sleep'. A quiet, 'good' baby may be ill. Most parents quickly learn to recognise their baby's different cries and respond appropriately. Ignoring a baby's cries will make her feel insecure and frightened. Table 4.1 on pages 107–8 details the main causes of crying and the role of the carer.

A baby who is crying often responds to the comfort of quick but gentle, rhythmical movements such as rocking, either in the carer's arms or in a pram. The speed of rocking movements (about 60 per minute) is thought to imitate the walking pace and heartbeat of the mother that a baby hears while in the womb.

KEY POINTS

■ You cannot spoil a baby in the early months of life by picking her up when she cries.

■ Research shows that babies cry less in the later months if carers respond to their cries and meet their needs in the early months.

CRYING AND THE OLDER BABY

Crying because of loneliness, pain and illness apply equally to the older baby as to the younger one. Additional causes may be separation from her mother due to illness or hospitalisation of either the mother or her baby.

Strangers and strange environments, such as initial attendance in a day care setting, may distress a baby (see also Settling in, Chapter 9, page 216).

Between six months and one year a baby becomes increasingly more mobile and interested in her surroundings. A stimulating environment will promote learning and discovery. However, with this stage of development comes frustration and often anger at the restrictions placed on her by adults. Rather than saying 'no' or 'don't touch that', adults should remove anything precious or potentially unsafe from the room or play area, allowing a baby to explore, touch and learn in safety. She may become cross trying to learn a particular skill or make a particular toy work. Leaving her to succeed on her own may be appropriate, but if she becomes very upset it is much better to help her.

It is important to provide a safe and secure environment by removing anything dangerous or unstable from a baby's reach.

PERSISTENT CRYING

Studies show that 1 in 10 babies cry persistently and are difficult to soothe and comfort. A medical check-up is advisable to make sure there is nothing physically wrong. Sometimes an allergy or infection, or hyperactivity, may be discovered but usually the baby is healthy. Most babies will grow out of it but some may grow into demanding toddlers. Persistent crying maybe linked to maternal depression.

Effects of crying on parents and carers
The effects of a crying, unsettled baby on her parents can be:
- exhaustion
- lack of confidence in caring for her, expectations may be shattered
- guilt at being unable to make her happy
- depression and anger – resentment of an 'over-demanding' baby
- worry – is something wrong with her (although the majority of babies are perfectly healthy)
- marriage or partnership and family life affected, isolation from friends
- danger of physical violence to the baby (studies in America show that child abuse often starts with a crying baby).

Table 4.1 The causes of crying in babies

Cause	Role of the carer
Hunger	Offer milk feed – water will not satisfy Is baby getting enough milk? Check weight Is help needed with feeding technique, for example, fixing correctly at breast, a larger hole in the teat? If mother is breast-feeding, suggest demand feeding Seek advice from health visitor **Remember!** A dummy will not soothe a hungry baby
Thirst (especially in hot weather)	Small babies – 30 ml (1 oz) cooled, boiled water Older babies – cooled, boiled water or well-diluted fruit juice from a cup Offer these drinks regularly in hot weather
Discomfort a) Dressing and undressing	a) Babies dislike being dressed and undressed and feeling cold air on skin. Keep disturbance to a minimum. Ensure room and clothes are warm and avoid chilling
b) Wet/soiled nappy	b) Change nappy. Follow guidelines for skin and nappy rash care and treatment and prevention of nappy rash (pages 84–5)
c) Too hot (damp around neck, face red)	c) Remove some clothing/bedding, but avoid chilling. Offer a drink of cooled, boiled water as above
d) Cold (whimpering, fretful	d) Check hands, feet and abdomen (tummy). Move to a warmer room, cuddle, try a warm feed **Remember!** Hypothermia (see page 185)
Loneliness/boredom	Physical contact needed – cuddle, use baby sling Talk to baby, play a music box or 'womb' tape Interest baby in household noises Rhythmical movements – rocking, baby bouncer Mobiles, activity centre, 'swipe' objects Put pram under tree or near washing line (do not forget the cat and insect net) Take baby for a walk or car ride **Remember!** Activities appropriate to age
Over-stimulation (loud noises, bright lights, too much bouncing, sudden happenings)	Check management Take baby to a quiet place Rhythmical rocking, patting Massage, stroking Sing to baby
Jerking and twitching (common movements in newborn babies – can cause them to wake suddenly)	Wrap up more securely, settle back to sleep
Colds and snuffles (breathing and feeding difficulties)	Medical care Nose drops Nasal care Drinks of cooled, boiled water *continued*

Table 4.1 The causes of crying in babies continued

Cause	Role of the carer
Colic	See Table 5.3, page 143
Allergies a) Cow's milk b) Infantile eczema	Always seek medical help a) Soya formula feed. Breast-feeding mothers should reduce intake of dairy products Revision of baby's diet according to medical instructions b) See page 89
Pain and illness (knocks, falls, burns, scalds, fever, diarrhoea, vomiting)	Medical care Safe practice, provision of safe environment Apply: management of illness, infections Knowledge of first aid Knowledge of workplace procedures See Table 7.2 on pages 173–4, and see Appendix: First Aid, page 257
Child abuse	Protection of baby, implement workplace and local authority policies and procedures Work with Child Protection agencies

Available help

Parents and carers should not be afraid of seeking help. Professional advice from the family doctor and health visitor can be useful. The self-help groups Cry-sis and the National Childbirth Trust offer advice on crying, as they do for sleep difficulties (see Sleep, page 97).

KEY POINT

- Research shows that persistent and troublesome crying may be helped by reducing the amount of stimulation the baby receives. Loud music and rattling toys, excessive lifting, patting and winding a baby should be avoided.
- Holding a baby in a quiet, dimly lit room may settle her. A soft light in the bedroom can have a soothing effect.
- Difficulties in sleeping and persistent crying may be effectively relieved by use of a complementary therapy (see page 109).

Activities
1   Choose a member of your group to contact Cry-is and find out about their support network.
    (a) How widespread is the network?
    (b) How big a need is there for Cry-sis?
    (c) How is Cry-sis able to help and support families?
    (d) Where would families find information about Cry-sis?

Complementary therapies

Complementary therapies are increasingly popular for the relief of symptoms of ill-health and to promote a feeling of well-being. Many of them have been used for thousands of years. Although they may be effective when used on their own, ideally they are used alongside traditional medicine in offering a holistic (physical, emotional, mental and spiritual) approach to medical and health needs. The better known ones include aromatherapy massage, homoeopathy, osteopathy, acupuncture, traditional Chinese medicine and reflexology.

REMEMBER!

Not all complementary therapies are regulated and their content may not always be known.

KEY POINTS

■ Care must be taken that any symptoms a baby experiences are thoroughly checked and assessed before any complementary therapy is given.
■ No complementary therapy or treatment should be given to a baby by a child-care worker without prior professional training.
■ Not all complementary therapists have specialist knowledge in treating babies. Parents and child-care workers must always make sure a therapist has specific qualifications, knowledge and experience of working with babies.

The two therapies described below may be beneficial for babies in certain circumstances.

AROMATHERAPY MASSAGE

Aromatherapy is an ancient, but controversial, therapy using 'essential' aromatic oils from a variety of plants, flowers and fruits to heal, relax, refresh and soothe the body and mind. Not all oils from these sources are suitable for aromatherapy and some are potentially dangerous and should in no circumstances be used. Others are unsafe for use on the skin as they may cause skin damage and allergic reactions. Well- known, safe essential oils used in aromatherapy include: geranium, jasmine, juniper, lavender, mandarin, rosemary, sandalwood and tea tree. However, essential oils are highly concentrated, powerful natural substances and must be diluted and blended with a'carrier' oil, such as peach kernel or sweet almond, when used on the skin. Two exceptions to this rule are lavender and tea trcc oils, both noted for their antiseptic, antibacterial and wound healing properties.

Different aromatherapy oils are used: in body massage; as compresses to aid healing of minor wounds, cuts, abrasions and superficial burns; as steam inhalants for relief of respiratory infections; and in beauty products, pot pourris and aromatherapy burners. Aromatherapy may also be effective as a healing aid alongside medical treatment for skin conditions such as eczema, but should only be used with the doctor's approval.

When aromatherapy oils are used in massage they are absorbed through the skin and into the bloodstream so circulating their effects throughout the body. Aromatherapy massage, using diluted 'essential' aromatic oils, can be a beneficial and safe therapy for babies in the hands of an experienced practitioner, helping to soothe and settle them.

KEY POINTS

- Anyone who does not have a sound knowledge of appropriate oils and how to use them safely with babies must **never attempt** aromatherapy.
- 'Essential' oils are highly concentrated substances and must be diluted and blended with a 'carrier' oil when used on the skin.

PAEDIATRIC CRANIOSACRAL OSTEOPATHY

Osteopathy is the practice of healing through manually adjusting the framework of the body. It is a state registered profession and is now widely used within the NHS. An osteopath manipulates, stretches and massages the musculo-skeletal system to relieve tension in muscles and ligaments and realign muscles and joints. Some osteopaths specialise in the technique known as paediatric craniosacral osteopathy – a subtle and sensitive therapy that gently manipulates and adjusts a baby's skull bones and releases uncomfortable tensions, so helping the healthy functioning of the whole body. A baby is subjected to many stresses during labour and birth as she is pushed and squeezed through the birth canal. The stresses can be particularly severe if the birth is traumatic or difficult, for example, a very long labour or a forceps or ventouse delivery. The moulded shape of the baby's head at birth (see Chapter 2, page 41) may disturb the nervous system and the cerebrospinal fluid surrounding it, causing discomfort and irritability, crying, sleep disturbance and feeding difficulties. Craniosacral therapy may relieve these symptoms.

Only a qualified paediatric osteopath should undertake this therapy.

Primary health care

Primary health care is health care and treatment provided in the community, as opposed to care and treatment in hospital. It is the basic foundation of community health provision in the NHS. Primary health care is concerned with promoting good health and preventing illness in families and communities.

THE PRIMARY HEALTH CARE TEAM

Many professionals make up the primary health care team (PHCT). They work together to ensure the best possible health for the community they serve. The core members of the team include family doctors, community midwives and nurses, practice nurses and health visitors. Other health professionals such as community paediatricians, school nurses and doctors, audiometricians, orthoptists and nutritionists, plus administrative staff, are complementary to the PHCT in extending community health care facilities.

The roles of some PHCT members who care for babies and their families are briefly outlined below.

Family doctors
Family doctors care for the health of the whole family, including sick and unwell babies. They refer babies to hospital (or other community health services) for specialist care and treatment. Many are also practitioners in preventive health care for children and:
■ care for an expectant mother before, during and after birth, including her postnatal examination at six to eight weeks
■ carry out periodic growth and developmental reviews for babies and young children, assessing their health and providing screening and immunisation programmes (see Immunisation, Chapter 7, page 169).

Community midwives
Community midwives have specialist training in all aspects of pregnancy and childbirth. They liaise closely with family doctors in caring for mothers both antenatally and postnatally. In particular, they:
■ monitor the progress of a pregnancy (check blood pressure and weight and test urine); check the position of the baby and listen to the heart-

beat; offer emotional support; and advise on diet, minor ailments, keeping healthy, and preparing for labour and birth through a programme of relaxation and breathing exercises

■ assist with home births
■ visit mothers and babies (whether a home or hospital birth) at home for at least 10 days after the birth. In particular they advise on all aspects of feeding (especially helping to establish breast-feeding), as well as skin and cord care. They take a blood sample for the baby's Guthrie and TSH tests (see Chapter 2, pages 51–2), check any abdominal or perineal sutures the mother may have and encourage her to continue with postnatal exercises.

Health visitors

Health visitors have a background in nursing and midwifery (or obstetric training) and an in-depth knowledge of child health and development. They are members of the PHCT, working in the community with people of all ages. However, they have special responsibility towards children under five years and their families. In particular they:

■ work with family doctors and community paediatricians in child health promotion and surveillance programmes
■ visit a mother and her baby soon after the midwife has completed her care, listen to any concerns the mother may have about the baby or herself and offer advice, support and reassurance, particularly to first-time mothers. They discuss all aspects of baby care (feeding, skin care, sleep pattern and the importance of immunisation) with the parents and are particularly interested to see how the baby is settling into the family
■ visit the family at home as often as necessary
■ invite mothers to bring their babies to the child health clinic for periodic developmental and health reviews, screening tests and immunisations
■ identify mothers who may be exhausted, depressed, unaware of, or unresponsive to, the needs of their babies. They can offer support and advice and bring in other professional help such as the family doctor or social worker
■ understand, and aim to alleviate, the difficulties experienced by families from different cultures in bringing up their babies and young children, especially those families for whom English is not their first language. They may be able to offer help through an ethnic link worker, cultural support group or information in their home language
■ screen babies for hearing and vision loss. Early detection is essential. Hearing difficulties can affect normal language development with

implications for social, emotional and intellectual well-being. Squinting, although seen in the immediate newborn period, can seriously affect vision if it persists
- identify babies and young children with special needs.

Health visitors are concerned with the holistic development of a baby. They help parents to promote all aspects of their baby's development, with particular emphasis on emotional attachments and parent–baby relationships.

CHILD HEALTH PROMOTION

Child health promotion has two approaches: encouraging good health and health surveillance.

Encouraging good health (primary prevention)
Good health is encouraged by: promoting breast-feeding and supporting mothers who breast-feed; guiding parents in providing a healthy balanced diet for their babies and young children; preventing dental decay (see Chapter 3, page 94); immunisations and health education (food hygiene, hand washing, etc.) to protect against infectious diseases – important factors in day care settings; accident prevention (accidents are a common cause of death in children); supporting parents in caring for their children; and offering help, when necessary, to lessen the possibility of emotional or behavioural difficulties in children.

Health surveillance (secondary prevention)
Health surveillance provides regular growth, development and health reviews; early detection of problems (including emotional and behavioural) and disorders; referral for specialist help; and screening for hearing and vision impairment, dislocated hips and undescended testes.

Screening
Screening is a test or examination for a particular condition or disorder that may be cured or treated. Early detection is important in preventing permanent damage and disability. A baby (through her parents) is offered several screening tests in her first year as part of the Child Health Surveillance programme. Further investigation is arranged if there is concern about any results. Screening tests must be carried out and interpreted correctly for them to be of value.

CHILD HEALTH SURVEILLANCE

Health surveillance for babies in the UK is provided within the primary care system by (mainly) family doctors and health visitors. Community paediatricians (see below) and midwives also have particular responsibilities. Babies are offered a care programme that aims to promote good health and prevent illness and disorders. To achieve this, a health visitor visits them in their own homes and also invites them to attend their local child health clinic. Whether in the home or the clinic, parents are helped and supported with feeding, weaning and child-care management routines. Most babies attend the clinic for their medical examination at eight weeks old, specific vision and hearing screening tests and for immunisations. Periodic health and development reviews are carried out in the home or in the clinic.

Community paediatricians

Community paediatricians are part of the Community Child Health Services. They are specialists in preventive health care for children and in care of the sick child. However, they do not provide antenatal and post-natal service for mothers.

KEY POINT

Child health and development clinics are for 'well' babies. If a baby is sick or unwell she will be seen in the usual way by her family doctor.

A child health clinic is usually based in a health centre, but it may be in a village or church hall, or a doctor's premises. Clinics should meet the needs of the families they serve with easy access and convenient opening hours – some are now open evenings and Saturday mornings. The premises must be safe with gates and a pram shed. Clinics should be child-friendly and clean, with adequate seating and provision for breast-feeding. Privacy is important for parents who wish to have a quiet discussion with their doctor or health visitor. A warm, welcoming atmosphere and friendly staff make the parents feel comfortable and provide a relaxed meeting place for exchanging news and views and comparing 'baby' notes. Many have crèche facilities and local information about play-groups, childminders, babysitting services and voluntary organisations displayed on a notice board.

GROWTH, DEVELOPMENT AND HEALTH REVIEWS

Reviews are offered at certain ages throughout the first year allowing the professionals and parents to assess a baby's progress together. The ages may vary slightly from area to area.

All reviews and assessments should take place in a relaxed and mutually trusting atmosphere. Parents know their baby best and have an important part to play in the exchange of information about her health and development. Any concerns parents may have about their baby should not be ignored.

A baby who is hungry, tired or irritable may not respond appropriately to examination and testing.

Parents should be asked questions relevant to the age and developmental stage of their baby and always given time to answer. Examples include: Do you have any concerns about your baby? How is her feeding/appetite? Tell me what she likes to eat? Describe her sleep pattern? How does she respond when you talk to her? What noises/sounds does she make? Does she appear to hear and see normally?

KEY POINTS

- Child care workers have a wide breadth of knowledge of child health and development, both from their studies and their day-to-day work with babies from diverse backgrounds and cultures. Consequently they are in a unique position to recognise any deviation from normal in a baby they are caring for.
- If you have health or development concerns about a baby in your care always discuss them with your supervisor or manager.

Typical review and screening tests schedule in the first year
- Neonatal examination by the hospital paediatrician or the family doctor: growth measurements, neonatal screening tests and 'top to toe' examination, including examination of the nervous system (see Chapter 2, pages 43–50). A neonatal screening test for hearing loss is available in some maternity units two or three days after birth.
- Eight weeks: repeat growth measurements. Hips checked, also testes in boys. Discussion with the parents about their baby's feeding and general progress. Observation of the baby's development and demeanour, and parent–baby interaction.
- Eight weeks to 6 months: opportunities for the family doctor to check the baby when seen for minor ailments and immunisations, and for the health visitor to talk to the parents and observe the baby during home visits and clinic sessions
- Six to 12 months: growth measurements; examination of heart and lungs; hips checked, also testes in boys (if undescended); observation of the baby, review of all-round development and emerging skills (gross and fine motor control, vocalisations and social behaviour); discussion with parents, listening to any concerns they may have.

Vision and hearing assessment

Questions asked: Do the parents have any concerns? Do they think their baby is seeing/hearing normally?

■ Six to 7 months: vision screening for squint and other vision problems.
■ Eight months: distraction test for hearing loss. (This test is likely to be phased out and replaced by more accurate and sophisticated neonatal testing.)

The baby will be retested or referred to a specialist if there are concerns about either test.

KEY POINTS

■ Growth measurements are plotted on a percentile chart (see Chapter 6, pages 151–2). The chart gives a picture of the baby's individual growth pattern in relation to the national average.
■ At all times, parents are involved in their baby's screening tests and developmental reviews. They keep their baby's Personal Child Health Record Book, in which information relating to her growth, health and development, and immunisation status is recorded.
■ If at any time, parents are concerned about any aspect of their baby's health or development, outside a regular review, they can arrange to see the doctor or health visitor.

REMEMBER!

■ Primary health care is health care in the community.
■ Family doctors, community paediatricians, community midwives and health visitors have particular responsibility to care for babies and their families.
■ Child health clinics are for 'well' babies.
■ Screening tests aim to detect and treat a disorder at an early age.
■ Health promotion includes encouraging breast-feeding and measures to prevent infection such as immunisation, hand washing and food hygiene.
■ Periodic health and developmental reviews are offered during the first year.
■ Parents know their babies best – always listen carefully to their concerns.

Activities

1 In pairs, try and make an appointment with a health visitor in your area. Ask her:
   (a) to explain the statutory duties of a health visitor;
   (b) to describe how she conducts her first visit to a new baby and the family;

Sure Start

Sure Start is a Government-funded initiative, launched in 1998, to improve the health, development and well-being of young children from birth to four years and their families. Sure Start programmes work with parents-to-be, parents and children in disadvantaged areas and aim to strengthen families and communities.

Local Sure Start programmes are concentrated in areas of high poverty and take into account the particular needs of the neighbourhood, and the different cultural needs of families. To date, over three hundred programmes nationwide have been approved and are delivering a range of services for families, including child care.

Programmes are run by local partnerships. A partnership includes family doctors, health visitors, midwives, education and child-care professionals, community volunteers, parents and others – all working together. While every Sure Start programme is structured for the particular needs of an area, all are likely to include:

- better antenatal support and advice, including help to stop smoking
- visits to all new parents within two months of birth to introduce them to Sure Start services. Support and advice on nurturing, guidance on breast-feeding, bonding, the importance of talking to and playing with babies

- more accessible baby clinics and advice on health, development, safety and prevention of infection
- improved quality of child care, more child-care places and a greater variety of provision
- support for parents, including parenting groups, advice on healthy eating and training for employment.

To achieve these goals, services already in existence can be extended or new services and facilities provided, for example:

- an increase in the number of health visitor sessions
- additional speech and language therapy
- more outreach visits and support for families in the home, family literacy sessions
- new play areas, a new play bus in rural areas
- grants for new toys and equipment
- setting up a parent support group
- advice and counselling
- further training for existing professionals and help for new workers and volunteers.

Activity

Research a Sure Start programme near your home, college or workplace. In what ways does the programme support (a) mothers and their new babies; and (b) mothers with postnatal illness?

'DELIVERING FOR CHILDREN AND FAMILIES'

The document 'Delivering for Children and Families' was published in November 2002 by the Government's Strategy Unit. It sets out measures to ensure affordable, good quality child-care provision is accessible to everyone. To this end, responsibility for Early Years, child care and Sure Start is being brought together within one interdepartmental unit. New funding and a new child-care strategy aim to ensure 250,000 more child-care places by 2006, new children's centres in deprived areas and expansion of existing Sure Start programmes – all designed to offer improved services and good quality support for parents, babies and young children. The Government's vision is to transform the way children's services are delivered so that the needs of babies and young children and their families, particularly the most vulnerable ones, are more appropriately met.

QUICK CHECK

1 Where is the best place for a newborn baby to sleep?
2 Describe the 'feet to foot' position? List **three** further points of safe practice relating to babies and sleep.
3 Give **three** reasons why a baby may not settle to sleep.
4 Give **three** reasons why a baby cries and the role of the carer in comforting the baby in each case.
5 What are the key points to consider in caring for a baby who is too hot?
6 What effect can a persistently crying baby have on her parent/carer?
7 What do you understand by aromatherapy? What is a 'carrier' oil?
8 For what particular problems might paediatric craniosacral osteopathy be beneficial for a baby?
9 Name the core members of a primary health care team.
10 Which member of the PHCT visits a mother and her new baby for at least 10 days after birth?
11 Describe the role and functions of a health visitor.
12 What are the functions of a child health clinic?
13 (a) In your own words, what are (i) screening and (ii) a health and development review?
   (b) At what age is (i) a baby's vision tested for any sign of a squint and (ii) a baby's hearing tested for any sign of hearing loss?
14 What do you understand by the Sure Start Government initiative?
15 Describe particular services likely to be included in the majority of Sure Start programmes.

5 INFANT NUTRITION

> **This chapter covers:**
> - **Breast or bottle?**
> - **Breast-feeding**
> - **Bottle-feeding**
> - **Weaning**
> - **Feeding problems**

Breast or bottle?

The choice between bottle-feeding and breast-feeding is an important one for any would-be parent and a decision is best made after careful consideration of all the health promotion information available. Pregnancy is an ideal time for information to be given about different feeding methods, as research tells us that parents are then especially responsive to new information. Remember, too, that social and cultural factors will also influence choices.

While it is important that relevant information is given to prospective parents, pressure should never be placed on a woman to choose any particular feeding method. A mother, who actively dislikes the idea, but who feels she 'has to breast-feed', may lose some of the joy of early parenthood.

KEY POINT

The decision on how to feed their baby is for the parents to make, and for carers and health professionals to respect.

Activities
1 What influences might affect parents' decisions between breast-feeding and bottle-feeding?
   (a) Which is cheaper?
   (b) How much equipment will be needed for each method?
   (c) What is the cost of a packet of formula milk?
   (d) How many packets will be required for one year?
   (e) How many bottles will be required?
   (f) What types and amounts of sterilising equipment will be required?

Breast-feeding

Breast-feeding is nature's 'designer food'; the milk is specific to each individual baby and although much can be copied in formula milks, the most important parts cannot. Breast milk changes as the baby grows and her needs alter.

BABIES' NUTRITIONAL NEEDS

Babies need food for energy, growth and repair of body tissues, the maintenance of body temperature, the building of bones and the transmission of nerve impulses.

The rate of a baby's growth is greatest in the first year of life, but especially in the first months – a baby will usually double her birth weight by 5 to 6 months and treble it by 12 months. The largest area of growth in these months is the brain. It is, therefore, very important that a baby's nutritional needs are fully met to allow this important development to take place.

SOURCES OF NUTRITION

Proteins, fats and carbohydrates
These all provide energy and promote growth. Proteins are found mainly in animal sources – meat, cheese, eggs, milk and fish, with smaller amounts in pulses, rice and nuts. Fats occur in dairy products, margarine and nuts, while carbohydrates are found in breads, cereals, potatoes and starchy vegetables.

Vitamins and minerals
Although these are required only in tiny amounts, vitamins and minerals are essential parts of complete nutrition. They allow the baby to use the

important nutrients – proteins, fats and carbohydrates – and they help in the development of the nervous and other body systems. They are found in a wide variety of foods and fruits.

KEY POINT

Breast milk is a complete food for the first months of life and no other nutrients are required.

HOW BREAST MILK IS MADE

The mature breast varies a great deal in size from one woman to another. Sizes of breast, nipple and areola (the surrounding area) are not related to the ability to produce milk successfully.

The important aspect of the nipple is its ability to become erect to allow the baby to attach herself or 'fix' at the breast. The milk does not leave the breast through a single channel at the nipple, but through the lactiferous (milk-producing) ducts leading from each of the lobes (see the diagram below). (There are between 15 and 25 ducts depending on the number of lobes.) The areola also has a number of small glands called Montgomery's tubercles, which become larger and more noticeable during pregnancy. They act like sweat glands and produce a fluid that helps to keep the nipple soft and supple – a natural moisturising cream that shouldn't be removed by washing with any soaps.

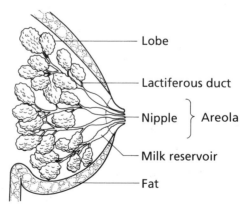

The lactating breast

HOW THE MILK IS RELEASED

Breast milk is released by the 'let-down' reflex (see diagram). Some women find this let-down sensation very strong, while others hardly notice it.

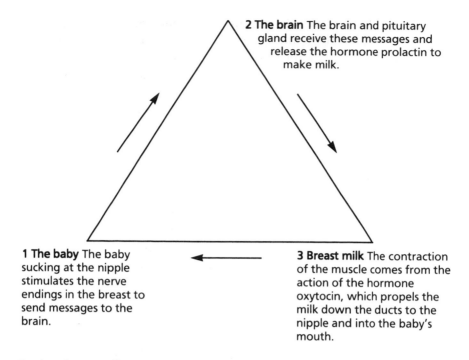

2 The brain The brain and pituitary gland receive these messages and release the hormone prolactin to make milk.

1 The baby The baby sucking at the nipple stimulates the nerve endings in the breast to send messages to the brain.

3 Breast milk The contraction of the muscle comes from the action of the hormone oxytocin, which propels the milk down the ducts to the nipple and into the baby's mouth.

The let-down reflex

Successful breast-feeding depends on 'supply and demand' – the more the baby feeds, the more milk is made. If this mechanism is broken, for example, by giving the baby 'extra' in a bottle, future under-production will result.

THE COMPOSITION OF BREAST MILK

Breast milk is a changing food – it adapts to meet the needs of the growing baby.

Colostrum
This syrupy, yellowish substance is the first milk made by the breasts. It starts after about the fifth month of pregnancy, and stays until about 10 days following the birth.

The purpose of colostrum appears to be to tide the newborn baby over, from her protected life in the womb, to the more exposed and potentially dangerous existence outside. It has a much higher protein content than later, mature breast milk. This is thought to be because:
■ the proteins contain many antibodies, which line the baby's intestines and prevent harmful bacteria from entering the bloodstream

- the high protein levels ensure that even the small amounts taken in will supply sufficient energy to allow the baby to sleep for long periods in the first days after birth.

For these reasons, even when not intending to continue, mothers are often actively encouraged to breast-feed for the first few days at least.

KEY POINT

There is no artificial replacement for colostrum.

MATURE BREAST MILK

When milk begins to be made in the breasts and 'comes in' on the second to fourth day, it is still mixed with colostrum and so looks rich and creamy. By the tenth day the mature milk looks thin and watery by comparison. The change in appearance does not mean reduced quality. The milk is natural and appropriate to the baby's needs.

By the end of the fourth week, it contains approximately a fifth of the protein of colostrum and more fat and glucose. The milk at the beginning, or 'fore', feed is high in the carbohydrate lactose, for a quick energy boost, and the latter, or 'hind', milk is higher in fat content for longer-lasting satisfaction for the baby. Human milk is almost completely digestible. The proteins are broken down into soft curds and quickly pass through into the small intestine. Water forms the liquid part of the milk.

All milks are poor sources of iron and babies depend on the stores laid down in their livers during pregnancy. These supplies will not be finished until the baby is four to six months of age. The high concentration of the sugar, lactose, and vitamin C helps in the absorption of iron.

> **Activity**
> 1 What special clothing will be required for a mother planning to breast-feed?
> 2 Which shops supply this?
> 3 What are the comparative prices with everyday clothing?

MANAGEMENT OF BREAST-FEEDING

A mother breast-feeding her baby will benefit from the advice you can give her when you answer any questions she may have. It is helpful for her to know that it may take time for her and her baby to get to know each other, and that although breast-feeding is natural, many first-time mothers, especially, need additional support to establish feeding patterns.

It is thought to be important for the baby to be put to the breast as soon after birth as possible. This 'skin-to-skin' contact helps the mother and her baby to develop a loving relationship and, in addition, the sucking helps to release hormones to contract the uterus.

The mother needs a comfortable position when feeding, for example, by lying on her side if her perineum is sore. Pain can lessen the let-down reflex and the flow of milk, so feeding in comfort is important. Chairs should give good support to the lower back, feet can be put on a stool if needed and privacy provided.

'Fixing' at the breast

The baby will use the rooting reflex to search for the breast. This can be achieved by stimulating the baby's mouth with the mother's nipple. The baby will then turn to the breast and suck. Take the baby to the breast and never force the breast into the baby's mouth.

The baby is correctly fixed at the breast when she has a mouth full, to include the lower areola – 'chewing' alone on the nipple will cause soreness. When successfully fixed, the baby's mouth will be wide open with her bottom lip curled back and some way from the base of the nipple (see the diagram on page 126) her cheeks will be full and her chin close into the breast. Initially there should be a short burst of sucking followed by strong, steady, deep jaw movements with pauses increasing as the feed progresses. The baby should be relaxed as she feeds with no other sounds than the occasional swallow.

If the baby's nose is pressing into the breast and causing her to come off frequently, reposition the baby so that her head tilts slightly backwards. Pressing the breast, to allow the baby to breathe, alters the shape of the nipple and should be avoided.

KEY POINT

After initially learning how to attach her baby a mother will feel comfortable when she is correctly fixed. This tells her that her baby is feeding in the right position.

Taking the baby off the breast

Allow the baby to come off by herself, when she has finished her feed. If necessary, the mother can put her finger into the corner of the baby's mouth to release the suction.

Frequency and length of feeds

Breast milk production (or lactation) is more easily established if the baby feeds soon after delivery. In the first few weeks of life, a baby who is

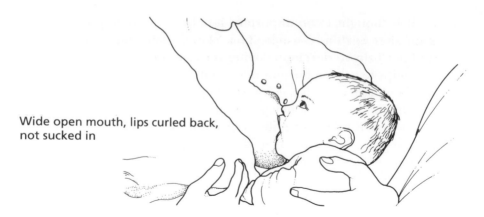

Wide open mouth, lips curled back, not sucked in

The baby fixed correctly at the breast

breast-feeding often feeds as frequently as every one to two hours. Some babies will get all the milk they require within five minutes, while others will take longer. It is important to let the baby decide the length of the feed so that she gets the rich, high fat 'hind' milk at the end of the feed that will satisfy her for longer. Feeding on demand limits the chances of the breasts becoming engorged or overfull with milk. It is not necessary for the baby to feed from both breasts at each feed, however, offering the other breast at the next feed would seem sensible.

Each baby is an individual and it is inappropriate to force her into a feeding routine for an adult's convenience

BENEFITS TO THE BABY FROM BREAST-FEEDING

■ Breast milk is suited to the baby's complete needs and digestion.
■ It is almost germ-free – straight from producer to consumer!
■ The nutritional content of milk contains protective antibodies particularly effective against diarrhoea and vomiting.
■ A breast-fed baby can get more cuddles from her mother.
■ Breast milk has a varying composition, which keeps pace with the baby's growth and changing nutritional requirements.
■ It reduces the incidence and severity of food and respiratory ailments.
■ Studies indicate a measurable increase in intelligence levels in babies who are breast-fed.

BENEFITS TO THE MOTHER FROM BREAST-FEEDING

■ Breast-feeding is thought to aid the mother–child relationship.
■ It is cheap.
■ It is often less work than bottle-feeding when well established.

- It aids in the contraction of the womb.
- It gives a sense of achievement of 'doing the best'.
- It is thought to help in the prevention of breast cancer.

BREAST-FEEDING DIFFICULTIES

Table 5.1 Common breast-feeding difficulties

Problem	Cause	Management
Sore nipples	a) Bad positioning	a) Check the baby's position at breast
	b) Nipples constantly wet	b) Expose nipples to air Change breast pads frequently
	c) Infections such as thrush	c) Treatment for both baby and mother
Cracked nipples	Failure to manage sore nipples	Discontinue feeding Feed from other breast Keep dry Expose nipples to air Treat superficial wounds by keeping moist, use small amounts of paraffin, or squares of paraffin-impregnated tulle, or purified lanolin, cover with a breast pad Resume feeding/check positioning
Engorgement (breasts overfull and painful)	a) Excess blood supply in early days	a) Baby-led feeding Bathing with hot and cold flannels
	b) Poor positioning	b) Check feeding technique
	c) Inadequate removal of milk from breasts	c) Use of firm bra Possibly manual removal of small amounts of milk
Blocked ducts (painful lumps in the breast, mother has no fever)	Poor feeding from baby or poor fixing	Correct fixing of the baby Regular, frequent feeds
Mastitis (infection or inflammation in a segment of the breast, possible fever)	Breast becoming overfull; inadequate feeding	Feed from affected side first Feed frequently Extra fluids to mother Bathe breasts with hot and cold flannels Possible treatment with antibiotics
Insufficient milk	a) Poor fixing	a) Check positioning
	b) Infrequent feeding	b) Baby-led feeding
	c) Use of complementary bottles	c) No bottles of milk
	d) Poorly nourished and overtired mother	d) Support mother, give good diet and sufficient fluids, check amounts of rest
Unsettled baby	Wet, tired, abdominal pain; difficulty in fixing	Check physical comfort Additional support at feeding

Remember! What the mother eats will pass through her breast milk. This will include excess alcohol, all drugs and even nicotine.

Bottle-feeding

Cow's milk is ideal for calves, but it is not the natural food for babies. Unmodified cow's milk, goat's milk and evaporated milk are all unsuitable for babies under six months, because:

■ they contain high levels of the protein, casein, which causes curds in a baby's stomach that are difficult to digest

■ they have high salt contents, which are potentially dangerous for young babies with immature kidneys

■ the fats they contain have a higher proportion of fatty acids, which are poorly absorbed and can hinder calcium absorption

■ the iron in unmodified cow's milk is poorly absorbed by babies.

All babies who are not breast-fed should be given formula milks, preferably up to 1 year. Formula milks have adapted protein and fat contents and are fortified with additional vitamins and minerals – the addition of iron is particularly important. Formula milks for new babies are almost all cow's milk-based. although if babies have difficulty in tolerating them, modified soya milks are available

CHOICE OF MILK

There are many varieties of formula milk available and they are continually being updated. Formula milks are primarily either whey or curd dominant.

Whey dominant formulae contain the protein lactalbumin that is easy for a baby to digest. These milks are particularly suited to the new baby and are nearest in composition to breast milk.

Hungrier babies may be given curd dominant formulae that contain the protein casein. The curds in these milks take longer to digest and the baby feels fuller for longer.

However, there is no difference in the calorie or nutrient content of the two types of milk. Often a baby will come home from hospital having been given a particular brand and, unless there is strong reason to change, it is sensible to continue with that brand to allow both the baby's digestion and her taste buds time to adjust.

For older babies from six months 'follow-on' milks have been produced, which can be used in place of cow's milk. These are less modified than new baby milks and are fortified with extra vitamins, iron and calcium, however, they have no nutritional advantages over new baby milks or breast milk.

Cow's milk intolerance

Some babies have difficulty in tolerating cow's milk products. This may be due either to the specific protein or to lactose (milk sugar). As a result milks have been developed in which proteins from soya bean have been used and the lactose has been changed to glucose. Medical advice should be sought before changing a baby to this type of formula to ensure that any symptoms – normally diarrhoea, rashes and cramp-like pains – are due to an intolerance and not some other cause.

If a soya-based milk is used, a baby may still develop a sensitivity to the protein. Extra care must be taken with dental health as the glucose in soya milk is particularly harmful to teeth. A cup should replace a bottle by 12 months to limit possible damage.

Activities
1 (a) Visit a chemists, or a specialist mother and baby shop. Research the different types of feeding bottles and teats that are available.
   (b) Prepare a talk to your group about the advantages and disadvantages of the different equipment you found.
   (c) How can a new mother discover easily whether the manufacturers' claims are accurate?
2 (a) Visit your local shops. What types of formula milk are available?
   (b) Do they have age recommendations on them?
   (c) Do you think the instructions for making up the feeds are adequate?
   (d) Are all the instructions in English, or are there instructions in different languages? If so, do they reflect those in your local community?
   (e) Look at the packaging. What might affect a parent's choice between the brands?

HOW MUCH FEED SHOULD A BABY BE GIVEN?

The calculation for the nutritional needs of small babies is: 75 ml of fully reconstituted feed for every 500 g of a baby's weight (2½ fl oz per lb) in 24 hours. The total feed is then divided into the number of bottles it is likely the baby will take in that time. For a new baby it is usually about eight feeds. Remember, however, that every baby is individual and that, like breast-feeding, a schedule should again be 'baby-led' to allow for changes in appetite.

REMEMBER!

- Inaccuracy in making up feeds is widespread.
- Over-concentration leads to excessive weight gain, too much salt and possible strain on the baby's kidneys.
- Cereals and sugars should never be added to bottles.
- Although under-concentration is less common, it can lead to poor weight gain, constipation and a distressed, hungry baby.

PREPARATION OF FEEDS

Keeping things clean

Whatever method of sterilisation is chosen, every piece of equipment should be thoroughly clean, including the work surfaces, jugs, knives, and especially your own hands, nails and clothes. Sterilisation (see the diagram below) is most commonly by a chemical agent. Any sterilising tank or container will need to be thoroughly washed every 24 hours and the correct concentration of solution achieved.

KEY POINT

Sterilisation is the complete destruction of all harmful bacteria. Preparing milk feeds for babies requires sterilisation of all equipment used.

1 Wash the bottles, teats and other equipment in hot water and detergent. Use a bottle brush for the inside of bottles. **Do not rub salt on the teats.** Squeeze boiled water through the teats.

2 Rinse everything thoroughly in clean running water.

3 Fill the steriliser with clean, cold water. Add chemical solution. If in tablet form, allow to dissolve.

4 Put the bottles, teats and other equipment (nothing metal) into the water. Ensure everything is covered completely by the water, with no bubbles. If necessary, weight down. Leave for the required time according to manufacturer's instructions.

The procedure for chemical sterilisation

Other non-chemical methods of sterilising equipment

Method	Efficiency	Costs	Dangers
Steam sterilisation	Up to eight bottles take 8 minutes Very effective	Unit required costs £30 approximately	Dangers of scalding from steam if unit is opened before cycle is complete
Microwave sterilisation	Up to four bottles in 10 minutes using effective steam principle	Special unit essential costing approximately £10, plus microwave oven	Not suitable for metal equipment
Boiling	Any number of bottles depending on the size of the saucepan All equipment must be fully submerged with no air bubbles for a full 10 minutes with the water at a rolling boil	Cheap with no expensive equipment required	Dangers of handling large quantities of boiling water must be considered carefully

SAFE PRACTICE

It is essential to continue sterilising all feeding equipment including spoons, measures, jugs, brushes, breast pumps etc. until the baby is nine months old. However, as milk is an ideal medium in which harmful bacteria can breed, it is safe practice to continue to sterilise bottles and teats, whatever the age of the baby, while milk is being given in this way.

General hygiene

Cleanliness is very important in the preparation of baby feeds. Infections can spread through the air and especially by touch through the hands. Germs live and breed easily in a warm nutritious world, such as milk. High standards of personal hygiene are, therefore, vital.

REMEMBER!

- Feeds should be prepared in a kitchen away from young children.
- Always check the temperature of the milk on the inside of your wrist, before giving a baby a feed.

1 Check that the formula has not passed its sell-by date. Read the instructions on the tin. Ensure the tin has been kept in a cool, dry cupboard.

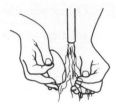

2 Boil some **fresh** water and allow to cool.

3 Wash hands and nails thoroughly.

4 Take required equipment from sterilising tank and rinse with cool, boiled water.

5 Fill bottle, or a jug if making a large quantity, to the required level with water.

6 Measure the **exact** amount of powder using the scoop provided. Level with a knife. **Do not pack down.**

7 Add the powder to the measured water in the bottle or jug.

8 Screw cap on bottle and shake, or mix well in the jug and pour into sterilised bottles.

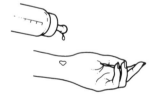

9 If not using immediately, **cool quickly** and store in the fridge. If using immediately, test temperature on the inside of your wrist.

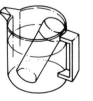

10 Babies will take cold milk but they prefer warm food (as from the breast). If you wish to warm the milk, place bottle in a jug of hot water. **Never keep warm for longer than 45 minutes** to reduce chances of bacteria breeding.

Note Whenever the bottle is left for short periods, or stored in the fridge, cover with the cap provided.

Preparing the bottle feed

- A baby should never be propped up with a bottle and left alone.
- Choking can easily take place.
- Siblings and unsure adults feeding small babies should be supervised at all times.
- Bottles should be used only for milk or cooled, boiled water – never add solids, sugar or use for fruit juices.
- Boiling liquids must never be passed over a small baby.
- A microwave oven is unsuitable for the warming of feeds, unless a special unit is used, as unexpected 'hot spots' can occur.

PROCEDURE FOR GIVING A BOTTLE

- Collect all equipment for the feed, before picking up the baby. Place the bottle on a tray and cover it. Keep it warm in a jug of hot water. Put bib, tissues and any other articles ready as well.
- Change the baby and make her comfortable. Wash your hands.
- Take the baby to the feeding area and sit in a comfortable position. This is a time for talking and cuddling the baby and is an enjoyable time, not to be rushed. Maintain eye contact and hold the baby firmly to give her a sense of security, using a similar position to that for breast-feeding.
- The baby should be held securely, with good eye contact.

The baby should be held securely with good eye contact

- Test the temperature of the bottle against the inside of the wrist.
- Test the size of the teat by turning the bottle upside down. The milk should flow freely at first – several drops per second.

- Stimulate the rooting reflex, by gently touching the baby's lips with the teat and then place the teat over her tongue and into her mouth.
- Check that milk is always present in the teat. This stops the baby becoming frustrated and sucking on air. Gentle tension on the teat helps her to keep sucking steadily.
- If the teat flattens during the feed gently draw it to one side to release the vacuum
- A feed usually takes about 20 minutes. Take a break after about 10 minutes to bring up the baby's wind and after the feed, let the wind come up again.
- Change the baby again, if necessary, and settle her comfortably.
- Clear away, wash utensils thoroughly and re-sterilise.
- Throw away any unused milk, formula or expressed breast milk.

Winding a baby
- Many old wives' tales are linked with bringing up a baby's wind.
- Air rises naturally in an upright bottle, so the baby, too, should be held upright, as this helps nature.
- Apply gentle, but firm pressure to the baby's stomach using the 'heel' of your hand, with the baby is on your lap, or by the front of the body if you are standing.
- Gently rub the baby's back.

This should result in natural winding.

If winding does not occur within a few seconds, it means that the air has continued on down the gastric tract and will be released in the nappy. Babies often expel wind spontaneously and can get distressed, not by the wind, but by the adult's over-eager efforts to help.

IS THE BABY HAVING ENOUGH FOOD?

Whether a baby is breast-fed or bottle-fed anxious parents often ask this question. Before deciding, consider the following:
- appearance and general behaviour
- weight gain – at first this should be 130–170 g (6–8 oz) per week for the first 4 months (breast-fed babies lose more weight after birth than bottle-fed babies, but this is made up by 10 to 14 days)
- alertness when awake, and falling asleep following a period of calm, after a feed
- warm and silky skin, firm and elastic to touch
- pink mucous membranes
- abdomen prominent after feeds, but not distended
- urine and stools passed easily without discomfort

- whether the baby moves and kicks well, cries for food (or if cold or insecure) but does not have prolonged crying spells
- sleeps well between feeds.

Stools give a good indication of the nutritional state of a baby:

- bottle-fed babies' stools are putty-coloured, formed and faecal smelling;
- breast-fed babies' stools are inoffensive, mustard-coloured and very soft.

Weighing

Carers can become exceptionally anxious over how much their baby weighs, so remember that although important, this is only one aspect of assessment of progress. Babies, too, will have spurts and lulls in gaining weight. Minor weights changes can be affected by variation in the times of the day when the baby is weighed, accuracy of the scales, differences between scales, if the baby is clothed or naked, or if weighed before or after a feed.

See Measurement of growth, page 147.

FALTERING GROWTH

Faltering growth is a term used to describe a baby who does not grow at the expected rate and fails to gain sufficient weight. The baby is often list-less, shows some developmental delay and can fall behind in her mile-stones – see Chapter 6 The developing baby.

The causes may be medical, but more commonly result from under-nutrition or mechanical feeding problems:

Possible reasons are:
- sucking difficulties, cleft lip or palate, and pre-term babies (see pages 45 and 62)
- poor absorption of the milk taken in – cow's milk intolerance
- severe illness that cause the baby to be too tired to complete a feed, eg heart problems, whooping cough
  Inadequate child care, including:
- insufficient or incorrectly made up feeds, over-dilution
- difficult mother–baby relationship – poor or delayed bonding and attachment
- maternal illness or depression
- poverty.

How a baby who appears to have faltering growth is managed will depend on the cause. The health visitor will be the first line of support and the baby and her family will be referred for medical assessment. Her growth and general progress will be carefully monitored and her weight checked at regular intervals on a percentile chart (see page 148). Families under stress may be offered a priority day care placement and social work support. For extra information see Influences on physical development, page 149, and Influences on intellectual, emotional and social development, page 157.

Weaning

When a baby is no longer satisfied with breast or formula milk and is taking large quantities of fluids, then weaning (the introduction of solid foods) may be considered. A baby is developmentally able to cope with solid food from 4–6 months. Her digestive enzymes, gastric acid and the absorptive capacities of her small and large bowel mean she can manage solid foods. She is also able to hold up her head, swallow, and digest and move food to the back of her mouth. Both the World Health Organisation and The Department of Health now recommend that as fully breast fed babies have their nutritional needs met completely and effectively by their mother's milk, weaning, before 6 months, is not advised. Before starting weaning check that an unsettled baby isn't bored or, perhaps, wants more cuddling, rather than early solid food. There is no evidence to support the idea that offering solid foods in the evening will help a baby to sleep through the night before she is really ready.

Early weaning is not recommended because:

■ a baby's digestive system is unable to produce all the enzymes needed to digest a wider diet
■ her kidneys are too immature
■ she may have difficulty in swallowing firmer textured food
■ early weaning can set bad eating patterns that can remain with the child in later life – the early introduction of diets high in fats and sugars can lead to obesity, diabetes and dental decay
■ the early introduction of solid foods may be linked to an increase risk of respiratory illnesses and asthma.

AIMS OF WEANING

■ To make the baby less nutritionally dependent on milk. For the baby at the age of one year, milk should provide about 40 per cent of the calorie intake. So, it still remains an important food source for the toddler.
■ To provide a variety of textures, purées and dices, which will enable the baby to join in family meals, so aiding her social and intellectual development.
■ To establish the acceptance of a variety of foods and flavours, setting healthy eating patterns throughout childhood.
■ To introduce iron into the diet. Human and unfortified cow's milks are

Weaning

poor sources of this mineral. During the first three to four months an infant has sufficient iron reserves received from her mother. However after 4–6 months of age, these reserves become run down and foods with good iron contents are needed in the diet.

■ To introduce a cup and spoon to the baby.
■ To provide and extend the learning experience for the baby, by introducing wider tastes, textures, smells, temperatures, consistencies and to promote fine physical skills and help social development.

Managing the weaning process

Weaning textures
Foods from 4–6 months should be:
■ smooth and runny.
Foods from 6–9 months should be:
■ puréed moving to mashed.
Foods from 9–12 months should be:
■ mashed moving to chopped.

Many mothers worry about this aspect of child rearing, so it is especially important that the carer is calm and confident herself. Weaning is an on-going process that the baby, parents and carers learn together.

It helps to remember that the nutritional content of early weaning is less important than the baby beginning to discover and accept, different flavours and textures.

In any learning process a baby should not be too tired or even too hungry. She will not yet realise that the contents of the spoon will satisfy her as the bottle or breast does, so some milk may be given before the spoon to help settle her. Allow plenty of time for her new experience and promote a relaxed atmosphere. The morning or early afternoon feeds are good times for introducing something new.

First weaning foods should be:

- gluten-free
- sugar-free
- salt-free
- of a sloppy consistency, for example, baby rice, mashed potato or banana, mixed with milk.

Use a sterilised, plastic spoon with a flat bowl that allows the baby to suck the contents off easily and initially offer a half to one teaspoon of a bland, warm savoury food.

After this first introduction the same food can be offered the next day – too many new tastes at one time can confuse a small baby and if something upsets her it is easier to discover the cause. Refusal may not mean dislike of the food itself, but of the new experience or the texture.

After two to three days when the baby is used to the new flavour and consistency, another food can be tried. If the first chosen weaning food is a baby cereal, the next food could be a purée of fruit or vegetable, for example purée of carrots. Babies appear to enjoy the very bland nature of cereals and there is a risk of a baby becoming overweight if too much is given.

As the quantity of solid food a baby eats increases, the amounts of milk offered may be gradually reduced so that by about the fifth week of weaning one of the milk feeds can be completely replaced by solids. As the milk is reduced, the baby will be thirsty and cool boiled water in a bottle (never sweet drinks that can cause dental decay) should be given Diluted pure fruit juices can be offered by a spoon and cup, egg cup or training beaker.

Babies do not need teeth to cope with more lumpy food as they use their hard back gums to manage lumps, and, from about seven months, pieces of hard foods such as crusts, peeled apple or a partially cooked carrot can be given.

KEY POINTS

- Supervision is important in weaning to limit the dangers of choking.
- Worries over salmonella mean it is no longer recommended that eggs, the white or the yolk, are used as weaning foods, and eggs should not now be part of a baby's diet until after one year of age.

As the baby becomes more actively involved, let her 'help' by holding a spoon as well. A baby can discover the textures and temperatures of her food with her fingers, as well as developing co-ordination skill in getting food into her mouth. Babies enjoy this part of meal times. Inevitably a mess can occur, so plan for this with bibs and protection of carpets etc. and allow her plenty of time. Learning to cope with lumps, experiencing different tastes and textures, developing hand–eye skills and eating in family groups are just as important as the nutritional aspect of weaning and should be encouraged. Always talk to her at meal times and try to widen her vocabulary by introducing new words such as 'hot', 'cold', 'thick' etc.

Research tells us that babies who are discouraged from playing with their foods, from developing the skills of self-feeding and those who are not offered different textured foods, may have related eating and other difficulties later in childhood. These may include difficulty in tolerating lumps, food refusal and dislike of messy play activities.

Each baby is an individual and some take to weaning more easily than others. One baby of six months may effortlessly accept a spoon and new foods, while another may not be ready for several months more. Ensure that you offer the baby the opportunity and make it a relaxed and pleasurable experience. Let the baby set the pace.

Vitamin supplements
It is advised that from six months of age a baby who has breast milk as her main drink should be given A and D supplements. In addition, it is recommended that all children between the ages of one and five need vitamin A and D supplements.

Activity
Make a list of new words that might be said to a baby of nine months during lunch time. What early maths and science ideas might be introduced at this time?

Cleanliness of weaning equipment
Sterilisation is no longer essential, as social cleanliness – a high standard of personal and domestic hygiene – is sufficient from nine months. However the baby should have her own bowl, mug etc., which is kept for her sole use. Everything can now be either washed thoroughly in a sink, or a dishwasher. The exception remains for bottles, which have contained milk. These should continue to be sterilised, as stale milk is a good source for bacterial growth and so a potential threat to health.

Babies with special needs
Babies with special needs may have difficulty in coping with either the amount or the consistency of a food and with swallowing. See Chapter 10 Feeding and mealtimes, page 254, for management.

Activity
Make a list of new words that might be introduced to a baby of 12 months during lunch time. What maths and science ideas might be learnt during this time?

RESTRICTIONS ON WEANING DIETS

When weaning their baby some parents wish to follow their own dietary codes, which can be affected by religious, cultural or personal beliefs.

Vegetarian diets

A baby whose parents do not wish her to eat meat or fish will need to be weaned using a combination of cereals, beans and seeds, dairy and soya produce, fruit and vegetables.

Nuts, which are a good source of protein, should only be offered as ground nuts from one year and preferably not until three years.

Quorn and textured vegetable protein (TVP) are unsuitable for babies as their salt content is too high.

Vegan diets

Diets for babies where no animal or fish flesh, or animal products are allowed, are challenging and you will need expert dietary advice. This will help to ensure that a nutritionally balanced diet can be achieved that includes sufficient calcium, vitamin B12 and protein for the developing baby.

Hindus and Sikhs

Fish, meat, eggs and foods containing them, are not permitted.

Muslims

Meat used must be killed by the Halal method and there are some weaning foods on the market that now meet this criterion. Pork and pork products are not permitted either.

Jews

Pork and pork products are not permitted and other meat must be kosher, from specialist butchers. Fish, which have fins and scales, can be used but not shellfish and eels. Any other products must be checked to ensure that animal products that are not kosher have not been used in processing, for example, biscuits made with animal fat and cheese containing rennet.

Chinese

Usually dairy products are excluded

Table 5.2 The weaning stages – a suggested plan

Stages	1	2	3	4	5	6
On waking	Breast- or bottle-feed	Breast- or bottle-feed	Breast- or bottle-feed	Breast- or bottle-feed	Breast- or bottle- feed	Breast- or bottle-feed/cup
Breakfast	1–2 teaspoons baby rice mixed with milk from feed or with water; breast- or bottle-feed	2 teaspoons baby rice mixed with milk from feed or with water; breast- or bottle-feed	Baby rice or cereal mixed with milk from feed or with water or pureed banana; breast- or bottle-feed	Cereal mixed with milk from feed or water; fruit, toast fingers spread with unsalted butter	Cereal, fish or fruit; toast fingers; milk	Cereal and milk; fish, yoghurt or fruit; toast and milk
Lunch	Breast- or bottle-feed	1–2 teaspoons pureed or sieved vegetables or vegetables and chicken; breast- or bottle-feed	Pureed or sieved meat or fish and vegetables, or proprietary food; followed by 2 teaspoons pureed fruit or prepared baby dessert; drink of cooled, boiled water or well-diluted juice (from cup)	Finely minced meat or mashed fish, with mashed vegetables; mashed banana or stewed fruit or milk pudding; drink of cooled boiled water or well-diluted juice in a cup	Mashed fish, minced meat or cheese with vegetables; milk pudding or stewed fruit; drink	Well-chopped meat, liver or fish or cheese with mashed vegetables; milk pudding or fruit fingers; drink
Tea	Breast- or bottle-feed	Breast- or bottle-feed	Pureed fruit or baby dessert; breast- or bottle-feed	Toast with cheese or savoury spread; breast- or bottle-feed	Bread and butter sandwiches with savoury spread or seedless jam; sponge finger or biscuit; milk drink	Fish, cheese or pasta; sandwiches; fruit; milk drink
Late evening	Breast- or bottle-feed	Breast- or bottle-feed	Breast- or bottle-feed, if necessary	Breast- or bottle-feed, if necessary		

REMEMBER! A baby who is breast fed has her nutritional needs fully met until she is at least six months of age – weaning is not recommended before this.

REMEMBER!

- Is the baby comfortable?
- Wash the baby's hands before and after meals.
- Is the baby well supervised?
- Do not add salt or sugar.
- Test food temperature with a separate sterilised spoon – no blowing or putting your finger in her food.
- Check for bones in fish and pips in fruit.
- Remove bib after meals.
- Modified milks should be used until the baby is one year old.

KEY POINT

Not all cultures use spoons and forks when moving babies from milk to solid foods.

FEEDING PROBLEMS

Table 5.3 lists the main problems associated with feeding.

Table 5.3 Problems associated with feeding

Problem	Signs and symptoms	Management
Allergies and intolerances	Faltering growth, diarrhoea and vomiting, infantile eczema/general rashes, wheezing	Liaise with medical advice/dietician Breast-feed if possible Use cow's milk replacement, if advised, for example, soya milk
Constipation	Small, hard, infrequent stools	Increase fluid intake Ensure feed not too concentrated No laxatives or sugar in feeds If weaned, increase fruit or vegetable intake Check to exclude underfeeding
Diarrhoea	Frequent, loose watery stools	Check hygiene of food preparation Give clear fluids and seek medical advice
Colic	Babies of (usually) less than 3 months cry and draw legs up appearing to have abdominal pain. Often showing distress at the same time of day – frequently early evening	Cause unknown Feed baby Check teat for size and flow, if bottle-fed Monitor feeding technique Reassure carer that pain is self-limiting Comfort baby with movement and cuddling Seek advice from health visitor
Overfeeding	Baby vomits/unsettled, passes large stools, sore buttocks, excessive weight gain	Seek clinic/health visitor advice Check re-constitution of feeds
Possetting	Baby frequently vomits small amounts, but gains weight and is happy	Condition self-limiting usually solved when baby is upright and walking Monitor weight
Underfeeding	Baby very hungry, wakes and cries; stools small and dark; poor weight gain; vomiting as a result of crying and air swallowing	Ensure feeds are correctly re-constituted If breast-feeding, check technique and mother's diet Increase frequency of feeds, before quantities

REMEMBER!

- Diarrhoea and vomiting can be serious in small babies, whatever the reason, and medical advice should be sought.
- A baby's feeding difficulties are stressful for parents – they will need your support.

QUICK CHECK

1 Explain why goat's milk and milk bought from the milkman are unsuitable for a new baby.
2 What would be the expected weight gain of a baby in the first six months of life?
3 'Milk is a food, not a drink.' Explain what this means.
4 What would you say to a mother when explaining that breast milk is about 'supply and demand'?
5 What is colostrum, and what are its special advantages?
6 How does breast milk change during a baby's feed?
7 What advice might you offer to a mother who says her breast-feeding baby is 'not getting enough milk'?
8 How could you ensure that a baby who is bottle-fed receives clean and safe food?
9 Calculate how much feed a baby of 3.5 kg will need in 24 hours.
10 How do you know whether a baby, breast-fed or bottle-fed, is receiving enough food?
11 An apparently healthy and happy baby loses a small amount of weight on a weekly clinic visit. What might be the reason for this?
12 Describe the differences in the stools of babies being breast-fed and bottle-fed.
13 Why is it important that a baby does not have salt added to her food during weaning?
14 How could you help a baby have a 'total learning experience' when being weaned?
15 Explain the difference between sterilisation and social cleanliness.
   (a) When would you move from one to the other?
   (b) In what special conditions would you continue to sterilise bottles?

6 THE DEVELOPING BABY

> **This chapter covers:**
> ■ An overview of general development
> ■ Physical development
> ■ The development of vision
> ■ The development of hearing
> ■ The development of language
> ■ Social, emotional and intellectual development
> ■ A summary of the stages of development

An overview of general development

Watching a baby grow and develop new skills is an exciting time. 'Signposts' or 'milestones' plot this progress and help parents, carers and professionals ensure that a baby is developing at the anticipated rate, for example, a baby would be expected to smile by six weeks and sit unaided by eight months. Within these patterns there are wide varieties of 'normal' development, for example, black babies usually have stronger muscle control at birth and their physical development remains ahead throughout the first year of life.

Often, babies appear to concentrate their improving skills in one specific area before moving on to extend another. A baby attempting to learn to crawl, for example, may 'practise' her speech less at this time. Gaining new skills, too, can often seem to be an uneven process with spurts and lulls. Babies will need the necessary stimulation when they are ready to master something new.

A baby's development is monitored in the following areas:
■ physical development
■ intellectual development
■ language development
■ emotional development
■ social development.

This is easy to remember if you take the first letter of each – PILES. Alternatively, from the headings social, physical, intellectual, cognitive and emotional, the word SPICE is used in a similar way to trigger a total view of development.

Many factors can affect a baby's development. These include inheritance (her genes), culture, health, opportunity, space and freedom and the most important developmental influence, which is the consistency and love from the baby's main carer.

One of the most important developmental influences is the consistency and love from the baby's main carer.

Physical development

Although babies gain complex skills at different ages, the pattern is always the same, for example – head control develops before sitting, crawling and walking (see the diagram below), cooing develops before babbling and single words.

Involuntary reflexes must be lost before controlled movements begin – see Examination of the nervous system on page 47.

In the development of controlled physical movement, gross motor skills come first, starting from head to toe, with large movement arriving before fine movement – the eyes and lips are the exception to this rule.

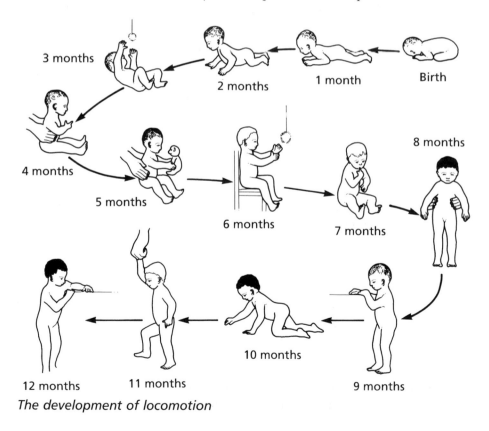

3 months

2 months

1 month

Birth

4 months

5 months

6 months

7 months

8 months

8 months

10 months

12 months   11 months

9 months

The development of locomotion

A baby will gain large and fine movements at the expected times depending on:

■ an undamaged nervous system – brain, nerves and nerve pathways;
■ healthy bones and muscles.

See Table 6.1 on pages 162–6, for a summary of the stages of development.

GROWTH

Growth – an increase in size, length and weight – is dependent upon a number of factors, as shown in the diagram on page 149.

Measurement of growth

Growth is measured and recorded on percentile charts (see page 148). Different charts are used for boys and girls, and for babies under one year two charts may be used.

One is for babies who are born pre-term, allowing head circumference and weight measurements to be recorded and charted from 20 weeks' gestation up to the expected date of delivery (EDD).

The second chart is used with the majority of babies and plots the growth of babies born from 30 weeks' gestation and up to 52 weeks or one year. Measurements of head circumference, length and weight are taken, and can be charted on the graph at regular intervals during the first year.

How to record

The birth measurement is an important starting point from which all other recordings are compared. A single measurement of a baby, which has no other measurement to compare with, is meaningless. It cannot indicate any deviation or growth pattern.

Accurate recording of the gestational age of a baby (the number of weeks spent in utero) must be the starting point from which other measurements follow. Three measurements are generally taken in babies born at term: weight, length and head circumference.

Weight

The birth weight is taken and recorded following delivery. Subsequent weighing should be undertaken with the baby naked, using regularly balanced, calibrated scales. This frequently takes place in the child health clinic by the health visitor.

Length

This may be difficult to record accurately in a small baby and two people are needed using a measuring mat with a head and footboard. The baby must be supine with one person holding the baby's head against the headboard and the second bringing the footboard up to the heels. The knees should be **gently** pressed down to help ensure the legs are flat.

Head circumference
This is especially important in the first six months of life. A non-stretchable, thin metal or plastic tape is placed around the largest part of the head, mid-way between the eyebrows and the hairline at the front and the most prominent part of the skull at the back.

Patterns of measurements
These three measurements are plotted on the percentile chart (see pages 151 and 152) Growth should follow a steady path on the chart and each baby will have her own individual pattern. An average-sized baby will generally follow the 50th centile line, a very large baby possibly above the 98th centile and a very small baby the 9th centile or less. There are variations according to a baby's ethnic background, African-Caribbean babies, for example, may be slightly above the 50th centile, while Asian babies may be slightly below it.

KEY POINT

All three measurements (height, weight and head circumference) should follow the same line, and if this does not happen further investigation will be needed.

REMEMBER!

All babies are individuals – Table 6.1 on page 162 and the photos on page 150 are just a guide to steps of development.

HOW TO RECORD ON A PERCENTILE CHART

- If starting a new record, select the correct chart for sex and gestation, or mark your results on the baby's existing chart if one is already in use.
- The age of a baby in weeks is shown at the top and bottom of the chart (see Percentile chart for girl's weight on page 151). Find the exact age of the baby at the time of measuring and mark this point and hold a ruler from top to bottom through this point.
- The measurements are indicated on either side of the chart in the margins, head measurements at the top on the left, the length in the middle in centimetres and the weight at the bottom in kilograms, both shown on the right of the chart.

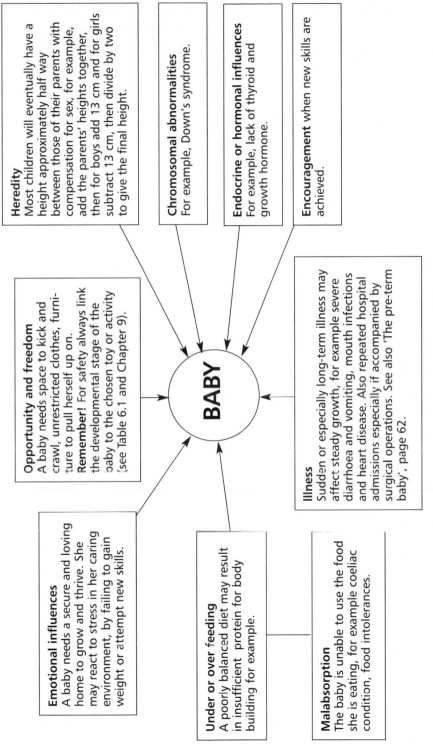

Heredity
Most children will eventually have a height approximately half way between those of their parents with compensation for sex, for example, add the parents' heights together, then for boys add 13 cm and for girls subtract 13 cm, then divide by two to give the final height.

Chromosomal abnormalities
For example, Down's syndrome.

Endocrine or hormonal influences
For example, lack of thyroid and growth hormone.

Encouragement when new skills are achieved.

Opportunity and freedom
A baby needs space to kick and crawl, unrestricted clothes, furniture to pull herself up on.
Remember! For safety always link the developmental stage of the baby to the chosen toy or activity (see Table 6.1 and Chapter 9).

Emotional influences
A baby needs a secure and loving home to grow and thrive. She may react to stress in her caring environment, by failing to gain weight or attempt new skills.

BABY

Illness
Sudden or especially long-term illness may affect steady growth, for example severe diarrhoea and vomiting, mouth infections and heart disease. Also repeated hospital admissions especially if accompanied by surgical operations. See also 'The pre-term baby', page 62.

Under or over feeding
A poorly balanced diet may result in insufficient protein for body building for example.

Malabsorption
The baby is unable to use the food she is eating, for example coeliac condition, food intolerances.

Key point Refer to 'Role of carer' in Table 6.1 on pages 162–6, and 'Toys and play' on pages 200–7.

Influences on physical development

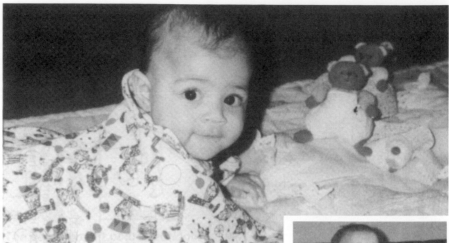

At about 5-6 months, the baby will rest on her forearms and try to get her chest off the ground

At about 8-9 months, the baby is able to crawl and explore by herself

At about 12 months, the baby is able to stand unaided

■ Using a rule, record the three measurements with a cross at the three points where they bisect the downward age line. Date these marks at the bottom.

■ Consider the baby's measurements against her expected curve. On percentile charts variations in the range of growth patterns are indicated with pink or blue lines (which can be solid, dotted or in blocks of shading), for each of the three areas of measurement. They provide a quick visual clue as to a baby's immediate progress against babies of similar age.

Special uses of percentile charts

Percentile charts are an important tool in assessing and monitoring the progress of babies who have faltering growth. Several sets of recordings at

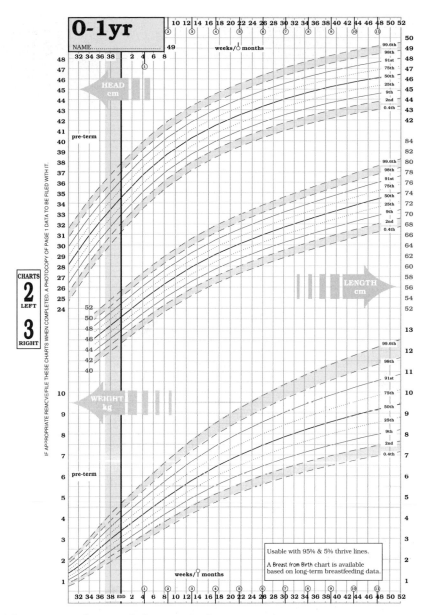

Girls pre-term (30 weeks' gestation) – 52 weeks

regular intervals are needed to give a clear picture of a growth pattern that is deviating from what is expected.

Hydrocephalus also can be detected. Here the spinal fluid fails to drain effectively from the membranes lining the brain and causes the head to swell. Regular monitoring of the head circumference allows prompt diagnosis and treatment, which can minimise possible brain damage.

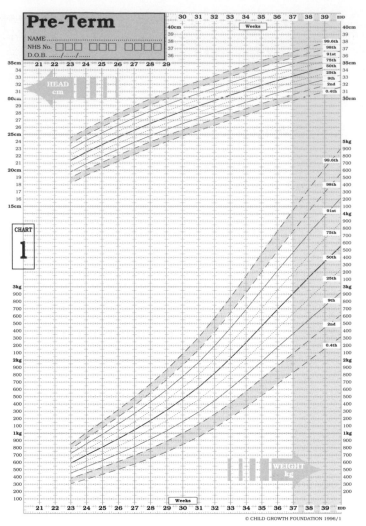

Boys pre-term (20 weeks' gestation) – EDD

REMEMBER!

Babies' measurements are charted from their gestational age (weeks spent in utero). This is especially important for babies who are born pre-term before their EDD (expected date of delivery), as it allows for adjustments to be made for their lack of growing time.

Activity
1 On the percentile chart for girls record:
   (a) birth-weight (40 weeks' gestation) 3.0 kg, length 50 cm, head circumference 34 cm;

(b) 2½ weeks, weight 6 kg, length 60 cm, head circumference 43 cm.
 2 What percentile curve did the three measurements follow at birth *and* at three months? Was there any measurement that might give cause for concern?

The development of vision

Babies can see from birth, but focus at about 20 cm – the distance from the baby to her mother's face when breast-feeding.

A newborn baby will turn to a source of light. By three months she will watch faces and look around her and, by four to six months, vision is thought to be similar to that of adults. Babies' eyes should be working together by this age and a squint, or 'lazy eye', must be investigated. Babies appear to respond to red and blue colours more eagerly than others. Choose toys that are big, bright and colourful to stimulate her vision, and use sounds to complement and explain everyday activities.

Important signs to watch for (if late or missing they may mean developmental delay):

- no eye-to-eye contact, especially with her mother
- does not smile in response to her mother, by 6 weeks
- does not follow the human face and bright objects, by 2 months
- abnormal eye movements
- does not reach for objects, by 6 to 12 months
- is not mobile and avoiding obstacles by 1 year.

REMEMBER!

Always take parents' concerns seriously.

The development of hearing

Hearing is difficult to test in the newborn baby, however, a baby should respond to loud noises by blinking or startling. She should turn to her mother's voice or a musical toy by three months of age and by nine months she should be able to find the source of a whisper.

Hearing and the development of speech are linked and babies who are hearing-impaired will make noises similar to any other baby until six months of age. A deaf baby is unable to experiment with sounds by practising and listening to their own efforts, so by six months they often become silent.

Stimulate a baby's hearing by using different tones in your voice. Make sure she can see your face when you talk to her, especially in the early months. As she begins to vocalise, give her time to respond and try not to deluge her with your voice without giving her an opportunity to vocalise in response.

Here are the important signs to watch for (if late or missing they may mean developmental delay).

Birth to 6 months:
- does not blink or startle at loud noises
- does not react to household noises such as vacuum cleaner, either by stilling or appearing to listen when they start
- does not smile responsively by six weeks – if the baby was born full term.

Infant from 6 to 12 months:
- does not turn to prime carer's voice across the room
- does not babble in conversation – vocalising decreases
- does not respond to own name.

REMEMBER!

Always take parents' concerns seriously.

The development of language

Even before birth, a baby is beginning to recognise her mother's voice and immediately after birth will be soothed by this sound. A newborn baby's cry is a reflex action to a variety of factors such as distress at the sound of sudden noises, or hunger. This will continue for several weeks, but by 3 to 6 weeks her cry will be used in specific situations, for example, to show hunger or thirst.

At 8 weeks she can detect human voices and responds differently to human and non-human forms. A baby will begin to coo and use vowels. Carers can help by changing their tone and the volume of their voices when talking to babies.

By 12 weeks the baby will recognise specific sounds, such as a spoon in a cup, and by 4 to 6 months will be using the consonants p, b, m, g, k, f, v, r and l. She will enjoy babbling and listening to the sounds she makes. She will use her sounds to attract attention and will enjoy the responses she gains.

KEY POINT

Always use everyday care procedures to promote language. Changing nappies, feeding and bathing are all times when interaction can take place.

Always:

- **tell** the baby what you are doing;
- **reinforce** with demonstration – for example, talk about and show her the clean nappy; tell her about her toes and tickle them to help her make the link;
- **describe** objects and activities, as you work, using such words as large, small, over and under.

The 'labelling' of objects and parts of her body like this will help her understand words, long before she is able to speak them.

By 6 to 7 months her language is becoming even more complicated and the baby is able to change from babbling to cooing, repeating sounds and altering loudness and length. She will enjoy the carer pointing out objects, games of throwing and the beginning of turn-taking. Always give her time to practise her sounds and respond by smiles and praise.

At 8 to 9 months the baby will mimic sounds and in another month repeat and copy sounds (known as echolalia), although they will not be understood. She will learn to point to objects and will be able to respond to simple requests, such as 'Give me the dolly'. She is beginning to link words to meanings, so reinforce this by repeating her words back to her.

Finally, by 12 months, the baby begins to have true speech and can use one or two words with meaning, but understands many more. She will enjoy simple books, with single known objects, and will repeat words spoken to her. The carer can help her develop her language skills by involving the baby in all her care, for example, by describing her clothes as she is dressed or explaining what she is having for her new weaning food. It is important to allow the baby time to both listen to the human voice and to practise her own developing skills.

KEY POINT

A baby will enjoy simple picture books with you for short periods at quite a young age. Choose books that show familiar objects to gain and keep her interest and reflect her own culture to her. Early pleasurable introduction to books can set good habits for childhood.

REMEMBER!

- Singing, too, promotes language development – introduce songs and rhymes from different cultures.
- A dummy is a comfort object useful in helping a distressed baby to sleep. However, always remove it when the baby is awake to allow her to practise her speech, and to develop her lip and tongue control.

Important signs to watch for (if late or missing they may mean developmental delay):

- mother or carers are not communicating with the child
- severe feeding difficulties
- at 3–6 months baby is silent most of the time even when alone
- limited response to noise, minimal eye contact
- by 6–9 months does not respond to play – has not babbled or has stopped babbling
- shows lack of rhythm and intonation when babbling
- no consistent response to noise
- by 9–12 months not trying to communicate by vocalising or pointing
- not responding to single words and simple commands
- not using a wide range of different sounds and intonations.

REMEMBER!

- Always take parents' concerns seriously.
- Language progress is dependent on effective hearing.

Activity 1

Develop your own personal resource file for songs, finger and action rhymes:

   (a) as you learn a new one write it down, with a description if necessary, for future use;

   (b) ask your placement colleagues, peers and friends to help you extend your repertoire;

   (c) especially valuable will be the songs and rhymes known by friends and colleagues from different parts of Britain and other countries.

Activity 2

   (a) With a baby of between 6 and 12 months, who is known to you and relaxed in your presence, tape-record his or her 'language' for a 5-minute period. Play this tape to your fellow students in college, ask them to assess the age of the baby from the sounds he or she is using.

   (b) Discuss ways of extending and promoting the language of the baby you chose.

Language (see page 154) **and eye contact**
Exposure to language, changing tones and pitches, explanations
Time for baby to practise words and sounds

Responsive care
Different cries recognised and responded to, for example hunger, loneliness, pain, boredom.
Giving positive responses to achievements, for example by smiling, clapping, hugging.
Regular care routines: for example bathing, mealtimes, play and social opportunities that are a family priority and give stability and structure.

Consistent, sensitive care
Effective bonding between mother and baby
Strong stable attachments.
Gradual introduction to wider social networks.

BABY

The meeting of basic physical needs
Food, warmth, cleanliness, safety, health, physical contact, including cuddling, rocking, games and comforters (special blankets, thumbs, dummies)

Stimulation of the senses
1) *Smell*, for example, food, flowers
2) *Hearing* (see page 153), for example, familiar sounds, music, voices
3) *Vision* (see page 153), for example, mobiles, faces, pictures
4) *Touch*, for example, holding, caressing, massage
5) *Taste*, for example, slowly developing range of foods and textures

Stimulation by toys and activities
Age-appropriate toys and games, for example, holding, manipulating, fitting and shaking toys, finger games, peek-a-boo, rhymes, board and picture books, familiar routines
Opportunity to explore own world by crawling, etc.

Influences on intellectual, emotional and social development

Intellectual, social and emotional development

These areas of development depend upon and influence each other (see Influences on intellectual, emotional and social development on page 157 and the table, A summary of the stages of development, page 162).

A baby needs to develop a special relationship with her prime carers – this gives her the security and the confidence to learn, to explore and begin happily to accept new situations and people. The first step in this process begins immediately after birth, with the mother and baby's emerging relationship, see Bonding, page 42.

ATTACHMENT

In addition to the vital mother–child bonding, the first relationships a baby makes with her main care givers are seen as very important in the development of her mental health. These relationships are called 'attachments'. Ainsworth and Bell (1970) described attachment as 'an affectional tie that one person or animal forms between himself and another specific one – a tie that binds them together in space and endures over time'.

There continue to be many theories about how and when attachment begins to take place, but most experts agree that it is a gradual process with the signs beginning to appear between six weeks and six months, and which develop in intensity over the following months. At about six weeks a baby will smile and respond more readily to her known adults than to strangers. By about six or seven months she starts to show a strong attachment to a specific care giver, usually her mother, and will begin to indicate distress when separated from her. She will look to her specific carer for encouragement, smiles and her physical presence for bathing, feeding and care routines. When crawling and exploring her new-found world she will repeatedly return to her main care giver for reassurance before setting off again to find other exciting things to explore. If the baby learns that her prime care givers respond and meet her needs consistently, in this first year, she is then able in her second and later years to have confidence in other adults and situations in the outside world.

It is thought that if a baby fails to make secure early attachments she will later find difficulty in making and maintaining relationships. This may lead to harmful effects on other developmental areas. Secure attachments give a baby stability and help her develop trust and confidence to explore, develop and learn. Babies who do not have their needs met effectively in this first year may superficially appear to separate easily from their known adults, or may alternate between distress and passivity. As they grow they can become anxious and reluctant to explore and play, and they may display behaviour problems later in childhood.

KEY POINTS

- Bonding is the parent's tie to their infant, occurring in the first hours or days of life, while attachment refers to the gradually developing relationships between the infant and primary carers.
- It was thought that the only primary attachment a baby made was with her mother, but research now tells us that multiple attachments can take place. However, the quality of these attachments remains vital.

A newborn baby is a social being, responding to a variety of stimulation and needing the company of other humans from birth. She learns quickly to recognise her mother's voice, the way her body moves and even her taste and smell.

The world is an exciting and fascinating place to her even if, initially, she understands little of it.

A baby shows her need to socialise with humans as early as two to three months by:

- attempting to imitate facial gestures – even by crying if her mother is distressed or angry;
- maintaining eye contact, and increasingly letting her eyes follow her carer around the room;
- moving her head to seek a social source;
- smiling responsively, from four to six weeks;
- crying;
- waving – often somewhat random movements;
- making noises of contentment from early weeks, and by cooing and gurgling from three months.

The skill and sensitivity with which a carer interprets such pre-verbal signs and responds to them is important in giving a baby confidence and security to try again. A baby who is ignored or handled insensitively is less likely to extend her social and intellectual skills easily. She needs reinforcement and reward for her efforts by you taking notice of her.

A baby in her first three months will respond randomly to a variety of other people, even strangers, but as she develops she shows that she has learnt to recognise specifically just a few special adults and by six months is anxious when separated from these known people.

If her mother or prime carer is near she will cry at strangers and reach out to be held by her familiar adult. This fear may not be so obvious if the situation is unfamiliar, the mother is absent and there are several strangers present.

- A baby is said to be attached when she recognises her prime carer and shows anxiety when separated – usually between six and nine months.
- This important sign tells us that the baby has learnt to discriminate and recognise people as separate individuals. Now she can begin to develop permanent meaningful relationships from her safe secure base – the attached adult.

In her early months when an object or person is out of sight the baby thinks they are gone for ever. However, towards the end of her first year object-permanence develops. A baby has learnt to understand that objects, although hidden and out of sight, still exist. This is an important intellectual concept for a baby as she now realises that even though her mother may be not immediately visible, for example in another room, she is still near.

Activity

Visit a parent/carer, baby and toddler group and ask to observe the children at play. If possible watch a baby of about nine months who is crawling.

1 How confident is she to leave her known adult?
2 How many times does she return to the adult during a session?
3 Record any non-verbal signs of anxiety – eyes following, pulling at adults' clothing.
4 How much vocalisation is taking place?
5 How much reinforcement is the adult giving the child – what happens if the baby does not earn a response from the adult?

MEETING EMOTIONAL, INTELLECTUAL AND SOCIAL NEEDS

A baby needs opportunities to extend her experiences, but she also can only achieve this successfully from a secure base. It is important that a baby is not flooded with large numbers of different people handling her, confusing her and possibly making her anxious. She will respond best by initially getting to know a few people well – her parents, grandparents, siblings and her child-care worker.

Respond to the signals she gives:
- smile back at her
- repeat her developing sounds
- name objects you use with her and repeat the words (labelling)

- respond to any distress, by attempting to understand the reason – feeding her, changing her nappy, giving her company and stimulation – and letting her see you while you work (see Why babies cry, page 105)
- meet her physical needs, ensuring she is warm, dry, comfortable and safe
- check that toys and activities chosen meet her changing developmental needs (see Table 6.1, Role of carer, on page 162 and Toys and play, page 200).

KEY POINTS

Important signs to watch for (if late or missing they may mean developmental delay):

- not smiling responsively with mother by 6 weeks
- lack of response by prime carers in responding to the baby's needs
- excessive crying
- lethargic and uninterested
- no stranger-anxiety by 6–9 months
- head-banging and rocking at 9–12 months
- faltering growth (see page 135).

REMEMBER!

Always take parents' concerns seriously.

Activity
A long-term baby study

The best way to learn how a baby develops is to observe. Find a friend or relative who will share their baby's progress with you and whom you can easily visit at home. It is best if they are in the final stages of pregnancy and you can discuss the coming birth with them.

1 Plan to record the progress of the baby fortnightly for the first six months of life and monthly until one year of age.

2 At the first interview record birth weight, length, head circumference and Apgar score (see page 38), as well as anything particular to your chosen baby, for example, the type of delivery and feeding method.

3 At each visit record what the baby is doing.
   - If she is sleeping, describe posture, noises, colour, etc.
   - Try to visit during a bathing session and at a feeding time.
   - As the baby grows, comment on her interaction with mother and siblings, if any.
   - Record types of toys used and whether you feel they were effective at arousing and keeping the baby's interest.

- Record any periods of illness and the outcome.
- Try to visit during a clinic development session with the mother and her baby, for example her six–eight week check or eight-month check. Record what happens and how the baby responds.
- Ask how the baby's hearing and vision are assessed, and observe when the baby begins to locate sounds, follow moving objects and focus.
- Observe the developing relationships the baby makes within the family. Record the signs of specific attachments.
- Chart the development of language – the sounds the baby makes. Perhaps record them on tape.

Accuracy is important and it is necessary to record exactly what you see and then compare the progress with Table, 6.1 A summary of the stages of development (see page 162).

Remember: always share your observations with the mother. Remember you are learning about the development of her baby, not judging her child care.

Table 6.1 A summary of the stages of development

Age	Development	Role of carer
Birth **4 weeks**	**Physical development** Will fix on faces and objects Eyes follow bright moving objects. Lies supine with head to one side. Drops objects in hands, which are clenched. Reacts to loud sounds **Language and social** Throaty noises Interested in faces **Learning and emotional** Reflex response, but becomes distressed to discomfort, for example cold. Enjoys feeding and cuddling Great need to suck Quietens when picked up	Talk to baby, change tone, describe events Baby enjoys mobiles and faces (visual range 8–10 in) Hold, touch, fondle Music, gentle movement Use baby's name Introduce to household noises and different rooms Change position of cot Use brightly coloured clothing and linen Hold firmly, talk and sing to baby when feeding Expect no set routine Feed on demand
8 weeks Posterior fontanelle closed	**Physical development** Controlled movement beginning to replace reflex responses. Turns from side to back. Begins to lift head briefly from prone position. Shows eye co-ordination to	Use wind chimes and mobiles the baby will see moving from room movement or own activity. Use bright colours in pictures placed in cot Place in supporting infant chair to watch adult's activity, or carry around. Use light

Table 6.1 A summary of the stages of development *continued*

Age	Development	Role of carer
	lights and objects, squinting less obvious. 'Listens' to bell and 'stills'	rattles, let baby kick without nappies Expose to different textures. Massage, and stroke limbs for example when bathing
	Language and social Begins to respond to adult's voice. Looks for sounds. Begins to coo and squeal with pleasure. Smiles in response to adult. Cries now begin to indicate type of distress	Talk and smile with baby, sing – allow time to respond
	Learning and emotional Begins to recognise familiar face, more interested in own world. Enjoys sucking	Talk to baby when feeding, hold close First immunisation (see page 169)
12 weeks Primitive reflexes now disap- pearing	**Physical development** Baby rests on forearms when prone. Basic crawling movements, may get chest off surface. Shows prefer- ence for sleeping position. Holds objects in hands brings to mouth, cannot release. Watches hands. Head control improved	
	Social and language Generally more sociable, smiles readily, babbles and coos. Stops when handled or sees known adult, turns head to follow. Enjoys play- ing when feeding. Stays awake longer	Encourage smiling, laughing Place on changing mat on floor
	Learning and emotional Recognises familiar faces and objects. Shows interest in own world and is aware of changes. Enjoys repetition of activities. Continues to enjoy sucking. Routine more settled, especially in sleeping	Continue to widen sound simulation Take on outings well-protected Develop rattle use, stimulate baby to attempt to reach for it and follow with eyes Immunisations programme continues
16 weeks Stepping and rooting reflexes go 4-5 months: birth-weight doubled	**Physical development** Eyes focus on small objects. Holds head up when pulled to sitting. Beginning to reach for objects. Turns to familiar sounds. Sits with support. Rolls from back to	Show baby mirror and encourage play Give soft squeezy toys of different colours and textures Water play in bath Continue with rattles Pat-a-cake, peek-a-boo games Repeat sounds at varying levels

Table 6.1 A summary of the stages of development *continued*

Age	Development	Role of carer
	side. Grasps with both hands. Everything taken to mouth	Repeat sounds at varying levels Introduce more gentle 'rough and tumble'
	Social and language Laughs and chuckles social-ly. Recognises mother, seeks and enjoys attention. Begins to respond to 'no'. Enjoys being propped up	Offer simple picture books, name items **Safety** Watch for toys too small, with loose fit-tings that might be swallowed
	Learning and emotional Enjoys attention, becomes bored when alone. Recognises bottle. More interested in mother, shows trust and security. Sleeps through the night, has defined nap time	Completion of primary Triple and HIB immunisations
26 weeks (7 months) 7–9 months: eye to eye contact Palmar grasp replaced by inferior pincer at 6–7 months Two lower central and lateral incisors appear	**Physical development** Sits alone for a few sec-onds. Bounces and weight bears when held in the standing position. Transfers objects, and places in mouth with one hand. Enjoys playing with feet. Bangs objects together, rolls over well. Possibly moving by rolling, or squirming **Social and language** Recognises strangers. Squeals, laughs aloud. Double syllable babbling, starts to say Ma, Da. Talks in 'own' language in conversation with adults	Provide toys to bang, stack and nest (round ones easier) Saucepans, spoons, 'safe' household equipment Continue with peek-a-boo, bye-bye, pat-a-cake Provide opportunities for developing large movement, space, firm furniture
	Learning and emotional Looks for objects that are out of sight. Curious, han-dles and looks at objects closely. Knows where sounds originate. Pulls toy with a string. Drops and picks up toys. Continues to 'mouth' and bite. Shows fear of strangers and is upset when mother leaves Continues to explore food. Enjoys sitting in high chair	Provide music and movement, simple repetitive rhymes Give pouring and squeezy toys to play with in bath Continue with picture books Extend outings to include animals, for example feeding the ducks Imitate animal sounds Let baby copy you – building bricks, etc. Allow time, no hurry Offer cup and extra spoon at mealtimes Strap into high chair, give finger foods but allow to 'play' with own food

Table 6.1 A summary of the stages of development *continued*

Age	Development	Role of carer
		Safety Look at wider environment, for example plugs, electrical equipment baby can reach with increasing mobility Encourage achievement
40 weeks (10 months) Four upper incisors – 9 months	**Physical development** Sits unaided, can regain balance. Manipulates objects with hands. Unwraps objects. Pulls to stand in cot, creeps. Uses finger and thumb to hold objects	Allow baby to make choices in play material Offer balls, dolls, pull and push toys, sand and water trays (well-supervised), building blocks, music
	Social and language Claps hands when asked. Knows own name, copies facial gestures and sounds. Smiles at self in mirror. Aware of environment, will play alone for considerable periods. Indicates likes and dislikes at meal and bed-times	Teach names of body parts Continue to extend experiences including types of foods, textures and tastes
	Learning and emotional Begins to imitate. More interested in books. Wishes to be more independent in dressing, feeding, etc. Enjoys achievement	Encourage baby to return affection
12 months 10–14 months: Anterior fontanelle closing Birth-weight triples Two lower lateral incisors, and four first molars appear by 14 months	**Physical development** Cruises around furniture, begins to stand alone, able to manage stairs. Begins to walk unaided. Turns pages in book. Builds tower of two blocks. Puts ball in box. May use spoon. Can release objects voluntarily. Shows preferred hand. Attempts to throw. Regular bowel movements	Motion toys Enjoys carrying and moving toys Continue with sand, water and music Continue to extend all activities and language
	Social and language Uses jargon, points to indicate wishes. Enjoys give and take games. Enjoys music, being noticed, having achievement clapped – will repeat for actions	Allow child-directed play in a safe environment

Table 6.1 A summary of the stages of development *continued*

Age	Development	Role of carer
	Learning and emotional Shows fear, anger, affection, jealousy, anxiety and sympathy. Determined in approach to play, increased concentration and attention. Some idea of space time and effects of own actions	Encourage self-feeding, use of cup and spoon Manage unacceptable behaviour with firm quiet 'no', distract if possible Give and encourage return of affection

QUICK CHECK

1 List **five** major factors that can affect growth.
2 Describe the sounds that a baby of six months makes.
3 Explain how you, the carer, can best help the language development of a baby of nine months.
4 What are the charts used to assess growth called and what three measurements are usually taken?
5 One racial group has advanced physical development – which one?
6 When would you expect a baby's first responsive smile?
7 What do you understand by the term 'attachment' and why are secure attachments essential for healthy emotional development?
8 What is meant by the term 'labelling' in language development?
9 To stimulate a young baby's vision what should you look for in toys?
10 What worrying signs might indicate a baby of six months was having visual difficulties?
11 List **six** major areas that are vital for social and emotional development in a baby.
12 You suspect that a baby of seven months is hearing-impaired. Give your reasons.
13 Define 'age-appropriate' toys, and say why they are important.
14 When should you anticipate 'stranger fear' in a baby?
15 There is one overwhelmingly important factor affecting the total development of a baby – what is it?

THE ILL BABY

Infection and immunity

A baby is particularly vulnerable to infection. When she was in the uterus she lived in a sterile world, with the placenta and amniotic fluid protecting her from many harmful organisms. Following birth, she has some protection passed on through the placenta and, if she is breast-fed, in the colostrum. This protection is called passive immunity. However, it lasts only for about six months. The baby's own ability to fight infection is immature and when the protection from her mother lessens she will become vulnerable to a wide range of diseases.

WHAT CAUSES INFECTION?

Germs are all around us, living on our skin and in our noses, throats and digestive tracts (stomachs and bowels). Usually they do not cause any harm. However, they can, under certain circumstances, cause outbreaks of common infectious diseases, and sometimes more serious illness.

There are three main types of organism and they are treated in different ways:
■ bacteria
■ viruses
■ fungi.

Bacteria
These are tiny and many can cause a variety of different infections, however, others are totally harmless. Innocent bacteria live perfectly happily in our bodies and provide useful functions, for example, in the large bowel, they help our bodies to break down and absorb food. However, if

these bacteria move to a different part of the body, they may sometimes cause infection.

If harmful bacteria invade, the natural defence mechanism of the body produces antibodies, which attempt to fight and destroy the bacteria.

If, in the future, the specific bacteria attack the body again it is able to reproduce these antibodies – this is called immunity.

Bacteria can be treated with some antibiotic medicines, although not all antibiotics are effective against all bacteria. The body can become resistant to certain types of antibiotics.

Viruses

These are much smaller than bacteria and enter the cells of the body, changing the way they work. However, the body can produce its own anti-bodies against some viruses and prevention through immunisation can be effective against others. Antibiotics are ineffective against viruses.

Fungi

These can occasionally cause infections, for example, nappy rash through thrush (candida albicans). Treatment is by anti-fungal medicine. Anti-biotics are usually ineffective.

KEY POINT

It is important for a doctor to know what is causing an infection so that the correct treatment can be given. Clues are provided by the signs and symptoms of the illness and by the taking of samples (for example blood or faeces) or swabs for laboratory investigation.

In addition to modern medicine, nature itself helps protect the young baby:
- the skin acts as a barrier to infection
- the stomach contents are acid and help to neutralise harmful bacteria that have been taken in accidentally
- the tears are antiseptic.

As the baby grows, she develops her own active immunity. When her body comes into contact with specific organisms her system begins to recognise them and produce antibodies to fight them. In the process of producing these antibodies she may be ill with the infection that particular organism is causing, for example, measles. However, when recovered, she is able to reproduce these antibodies if she encounters the specific organism again. One antibody is effective against only one specific organism and not a variety.

Immunisation

We can reproduce active immunity, artificially, through programmes of immunisation. Minute, weakened doses of the live disease or poisons from the specific disease are given to a baby, often over a series of months. This allows the baby's own defence mechanism to produce the necessary antibodies to fight the disease should she come into contact with it again.

Immunisation programmes in the UK have resulted in most of the diseases, from which children can be protected, becoming rare.

Even so, children continue to need immunisation protection as:
- the diseases remain serious and can be fatal when they occur
- the diseases arc common in many parts of the world
- increased travel and migration around the world means potential access to a wide range of diseases
- a reduction in the numbers of babies completing immunisation programmes means the diseases could reappear in the UK.

SAFE PRACTICE

To ensure that the baby is able to produce these new antibodies safely, it is important that she is fit and well at the time of her injections. Advice from a GP should be sought before immunisations if the baby:

- is unwell, or has a fever
- is taking any sort of medication or having hospital treatment
- has reacted severely to certain medicines
- has untreated malignant diseases or altered immunity
- has had a bad reaction to a previous immunisation, for example, developed a fever, had a swollen, painful lump at the injection site
- has suffered severe allergic reactions
- has close relatives who have had convulsions.

SAFE PRACTICE

Polio vaccine is a live virus and is excreted in the stools. Only carers who have been vaccinated within the last 10 years should handle soiled nappies of recently immunised babies. Strict personal hygiene, especially hand-washing after nappy changing, is essential for up to 6 weeks after the last polio vaccine dose.

ANXIETIES OVER VACCINE SAFETY

Over recent years there have been many health scares over the safety of vaccines and the resulting fears have led to a drop in the level of immuni-

Table 7.1 Immunisation schedule

Disease	Name of immunisation	How given	When it is given
Hib (haemophilus influenza type b) ⎞			
Diptheria ⎟			
Tetanus ⎟	DTP – Hib	All in one injection	2, 3 and 4 months
Whooping cough ⎠	Meningitis C	Injection	2, 3 and 4 months
Meningitis C	Polio	Oral drops	2, 3 and 4 months
Poliomyelitis			
Measles ⎞			
Mumps ⎟	MMR	All in one injection	12-15 months
Rubella ⎠			
and pre-school booster			

Key points

■ High incidence In areas where there is an increased risk of certain diseases, alterations in the timings of immunisation may be made. Additional early protection may be offered against individual illnesses, for example, tuberculosis, see page 40.

■ In the first 4 months of life a baby will have 6 separate injections over a period of 3 months. Three oral doses of polio vaccine will be given at the same time. These must all be complete for a baby to be fully vaccinated against the diseases.

■ In the second year of life at 12-15 months one dose of MMR is given by injection to achieve immunity for measles, mumps and rubella.

■ Immunisations against diseases are often given in combined doses over a period of time. This avoids babies having unnecessary, multiple injections and provides maximum protection when they are at their most vulnerable.

■ A written record of the immunisations a baby has received is given to the parents.
(See Table 7.2, Infectious diseases on page 173 and Table 7.3, Common ailments in babies on page 182 for information about the diseases immunisation can protect against.)

sation. In the past, unfounded worries over whooping cough vaccine led to three major epidemics of whooping cough, which resulted in the avoidable deaths of around one hundred children.

Currently the MMR vaccine has been the subject of debate and anxiety for parents. In small studies in England it has been linked to autism and Crohn's disease (a disease of the bowels). The incidence of Autism, where children in early years begin to demonstrate severe developmental difficulties, has been increasing and the reasons are not fully understood. Autism begins to appear at between one and two years of age, the time the MMR injection is given,. Extensive international research, however, has been unable to make the link between the vaccine and these two conditions. Currently over 500 million doses of the vaccine have been given world-wide in 90 countries over 30 years and the World Health Organisation describes the MMR as having an outstanding safety record.

Many parents have requested separate doses of MMR, for measles, mumps and rubella. However, it is felt that this potentially may leave a baby at risk as three independent courses would take longer to complete, leaving a baby vulnerable to the diseases. History tells us that subjecting a baby to additional injections often means that courses remain incomplete as parents fail to complete the programme.

The diseases MMR protects against are not insignificant.

- Measles can be a serious illness, often associated with fatal complications.
- Mumps can cause deafness, sterility in males and was the largest cause of viral meningitis in children.
- Rubella vaccine prevents serious harm to the unborn child. This includes brain damage, physical difficulties, deafness and blindness,

KEY POINTS

- Even though MMR is not given until the second year of life anxieties and concerns need to be addressed early.
- Making the decision to have a baby immunised is not easy and parents must have access to full and accurate information.

After immunisation

Following any immunisation side-effects may occur. These are usually minor and easily treated with the correct dose of infant paracetamol, however, always check first with a health professional, if you have worries.

Following DTP-Hib the baby may:

- be irritable within 48 hours
- have a mild temperature.

Following MMR:
- after a week to 10 days some children develop a fever and a measles-like rash
- 3 to 4 weeks after the injection a child may occasionally get a mild form of mumps
- 6 weeks after the injection a child may get small, bruise-like spots.

KEY POINT

Children who complete their courses of immunisations help protect other children who are vulnerable and cannot have immunisation themselves, for example:

- children who have immune problems of their own, ie leukaemia
- children who are having treatment for cancer
- babies who may catch the diseases from siblings before they can be protected
- pregnant women and their unborn babies.

Activity
You are employed as a nanny in a home with a new baby.
1 What professional reasons and arguments might you put forward to the parents for the benefits of immunisation?
2 Research what homoeopathic immunisations are available.
3 Discuss the advantages and disadvantages of conventional medicine versus the homoeopathic approach with your fellow students.
4 How has the effectiveness of homoeopathic immunisation schemes been evaluated?

INFECTION, WHAT CAUSES ITS SPREAD?

Infections are spread:
- by droplets through the air – coughing, sneezing
- by direct contact – skin to skin, dirty hands
- via the digestive tract – poor personal hygiene, infected food
- by animals – they can carry diseases that do not harm them, but are potentially dangerous to humans, for example, blindness from the worm toxocara carried in the faeces of some dogs and cats.

REMEMBER!

The spread of infections is aided by warmth, moisture, food and time.

Table 7.2 Infectious diseases

Disease	Cause	Spread	Incubation period	Signs and symptoms	Rash or specific sign	Treatment	Complications
Diphtheria	Diphtherus bacillus	Direct contact	1–6 days	Sore throat, slight temperature, prostration, pallor	Grey membrane in throat	Rest, fluids diphtheria antitoxin, antibiotics, diphtheria toxoid	Paralysis of muscles, throat obstruction, heart involvement
Scarlet fever	Haemolytic streptococcus	Direct contact; droplets; indirect contact	2–5 days	Sudden onset of fever, sore throat, vomiting, 'strawberry' tongue, flushed cheeks, pallor around mouth	*1st or 2nd day:* Bright red rash with raised pinpoint spots behind ears, spreading to trunk, arms and legs, skin peels after 7 days	Rest, fluids, observation for complications, antibiotics	Middle ear infection, kidney infection, heart involvement
Tonsillitis	Streptococcus or staphylococci	Direct infection; droplets		Very sore throat, white patches (pus) on tonsils, swollen glands in neck, aches and pains in back and limbs	No rash	Rest, fluids, medical aid – antibiotics	Middle ear infection
Measles	Virus	Direct contact; especially droplets	10–15 days	Misery, high temperature, heavy cold with discharging nose and eyes, later harsh cough, conjunctivitis	*2nd day:* Koplik's spots – white spots inside cheek *4th day:* dusky red, patchy rash starts behind ears and along hairline, spreads to face, trunk and limbs	Rest, fluids, sponging to reduce temperature, dark room if photophobia	Eye infection, chest infection, middle ear infection, encephalitis

continued

Disease	Cause	Spread	Incubation period	Signs and symptoms	Rash or specific sign	Treatment	Complications
Poliomyelitis	Virus	Direct contact: especially droplets; indirect contact: food or water	5–14 days	Sudden onset of headache, stiffness of neck and back followed by paralysis	No rash	Rest, medical supervision	Permanent paralysis
Rubella (German measles)	Virus	Direct contact; droplets	14–21 days	Slight cold, sore throat, slight fever, enlarged glands behind ears, pains in small joints	*1st day:* Rash-like sweat rash, bright pink; starts at roots of hair; may last 2–24 hours	Rest if necessary (mild disease)	None unless patient is pregnant woman; virus can seriously affect foetus in first 12 weeks of pregnancy
Chicken pox	Virus	Direct contact; droplets	7–21 days 14–21 days	Slight fever, irritating rash	*1st day:* Red spots with white raised centre on trunk and limbs, mostly very irritating	Rest, fluids, lactocalamine or solution of bicarb. of soda on spots	Impetigo
Pertussis (Whooping cough)	Haemophilus pertussis	Direct contact; droplets	10–14 days	Heavy cold with fever followed by cough	*2 weeks:* Spasmodic cough followed by characteristic cough and vomiting	Rest, supporting during bouts of coughing, feed after bout of coughing	Bronchitis, bronco-pneumonia, haemorrhage due to strain of coughing, prolapse of rectum, mouth ulcers, debility, encephalitis
Mumps	Virus	Direct contact	7–28 days	Fever, headache, swelling of jaw in front of ears, difficulty opening mouth	No rash	Rest, bland fluids through straw	Orchitis (inflammation of testicles), debility, encephalitis (rare)
Infective hepatitis (Jaundice)	Virus	Direct contact especially droplets; indirect contact: food or water	23–25 days	Gradual onset of headache, loss of appetite, nausea, urine dark, faeces pale putty colour	*5th–7th day* Yellow skin, itching, also yellow conjunctiva	Fluids with glucose, fat-free diet, isolation	Liver damage, meningitis

Source: J. Brain and M.D. Martin, *Child Care and Health for Nursery Nurses*, 3rd edition (Nelson Thornes, 1990)

Preventing the spread of infections

Careful personal hygiene is important in limiting the spread of infection. Hands must, therefore, always be washed carefully before handling babies, following nappy changing and before feeding and meal times. Cover your mouth when coughing and sneezing, and maintain your own health.

■ Ensure your own immunisations are up to date.
■ Wear clean personal clothing, or use regularly changed aprons/overalls.
■ Discourage visitors with coughs and colds from contact with very young babies.
■ Keep a high standard of routine cleanliness, particularly in the toilet, kitchen and nursery areas.
■ Maintain careful heat regulation in a nursery, using a fixed wall thermometer with the temperature maintained at 20°C (68°F).
■ Have good air circulation to help dilute germs and prevent them breeding.
■ Dispose of soiled nappies, dirty clothing and dressings into covered bins and sealed bags. Flush vomit, excreta and used tissues down the lavatory (see page 225–6).

KEY POINTS

■ Poor hand washing is thought to be one of the major causes of cross-infection.
■ Hands must still be washed before and after using gloves.

Signs and symptoms of the ill baby

It is an enormous responsibility to care for a baby who is unwell and unable to say where a pain is, or how she feels. The carer who knows a baby well will notice worrying signs and changes in behaviour early (see the diagram on page 176). This is important as babies under six months can rapidly become worse and what might, at first, seem a minor illness could quickly become life-threatening. Generally, the younger the baby, the wiser it is to be cautious.

REMEMBER!

Telephone numbers to display prominently in case of an emergency:

■ the baby's parents
■ the baby's doctor
■ the health visitor
■ the hospital.

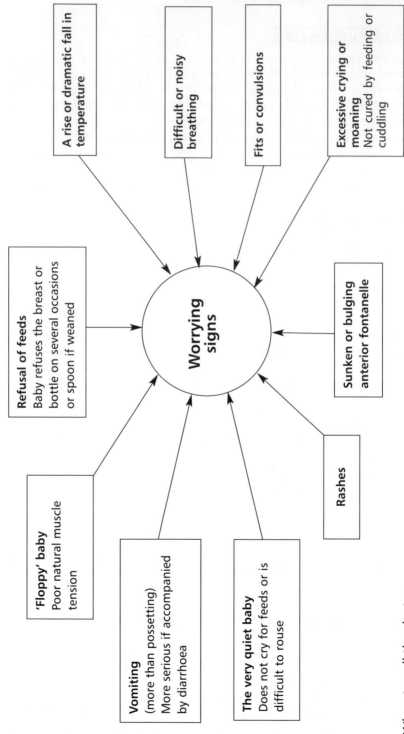

A rise or dramatic fall in temperature

Difficult or noisy breathing

Fits or convulsions

Excessive crying or moaning
Not cured by feeding or cuddling

Refusal of feeds
Baby refuses the breast or bottle on several occasions or spoon if weaned

Worrying signs

Sunken or bulging anterior fontanelle

'Floppy' baby
Poor natural muscle tension

Rashes

Vomiting
(more than possetting)
More serious if accompanied by diarrhoea

The very quiet baby
Does not cry for feeds or is difficult to rouse

When to call the doctor

RAISED TEMPERATURE AND FEVER

The body shows that it is under attack by raising its body heat, producing a temperature and increasing its heart and breathing rates. Pulse and respiratory rates in a baby are difficult to measure; both are naturally quite rapid and have a wide range of 'normal':

- newborn, pulse 70–170; respirations 30–50 per minute
- 12 months, pulse 80–160; respirations 26–40 per minute.

These rates tells us how hard the lungs and heart are working. It is helpful to practise pulse-taking before attempting it on an ill baby.

KEY POINT

Observation of a baby's behaviour, together with accurate recording of temperature, is the most helpful indication of progress in a baby who is ill.

Activity

Practise counting a friend's pulse and respiration.

1   First take the pulse rate – where an artery crosses a bone, use your first and second finger, not your thumb as you have your own pulse there. Try at the base of the thumb in the depression above the wrist, or at the temple.

Using a watch with a second hand, count the beats for a full minute. Was the beat regular, strong, easy to feel?

2   'Pretend' to continue taking the pulse, but instead watch the rise and fall of the chest and count each complete breath (in-and-out is one respiration).

Ask your friend if they were aware you were counting their breathing and if it affected their ability to act 'normally'.

Remember, it is very difficult to obtain accurate measurements of respiratory rates if an adult or older child is aware that they are being recorded.

It is thought by some that the raising of the blood heat (or temperature) is an attempt by the body to destroy harmful substances. The heat, or temperature control, mechanism is in the brain and this can appear out of control when a baby is suffering an illness. Babies and young children produce very high temperatures quickly.

Observation will tell if a baby is feverish by a change in her colour (usually increased), or occasionally by unusual pallor. The easiest place to check if a fever is present is to feel the baby's forehead. This is the area of greatest heat loss (the hands are frequently cold even in an ill baby).

A thermometer can be used to give an accurate reading of the level of temperature; they always show measurements in Centigrade and often Fahrenheit as well.

F = Fahrenheit	C = Centigrade	
95	35.0	
96	35.6	
97	36.1	Baby may be
98	36.7	underheating
98.4	37	
- -		-Normal
99	37.2	
100	37.8	
101	38.3	
102	38.9	Baby overheating
103	39.4	
104	40	
105	40.6	
106	41.1	

Measurements on a clinical thermometer

Parents and carers, who know their children best, are often alerted too by changes in general behaviour (see When to call the doctor on page 176).

SAFE PRACTICE

Glass thermometers that contain mercury and could break should never be placed in a baby's mouth. Newer safer ways of measuring fever are now used.

How to take a temperature
Digital thermometers
Increasingly, unbreakable, easy to read, battery-operated digital thermometers are used. Often these bleep to indicate when the temperature is measured.
■ Check the thermometer is registering nought.
■ Place the slender tip between two bare skin surfaces, preferably in the armpit.
■ Leave for the time indicated on the thermometer.
■ Read the result.
■ For temperatures taken in the armpit another degree should be added to the result.

Special plastic temperature strips
These are placed across the forehead and are easy to read changing colour to indicate fever levels. They are, however, less accurate.

Other methods of measuring temperature
In hospitals, tympanic thermometers are used with older babies. The eardrum, which is close to the brain, is one of most accurate areas for measuring a baby's temperature. A funnel-like attachment is placed gently in the outer ear and the temperature is recorded within a few seconds – a buzzer sounds when the reading is accurate. A disposable filter is attached to the funnel and is changed after use, reducing the chances of cross-infection. This method is especially valuable with restless babies, as it is quick, safe and very accurate.

KEY POINT

Whatever method is chosen, the result and time, when the temperature is taken, need to be written down.

Care of the ill baby

MANAGEMENT OF FEVER

Fever in a baby can occur quickly and mostly there are no ill effects. However, in a few babies over six months a high temperature may trigger a fit or febrile convulsion. If this happens, the baby becomes stiff, twitches and rolls her eyes, she may go blue and foam at the mouth, and lose consciousness. It is a frightening experience, although not dangerous. Babies who fit with high temperatures usually grow out of them with no harmful effects. It does not mean the baby has epilepsy.

There is little that can be done once a convulsion is under way except to ensure the baby does not harm herself if she thrashes about. It is dangerous to force anything between the gums to stop the tongue being bitten. Medical advice should be sought. Follow the advice below for prevention.

Prevention of febrile convulsions
- Keep the room airy and cool.
- Remove the clothes and gently sponge with tepid, not cold, water. Allow to dry naturally – this will bring down the fever.
- Do not allow her to get too cold and shiver – this will force the temperature up again.

- Ensure any previously prescribed medication is given at signs of fever.
- Observe and supervise the baby carefully.

REMEMBER!

If you feel the baby has a high temperature remember it is dangerous to wrap her up to keep her warm – this will increase the risk of convulsions.

ROUTINE CARE OF AN ILL BABY

An unwell baby will feel frightened and will show her distress by changes in behaviour and an unsettled routine. She may regress in social development, for example, an ill baby who previously settled well into day care may cling and cry when separated from her parents. At this time it is especially important known adults – her parents or key worker, undertake her care.

While unwell let the baby show how she wishes to be cared for – she may feel the need for extra physical attention, cuddling etc. or she may appear more settled resting in her own cot and allowing her body to fight the infection. You might find her fractious, wakeful and disrupted in her normal sleeping patterns. Extra supervision will be needed in case her condition worsens, or she vomits unexpectedly. However, it is comforting to remember that babies have the ability to recover quickly from minor illness and usually return to their normal routines speedily.

A fractious baby only needs a top and tail but a bath, although not essential, may make her more comfortable, together with clean clothes and bedding. Do not force solids on to a previously weaned baby. All she will need is extra fluids, perhaps cooled boiled water, with the addition of

An unwell baby may need extra physical attention

part of the strained juice of a freshly squeezed orange. An unwell baby who has finished breast-feeding often feels the need for the breast for comfort again.

Try to keep visitors to a minimum and attempt to stop siblings, or other children wanting to hold and play with a baby when she is unwell.

KEY POINTS

- Anything unusual in the way of vomit or nappy contents will need to be shown to a doctor.
- Always observe carefully an ill baby.
- Record and chart her temperature if requested.
- Keep parents fully informed of any changes.

Medicines that are prescribed for a baby will almost always be in liquid form, and must be given carefully and accurately, according to instructions. Never put medicines into a bottle of milk; this may make the baby refuse a normal feed. Luckily most medication for babies is pleasant tasting and when offered from a spoon is taken readily.

SAFE PRACTICE

When giving medicines to an ill baby you should know the answers to these questions:

- How often should it be given?
- Should you wake the baby if she is asleep?
- Do you have the correct-sized spoon, sterilised?
- For how long a period should you give the medicine?
- What should you do if the baby is better before the medicine is finished?
- At what temperature should the medicine be stored?
- Should the medicine be given before or after a feed?
- Are you sure the correct baby's name is on the label?
- What are the side-effects that you need to look for?
- Can you be certain that other children in the house cannot take the medicine?
- What should I do with any medicine left over?

If you cannot answer all the above questions, seek further advice.

Activity
Find out how much information about the administration of children's medicines is available on 'over-the-counter' products.
1 Where would you go for advice and information?

2 On the actual packaging are the instructions clear, simple and easily understood?

3 How many languages, other than English, are there on the packaging?

Common ailments in babies

The table below summarises the common ailments that can affect babies.

Table 7.3 Summary of ailments of babies

Condition, causes, signs and symptoms	Role of the carer
Colds and snuffles Viral infection of the lining of the nose, clear discharge is more serious in very tiny babies due to difficulty in mouth breathing – no cure	Small frequent feeds, possible use of nasal drops from doctor to clear nose Gently wipe any discharge from outer nose
Coughs Viral infections, occasionally bacterial. Often associated with colds. Mucus drains down the back of the throat, cough more at night, may accompany other illnesses, measles for example **Note** A cough is a reflex response to remove irritation from the lung, so a cough might indicate an inhaled object	Keep air moist, for example use steam kettles. Only give prescribed medicines Supervise especially if accompanied by vomiting Seek further advice if baby fails to improve, or if there is any 'noisy' breathing
More serious chest infections: *Bronchitis* Infection of both upper and lower air passages. Temperature, runny nose, 'rattly' cough, worse at night. Can be viral or bacterial.	As for treatment of cough Observe to ensure condition does not worsen Give prescribed medicine
Bronchiolitis Initially a viral illness affecting all the tiny air passages in the lungs. More common in winter. Cold-like symptoms. 'Fluid' or 'bubbly' cough. Possible breathing difficulties shown by blueness of lips, etc.	Seek medical help Watch for any breathing difficulties Usually admitted to hospital for oxygen treatment and fluids by tube into stomach or into a vein
Pneumonia Bacterial or viral infection of the lower air passages, the alveoli, resulting in part of the lung being 'blocked' by infection, reducing air capacity of lung. High temperature, fast noisy or 'grunting' breathing. May or may not have cough	Can be treated at home with antibiotics or more usually in hospital Small, frequent feeds, delay weaning, increase fluids Monitor carefully Follow medical advice

Table 7.3 Summary of ailments of babies *continued*

Condition, causes, signs and symptoms	Role of the carer
Croup Babies over 6 months can develop noisy breathing from a spasm of the larynx (upper air passages in the throat). The larynx swells with the spasm and can become narrow, causing a noise as the air tries to get through. Worse at night, baby may become blue as she get less air	Babies usually admitted to hospital, some less serious can be helped by keeping atmosphere steamy with kettles In emergency use bathroom with hot taps turned on Comfort babies, as frightening
Otitis media Infection of the middle ear. Common in babies as their Eustachian tube (leading from the back of the throat to the middle ear) is short and babies spend more time lying down. Increased risk of food and infection travelling into ear. Baby ill with fever, vomiting, diarrhoea, screaming and crying with pain, possibly pulling at ear if older	Give prescribed antibiotics Comfort baby Ensure follow-up visit to doctor to monitor healing and hearing No swimming with head under water **Note:** Commonly confused with 'glue ear', which is less acute and less likely to occur in a 0–1-year-old baby
Vomiting This is a sign that the stomach is not tolerating food. This may be a minor problem or more serious if associated with diarrhoea (see below)	The amounts the baby is vomiting will have to be judged, as well as colour and how the vomiting occurred. Is the baby still hungry and fit and well? Usually if vomiting alone, it may be a temporary feeding problem (see page 143) The baby's stomach will need to be 'rested' by giving fluids only, for 24 hours – either prescribed solutions or boiled water. Medical advice should be sought
Diarrhoea Frequent loose stools If accompanied by vomiting, this may indicate an infection and lead to dehydration (loss of fluid) which may be serious, and is indicated by a sunken fontanelle, dry skin and very little urine	Seek medical advice and follow treatment plan Monitor hygiene practice Ensure soiled nappies are disposed of safely Monitor cleanliness of feeding equipment Delay any weaning plans
Colic Affects many babies. Specific periods of the day, often early evening, baby cries for some time. Pulls legs up onto stomach and appears in pain. Difficult to comfort. Baby thrives in all other respects	No single cure Generally settles by 3 to 4 months Comfort baby by rocking and cuddling Non-nutritive sucking often helps, for example dummy

Table 7.3 Summary of ailments of babies *continued*

Condition, causes, signs and symptoms	Role of the carer

Pyloric stenosis

Often, but not always, affects male babies of around 6 weeks. Hungry baby, feeds eagerly, but immediately returns feeds, effortlessly and with force – up to several metres in distance. The muscle at the exit of the stomach is thickened and does not allow food to pass. The baby can quickly dehydrate

Report symptoms quickly, with description of type of vomiting
Baby admitted to hospital for simple operation to enlarge ring of muscle

Intestinal obstructions

Any condition that stops fluids from going through the digestive tract is potentially very serious. The baby will vomit, may fail to pass urine, and have only a few stools, which are hard and small. The causes may be several, but the main one in a tiny baby is when the gut telescopes inside itself, then swells and causes an obstruction (intussusception)

Observe and report signs and symptoms quickly
Baby will be admitted to hospital

Meningitis

A severe infection of the membranes that cover the brain and spinal cord. Causes can be many. The baby may vomit or refuse feeds, have a high temperature but possibly have cold hands and feet. She may have neck stiffness, high-pitched moaning, whimpering cry, blank, staring expression, pale blotchy complexion, be fretful and not like being handled, be lethargic. The fontanelle may be tense or bulging. The most severe, caused by the meningococcal bacteria, is also accompanied by a rash. This rash does not disappear when a glass is pressed over it. Bacterial meningitis has a dramatic and sudden onset. The condition can be fatal and cause long-term brain damage, hearing and visual problems. If the meningitis is viral in origin the baby may only be ill with flu-like symptoms and will rapidly recover

Help prevent condition by ensuring baby has HIB and meningitis C immunisations
Good knowledge of the baby will aid early recognition in an unwell, fractious child
Seek urgent medical help
The condition worsens rapidly

**Sudden infant death
(Cot death syndrome)**

A previously fit and well baby is found dead in her cot, with no obvious cause. Usually between 1 week and 2 years of age, the peak time is 3 months. No single cause but certain factors increase risk:
(a) sleeping prone

Ensure baby sleeps supine
Do not overheat, use blankets not duvets, no cot bumpers
Always place in the *feet to foot* position – baby placed on back with feet at the foot of the cot with

Table 7.3 Summary of ailments of babies *continued*

Condition, causes, signs and symptoms	Role of the carer
(b) overheating. Also increased risks: winter months, male babies, multiple births, untreated minor ailments, over-concentrated artificial feeds, smoky environments	the bedclothes over this lower part *only*, so the baby cannot slip under the clothes during the night Never cover baby's head while sleeping Use a firm, flat, mattress that can be kept clean easily Keep thermometer fixed on nursery wall – temperature constant 20°C (68°F) day and night Promote breast-feeding Avoid smoking and smoky atmospheres Promote pre-conceptual health education Support families who suffer such a tragedy Always seek medical advice if the baby is unwell Liaise with health professionals (see *Bereavement*, Chapter 2, page 67)
Neonatal cold injury/Hypothermia Baby has a false appearance of health with a good colour. Lethargic, runny nose, swollen hands and feet, cold to touch. Usually only happens in early months, pre-term babies more at risk	Prevention important, careful child-care practice Keep thermometer fixed on nursery wall – constant 20°C (68°F) Observation If occurs, raise temperature by wrapping baby loosely in warmed blankets and by cuddling *No* direct heat – raise temperature slowly Offer glucose (sugar) feeds Seek medical help urgently
Roseola A common viral illness with fever and rash, occuring usually after 6 months. Baby has high fever but does not appear unduly ill. After 3rd–5th day fever lessens and rash appears. Rash consists of multiple small, red, flat spots – whitening when touched. Most common on the trunk but also to a lesser degree on the face and extremities – rash lasts between a few hours and 2–3 days.	Virus passed through saliva, so care with sterilisation of feeding equipment essential No medication required Routine fever management

QUICK CHECK

1 Name the **three** organisms that can cause illness.
2 How does nature help a baby protect herself from infections?
3 Describe 'artificial active immunity'.
4 Which signs and symptoms indicate that it would advisable to postpone starting immunisation in a baby?
5 Why does a carer need to ensure especially strict personal hygiene when handling the nappy of a baby who has recently received polio vaccine?
6 'DTP – Hib, and MMR' – what do these initials stand for?
7 What extra protection might be given to a baby born in an area where there is a high incidence of tuberculosis?
8 Explain how you should dispose of soiled dressings, vomit and excreta.
9 Describe how you can limit 'cross-infection' in the nursery.
10 List **10** worrying signs showing a baby may be unwell and that a doctor is needed.
11 A baby is running a fever. What initially should be done?
12 Explain why diarrhoea and vomiting are so worrying in a tiny baby.
13 Name **two** factors that are thought to increase the risk of sudden infant death syndrome and describe the recommended sleeping position.
14 What is the special feature about the rash caused by meningoccocal meningitis?
15 Describe how a baby's behaviour and development might temporarily change with illness.

8 EQUIPMENT, TOYS AND PLAY

> **This chapter covers:**
> - **Planning for a new baby**
> - **Basic equipment**
> - **Clothing**
> - **Nappies**
> - **Toys and play**

Planning for a new baby

There are many things to consider when selecting and choosing equipment for a new baby. This is a time of great excitement and importance in the life of any family, and the advice and skill of a child-care worker can sometimes help in making these decisions. Families are under considerable pressure from many sources. This includes advertising, which can be very persuasive in attempting to convince new parents of the need to purchase widely and unnecessarily.

Consideration of the following points will help to decide priorities.

- **Lifestyle** Choices made will depend on families' circumstances. For example, different equipment will be needed for working parents living in a flat in a high-rise block who will take their baby to and from day dare to a family employing a nanny, with a house that has plenty of space and a large, safe garden.
- **Space** How much is there and of what type? For example, will the baby go straight into her own room? Or will she share with another sibling or with the carer?
- **Cost** How much money can be spent? Are there tight budgetary constraints?
- **First or subsequent baby?** If this is not the first baby, is some equipment still safe, available and suitable?
- **Safety** What safety marks should be looked for? What specific safety equipment should be bought? What if the equipment is second-hand?
- **Flexibility** How long will various pieces of equipment last? Will the baby outgrow them before good use has been made of them? Will the equipment receive enough use to justify buying it?
- **Appearance and comfort** Is the equipment pleasant to look at? Will it visually stimulate the baby? Will it please the carer?

- **Durability** Will the chosen equipment stand heavy use from baby and toddler, and perhaps further children? Is it well built?
- **Maintenance** Will the equipment be easy to look after? Are replacement parts available?

All of these areas will need to be discussed before buying.

Basic equipment

A baby needs equipment for:
- sleeping
- bathing
- feeding
- playing
- moving around.

SLEEPING

The early months

Where a baby first sleeps depends on the parents' preference.

In the first weeks of a baby's life many wish to have their baby sleep with them in their own bed, finding this convenient, comforting and making night feeds easier. For safety reasons, though, it is not advisable if the parents are very tired, smoke or take drugs, or have taken alcohol or medication, which can make them sleep heavily. Care too must be taken to avoid overheating (see Chapter 4 and Sudden infant death on page 184).

Many new babies sleep happily and safely, immediately after birth, in a conventional cot (see page 190). Some carers feel that, early in life, a baby may feel more secure in the close environment of a Moses basket, carrycot with its transporter or stand, or crib. Apart from cribs, these are portable and have the advantage of providing a familiar sleeping place for a baby when away from home.

After a choice is made check it:
- is sturdy and strong
- has washable, non-glare lining fabrics or materials
- has a firm, well-fitted mattress with a waterproof cover
- has light, washable sheets and blankets of natural fibres –cotton or wool and cotton mixture – no duvets
- has no pillows, cot bumpers or baby nests.

In addition, note the following:

Moses baskets

- Must not be used when a baby is active and wanting to roll, usually three to four months.
- Can only be carried if the handles are secure and meet in the middle.
- Ensure it is placed on a safe surface or floor away from other children or any animals.

Cribs

- Always check the manufacturers' recommended weight limit.

Carrycot, transporter and or stand

- Ensure the height is comfortable for the carer. The total weight should not exceed 9 kg (20 lb), safety number BSEN 1466 (1988).
- Ensure it is stable and placed on a firm surface, away from other children or animals.

SAFE PRACTICE

When carrying a baby in a Moses basket or carrycot special care should be taken. Carers can trip on stairs, catch feet on toys or loose carpets, and the baby can fall out or be dropped.

From about six months – daytime

A flexible transport system is usually needed to meet both the developing needs of the baby and the mobility and lifestyle of the carer. There are constantly new and changing products on the market from which to choose. Many pushchairs now have multi-functions, which can meet a variety of parents' requirements in one piece of equipment. There no longer the need to buy a separate pushchair and pram. Babies over six months can often sleep for short periods in a semi-reclining position, however, some models of pushchairs now allow a baby to lie flat rather than angled. This is more comfortable, particularly when a baby may spend some time in a pushchair when shopping or on outings, for example. Carers, too, look for pushchairs that can be easily folded and carried when not in use. All should come with waterproof coverings, a fixed safety harness and trays for carrying shopping.

In addition flexible options include pushchairs that allow:

- the position to be easily swapped for the baby to face forwards or backwards, as the mother/carer decides
- the 'body' to be removed so the baby can continue to sleep, without being disturbed
- twins and children of different ages to use pushchairs, either side by side or one in front of the other.

Conventional strollers, pushchairs and prams, however, are still widely available.

SAFE PRACTICE

Whatever type of pushchair or pram is chosen it is important to ensure the following.

- Brakes are easy to use and are tested regularly.
- Seats for toddlers are not placed on the less substantial bodies of carrycots – if used on pram bodies, they should be placed at the back of the pram body to prevent toppling over, or used only as recommended by the manufacturer.
- Shopping, if hung from the handles of a carrycot or pushchair, can cause imbalance. It is safer to place shopping on a special tray under the pram and over the wheels.
- Fixed harnesses are attached when any pushchair or pram is purchased and are always used when a baby is sitting.
- Cat and insect nets are used on prams for all babies sleeping in gardens, or in homes with a pet cat.
- The weight of the baby matches the recommended weight for the transporter or pushchair you are using.
- If 'use-by age' advice is given, remember that a baby's development will vary and following weight recommendations is safer.

Cots for longer sleeping periods and night time
These will be the main sleeping place for the baby, allowing room for growth and movement. They need to be able to withstand several years of hard wear.

SAFE PRACTICE

- Cot bars must not be more than 76 mm (3 in) apart.
- Safety catches must be childproof.
- Mattresses must fit snugly with no gaps.
- If it has been repainted, check safe paint was used and any transfers cannot come off.
- If wooden, check for splinters.
- Check the cot's stability.
- Do not allow toddlers to climb in and out of cots.

KEY POINT

- If the cot is second-hand, it is still advisable to buy a new mattress.

SAFE PRACTICE

- Change bed clothing frequently (see Care of clothing, page 197).
- Keep the cot clean and wash it regularly.

BATHING

Most newborn babies prefer the smaller environment and security of a specific baby bath. These are usually plastic, coloured and easily transported for cleaning and filling. They can be used with the fixed base purchased for the carrycot, or placed in an adult bath or even moved to a warm sitting room.

Some carers prefer to use the adult bath, especially if there is an older sibling and the baby can either be bathed before her sibling, or with them when older. In this case a non-slip mat is a good investment. Some method for checking the warmth of the bathroom is necessary and possibly an additional fixed wall-heater may be needed.

Babies, wherever they are bathed, will need their own towels, face cloths and mild, perfume-free toiletries.

Two buckets, with lids, are needed, one for soiled baby clothes and the other for soiled nappies. See Chapter 3 for more information on bath time management and equipment.

INFANT NUTRITION

Whether a mother decides to breast-feed or bottle-feed her baby, certain equipment should be ready for the newborn. Bottles, teats, lids and sterilising equipment are essential not only for giving feeds, if required, but also for cooled boiled water to quench thirst and possibly for expressed breast milk too.

If the baby is to be bottle-fed remember that a newborn baby may require 10 or more feeds in 24 hours and the number of bottles bought need to be with this in mind. See page 128.

If the mother is going to breast-feed her baby, she will need support bras and breast pads to make feeding more convenient and a comfortable chair in which to feed, cuddle and talk to her baby.

As the baby grows and begins to sit she will need a chair for her meal times. Various combinations are available from reclining adjustable low chairs to the more conventional high chairs suitable for a baby who sits securely at about nine months.

Whatever is chosen, check:
■ there is an attached integral harness and crotch strap, in good condition
■ the chair can be easily cleaned, with not too many nooks and crannies for food to become lodged
■ there is a large, firmly fixed tray attached
■ the seating is comfortable
■ the chair conforms to the BS 5799 safety standard.

PLAYING

Initially the most important play for a new baby will be the interaction she has with her parents. Play is discussed in detail on pages 200–6.

MOVING AROUND

Babies always need safe transportation and this includes their first journey home from hospital. It is illegal to allow a baby to travel in the front of a car unless secured in a suitable car seat. Although not illegal for a baby to travel unsecured in the back, in their parents' arms for example, it is not recommended. Infant car seats are classified according to the weight of the baby and most infant models are suitable for babies weighing up to 13 kg (2 stone).

Car seats will have upper weight limits indicated on them; these must always be checked and matched against the weight of a growing baby. Not all car seats will fit all cars.

SAFE PRACTICE

- Cars with airbags must never have child seats in the front passenger seat.
- The safest place for an infant is in the centre of the rear seat to protect from side impact crashes.
- The outside rear seat is the second safest seat.
- The front passenger seat is the least safe.
- A baby is safer facing rearwards, so should be kept in this position as long as possible.
- Always check the instructions for fitting a seat have been followed exactly. Many shops offer a free infant-seat fitting service by trained staff.
- Always check any harness is firmly adjusted each time it is used.

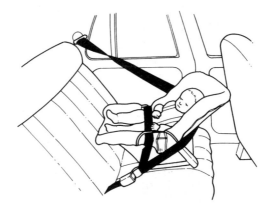

Secure the baby on the back seat in a recommended baby carrier

There are a variety of models of seats from which to choose. Some are light and portable, allowing an infant to semi-recline and incorporating a carrying handle to help move the baby easily from the car. This type uses the adult seat belt, to hold it in place, and can be used either in a back or front seat.

Some seats are designed to remain permanently in the car and these are usually forward facing and fitted in the rear of the car for babies when sitting comfortably, and from 9 kg (20 lb) or nine months of age.

Slings

Baby slings, worn on the front of the parent's body, are often used in the first few weeks after birth. Their advantage is the close body contact they give between mother or father and baby. When the baby begins to gain weight, however, they can put considerable strain on the carrier. Safety must be borne in mind when choosing what activities to undertake when carrying a baby in a sling.

In some cultures babies are carried well into the second year of life on their mother 's backs, giving them a good view of the world, close contact with their mothers and allowing freedom for the mothers to continue their own work. The weight is in a more natural position, causing less back strain. In the UK metal-framed baby carriers fulfil a similar function.

A baby carrier allows a good view of the world

Pushchair or pram?

Parents will have to decide their own priorities when deciding whether to buy a pram or a pushchair or a combination model. Table 8.1 summarises the main points.

Table 8.1 The advantages and disadvantages of prams, pushchairs and combination models

Advantages	Disadvantages
Pram	
Good protection against wind and rain	Expensive
Suitable for sleeping comfortably	Too large for use on public transport
for long periods	Heavy
Can be used with a toddler seat	Will need a cat net
Shopping can be placed underneath	Bulky for storage
Often used for several babies, especially in day care	
Pushchair	
Baby or toddler has good vision	Baby vulnerable to dogs, etc.
Easy to handle. Lighter	Possibly less comfortable
Suitable for use on public transport	Some models unsuitable for a baby under
Less expensive than pram	6 months
Easier storage	Only for one child at a time
Often able to fold easily	Limited opportunity to carry shopping
Easy, one-handed portability	or extra equipment
	Not all models allow a baby to lie flat, so unsuitable for long periods of sleep
Combination models	
Highly flexible from birth to toddler stage	Expensive
Can provide a comfortable, supportive sleeping area	Often not really suitable for use with a toddler seat
Baby can be placed face forwards, or face towards carer	Sometimes limited area for carrying shopping
Models have different features so parents can choose to suit their own requirements	These may not be as effective in performing all the tasks as a piece of equipment designed for a specific purpose
Some multi-purpose combination pushchairs can also be used as car seats and carrycots	

Activity

Visit a local baby shop or department store and research the variety and types of prams, pushchairs and combination models on sale.

1 Compare prices of the models.

2 What special features do you see that you would consider helpful for:
  (a) busy parents;
  (b) meeting the changing needs of a growing and developing baby?
3 What current developments in safety factors are now included on this type of equipment?
4 Do the cat/insect nets on sale fit snugly all types of prams and pushchairs in which a baby may be left to sleep?

SAFE PRACTICE

For prams, pushchairs and combination models check the following.
- Are the brakes out of reach of small fingers?
- Do the brakes on pushchairs and combination models with swivel rear wheels work simultaneously?
- Are there two locking devices: one manual, one automatic?
- The tyres cannot puncture.

SAFETY

Good child-care practice means planning in advance to meet a baby's developing needs safely and anticipating her development. An immobile

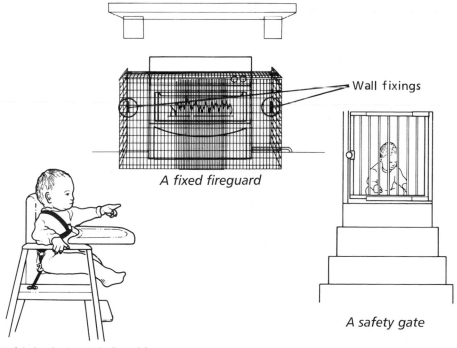

Wall fixings

A fixed fireguard

A safety gate

A high chair with fixed harness

newborn baby will soon roll, crawl and reach out for objects. Safety equipment is essential and needs to be a spending priority. Always buy products made to a recognised standard which carry a British (BS) or European (EN) number. Basic equipment is widely available and should include the following:

Other important safety equipment
- Functioning smoke alarms (always check regularly).
- Non-slip bath mats.
- Baby monitors.
- Fixed fireguards and radiator guards.
- Safety harness for high chairs, pushchairs and prams.
- Socket covers.
- Safety glass or safety film for glass for windows and doors.
- Safety locks and catches for doors, windows, cupboards, fridges and toilets.
- Corner protectors for tables and low units.
- Anti-slam door stops.

REMEMBER!

The biggest cause of death in children under five years in the home is by fire, so always ensure a functioning smoke alarm is fitted.

Activity
Visit a selection of shops. Decide which large pieces of equipment you think are the minimum a new baby will need. Consider: price, quality, safety, comfort, appearance/design, size.
1 Choose one set of essential equipment suitable for a baby coming to a small home, such as a one-bedroom flat.
2 Choose another set of essential equipment for a home that is spacious and well equipped with labour-saving devices.
3 Justify your choices to the parents or carers, presenting a list of the costs and the reasons for your decisions.
4 How would you care for and store such expensive equipment?
5 How often would it needed washing, servicing, and brake and stability checks?
6 What advice might you give to help prolong the life of such equipment?
7 Record the relevant safety number for each piece of equipment.

Clothing

When buying clothes for a newborn baby remember the following.

- She will require many changes of clothing in the first months after birth. Babies dislike dressing and undressing, so choose clothes that are easy to take on and off, that allow for ease of movement. Clothes with fussy bows and buttons are often uncomfortable.
- Initially, a baby will need vests, sleeping suits (babygros), jackets, booties, bonnets and gloves, depending on the season.
- If clothes have been knitted by relatives check that the tension is firm and any lacy patterns do not have holes, which could trap tiny fingers.
- Clothing must be safe for the baby as she grows and becomes mobile.
- Comfort is best achieved from natural fabrics – cotton or cotton and wool mixtures – that are absorbent.
- Low flammability qualities are important – look at the symbols in the clothing. Remember, too, that nylon may not flare but it can melt and cause serious burns.
- The baby will also need protective clothing when she is outdoors in her carrycot or pram.
- Shoes are unnecessary until a baby is walking unaided and sturdily outside, often in the second year of life.
- Any socks, gloves, stretch suits or baby slippers should be non-restrictive to the small and delicate bones of the baby's foot.
- As the baby becomes more mobile it is essential that continual reviews are taken that clothing is of the correct size to allow her to develop skills in crawling and walking safely, and with freedom.

KEY POINT

Clothing and bedclothes made of 100 per cent terry towelling for babies up to three months old must carry a label showing whether or not the garment has passed the low flammability test.

REMEMBER!

Anticipate changes in weather – light layers that trap the air are better insulators than one thick jacket. You can also manage her temperature more easily, preventing underheating or overheating.

Care of clothing

The skin of a baby in her first year of life is especially sensitive and vulnerable to the products used in laundering clothes and bed linen, as her clothes will require above average washing from such things as leakage from her nappy and minor vomiting after feeds. Remember to:

- use non-biological – enzyme-free – soap-based, washing powders
- always rinse clothing thoroughly
- limit the use of fabric conditioner to the minimum. If a conditioner is used make sure it is perfume free
- soften clothing and bed linen effectively and more gently by tumble drying or line drying in the open air
- check you understand the term 'low flammability'
- learn the different laundry symbols on washing powders and compare them with the laundry instructions on the baby's clothes.

Activities

You need to be aware of the wide range and choices of first clothing available for a baby – the layette.

1 Devise, list and cost a minimum set of clothing a baby might need.
2 Write a short introduction about your choice and then visit two different shops in your area – preferably one more 'expensive' and one chainstore outlet.
3 Cost the items included in your lists.
4 Compare the total cost of the two shops with comments on quality. Say which layette you consider gave value for money.
5 Write an account in 300 to 400 words of the importance of comfort, safety and design factors of the clothes. Remember to include types of materials, ease of laundry and the simplicity of dressing and undressing, including the types of fasteners.
6 Describe how you would launder wool and wool-mixture clothes.
7 Discuss the layout of the two shops you visited and comment on how easy it would be for a parent with a pushchair and toddler to visit.

REMEMBER!

Choose clothing colours to stimulate the vision and interest of a baby.

Nappies

Traditional reusable nappies are made of terry towelling squares, which are folded to fit the baby, secured with a pin, and covered by waterproof pants or ties. More modern nappies come in a range of sizes and are made of layers of shaped soft cotton, with elasticised waist and legs, and popper or velcro fastenings. They can consist of one or two pieces, either incorporating an outer waterproof layer, or with a separate outer water-proof wrap.

Disposable nappies are highly absorbent and effective at keeping a baby dry. They also come in a variety of sizes suitable for babies and toddlers. Busy working mothers find them convenient and effective. However, they are expensive and bulky and also have a significant environmental impact. Currently it is thought eight million nappies daily enter the waste stream in the UK.

Whatever choice is made, remember that a very young baby will need changing many times in a 24-hour period and a considerable amount of money will be spent on this aspect of baby care.

Cleaning solutions and lidded buckets for safely storing soiled reusable nappies before washing will be necessary. A padded waterproof baby-changing mat provides a carer with a clean and readily available surface for nappy changing, whenever it is needed, and is a useful additional piece of equipment.

Carers will have to decide whether to use reusable or disposable nappies (see Activity below).

Activity

You are employed as a nanny. You have been asked your opinion on the merits of reusable nappies against disposable nappies. What would you say? You will need to research your answers, including the following questions.

1 Consider short-term and long-term costs, remembering many children will be using nappies for three or more years. How many should be bought and of what sort?
  In considering costs, include the expense of washing machines, dryers, powders, electricity etc.
2 If the family is living in cramped accommodation, think about storage of large packets of nappies, and the possible problems of collection etc.
3 Is there a nappy service available locally? What is it and what are the costs?
4 Think of the effects on the environment of both disposable nappies and of the chemicals used in the laundry of reusable nappies.
5 Which nappies do you think will be most comfortable for the baby?
6 Which are the most suitable for the delicate skin of the newborn? Give evidence to support your views.
7 Is the lifestyle of the carers more suited to one type of nappy than the other?

Toys and play

In her first year a baby changes more quickly than at any other time of her life. At birth, she has random, reflexive, uncontrolled movement, however, by one year she is sitting, crawling and cruising. Her fine motor development has advanced to allow her to pick up delicate objects between thumb and forefinger and to begin to feed herself (see the table, Summary of the stages of development, page 162).

She has made enormous intellectual growth. Toys and play, therefore, must respond and complement these changes.

BIRTH TO THREE MONTHS

At birth a baby can react to noise, light and touch. However, the richest sensory experience for her will be in the close contact she has with her carer. She will respond to skin-to-skin contact, the sound of her mother's voice (the baby's hearing is acute) and especially to her face. Cuddling, talking and singing to a new baby will all be highly pleasurable for her.

She will enjoy using her developing sight and hearing. Mobiles hung over her cot, changing mat, or attached to her relaxing chair, will attract her attention. They should be placed within her field of vision, approximately 20–25 cm (8–10 in) from her face. They should move freely and be of different shapes and colours. Bells and chimes will add variety and stimulate her hearing. Toys, which incorporate mirrors, will be a great source of fascination, even though she will not yet recognise her own reflection.

Ensure the baby's world is visually stimulating. Move the cot or changing mat to different areas of the room and use brightly coloured clothing and linen to attract her attention. On warm days place her pram under a tree to see the leaves sway in the breeze or tie coloured balloons from a branch to move in the wind near her face.

At around three months fingers are interesting and the baby will clasp and unclasp them before her eyes

THREE TO SIX MONTHS

Voluntary movement is slowly replacing reflexive behaviour so the baby now needs things to hold as well as to look at. If a rattle is placed in her hand she can hold, but not yet look at it, at the same time. Toys should make sounds to accompany movement.

The baby will discover these play materials, not only from her hands, eyes and ears, but also from her highly sensitive mouth, where she receives information about taste, textures, shapes and the hardness and softness of the objects. Light rattles are ideal toys at this stage. Variety in play is important, so toys should incorporate different textures, be light, easy to hold and move, and made of different materials. Playmats, which include flaps, squeaks and safe chewable attachments, are ideal. Small toys strung across a pram, or as part of an activity arch will allow a baby to try swiping and grasping.

By 6 months the baby will have discovered her feet, but she will still try to put them in her mouth

SAFE PRACTICE

■   Nothing should be cracked or broken.
■   Ensure pieces of the toy cannot be torn or broken off.

- Everything should be washable or disposable.
- Take care with dyes, paints, transfers and stickers.
- Ensure toy fillings are non-toxic, and cannot escape, be torn off or swallowed.

KEY POINT

Concerns have been raised that softening materials used in the production of plastic toys – 'phthalates' – might be detrimental to babies' health. Currently there is a temporary ban from the European Union on their use in toys that involve sucking or chewing, e.g. teething rings, dummies and some soft toys. The situation is at present under review.

A baby at this age will enjoy the freedom to lie on a firm, safe surface and explore her developing movements, kicking without a restricting nappy, playing with her fingers and hands, and by six months her toes and feet.

The baby is developing her communicating skills and will enjoy listening to her own voice and that of her carer. She will continue to enjoy songs and movement in the adult's arms. This is the time, too, to start interactive games such as 'This little piggy'.

KEY POINTS

- Always allow time for her to practise her sounds and developing skills.
- Show your approval with smiles and gesture.

SIX MONTHS TO ONE YEAR

The baby will, by now, be sitting with support, progressing to sitting unaided and able to play with her toys around her. She will be moving by rolling, squirming, and eventually crawling, cruising and walking.

The baby will enjoy her bath and the toys and play, which go with bath time, so reflect this in your choice and planning. Her environment is exciting and she will explore it eagerly, emptying cupboards, stacking cans, playing with saucepans etc.

She will begin to 'use' her playthings too, for example, 'brushing teeth' and to imitate, not only actions, but also sounds. She will enjoy putting objects in and out of containers, and knocking down piles of bricks. Towards the end of the first year she will begin to attempt to build towers with bricks herself.

She will enjoy looking at her reflection in a mirror, familiar photographs and her 'own' possessions, for example, a plate with her name on it.

Bath time is an occasion for water play with containers for pouring, floating, sinking and bubble play. A happy bath time enables a baby to become confident in water in preparation for swimming.

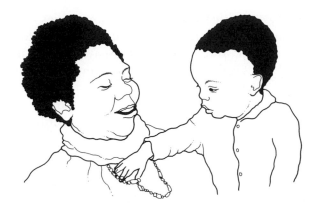

The baby is attracted by the colours and shapes of the beads around her carer's neck. She is confident in her arms to reach and explore them

At this stage the baby is increasingly interested in the outside world. Outings and visits in the pram or pushchair will enable her to enjoy the changing scenery, see animals, visit shops and parks. The carer can extend the world for the baby, talking and explaining the new experiences to her. The baby will enjoy repetition of outings to known favourites, too, for example, feeding the ducks in the park.

As soon as she is a confident crawler, the baby will have much pleasure in crawling for its own sake, reaching toys and interesting things that previously have been out of reach. She will enjoy push/pull toys, rolling balls, banging drums and tearing paper, putting objects in and out of boxes, lifting lids and playing with toys that stack. At this stage of her development,

Water play

you need to provide stimulating opportunities, as well as constantly watching and monitoring the environment for safety. She will have no concept of danger, and although she may repeat a firm 'no' she will not understand the implications or remember this instruction if something else tempts her curiosity.

If she is beginning to toddle she will enjoy using firm furniture to progress around the room and, when more confident, push along baby walkers.

Activity

Create a treasure basket for a baby who is not yet crawling but who sits steadily when unsupported. A treasure basket provides an exciting opportunity for a pre-mobile baby to enjoy, explore and learn. It should offer stimulation in all areas, but especially in sensory, physical and emotional development.

1 Choose a wicker basket – no sharp or jagged edges – that is strong and durable.
2 Fill it with about 15 to 20 safe, challenging and stimulating natural articles for a baby – for example, an orange, a wooden spoon, a large fir cone etc. Aim for a variety of shapes, textures, weights, colours and materials. Aim to provide stimulation for all the baby's senses.
3 Allow the baby to play with it on her own, or with a friend.
4 As the adult, you should stay near but do not intervene unless she is anxious and needs reassurance.
5 Write three observations of the baby playing with the contents.
6 Write an evaluation of the activity, justifying your treasure choices and comment on any changes you would make when the basket is used again.
7 How successful were you in your aims of stimulating and challenging the baby?

If the treasure basket is being used in a day care setting keep other young children away while the basket is in use. Not only will this allow the baby to explore and play unhindered, but may prevent some articles becoming unsafe with boisterous toddlers throwing or banging them with force.

KEY POINT

■ Offering a treasure basket to a baby at the correct developmental stage is essential if she is to gain maximum benefit from it. If the baby is insecure in sitting unaided she will tire easily and lose interest in the basket and be unable to reach, pick up and manipulate objects without toppling over. If, however, she is crawling then she will move away to other interesting and new areas.

- For the most effective use of a treasure basket a baby needs to be able to sit securely and confidently for some considerable time, but before she is fully mobile.

REMEMBER!

A baby learns by discovery, so safety is always important. When purchasing or making toys always consider the following points.

- Toys should be strong, well made and unbroken.
- Toys should not contain small parts that can come loose and be swallowed.
- Materials chosen should be durable, strong and not break leaving sharp edges or splinters.
- Materials must be non-toxic and non-flammable. They should not contain PVC, dyes that rub off or toxic paint.
- Take care with toys with small holes that might trap fingers, or toys that are hard enough to hurt, if dropped or banged on fingers or toes.
- Toys for new babies should not have long narrow parts to reach to the back of a baby's throat, and should never be attached around a baby's neck on a string.
- When a baby is playing with paper ensure that she does not chew off small pieces and choke on them. Furry toys should have short, not long hair.
- Wooden toys need dovetailed, not nailed, joints, or joints fixed with tightly fastened, counter-sunk screws.
- Toys marked BSEN 71–BS 5665 have met the highest British and European Union safety standards for toys.
- The 'CE' mark is mandatory for all toys sold through the EU and indicates toys conform to EU law. However, it does not mean that individual toys have been tested for safety.
- The 'Lion mark' on toys indicates quality and safety and is used by members of the British Toy and Hobby Association

KEY POINT

Supervision is essential.

Your skill is to allow a baby the opportunity to experiment, practise her emerging skills and to discover, within a non-smothering, but safe environment. Always consider her developmental stage.

By the end of the first year of life, a baby's play has made enormous strides and by the age of one, she is enjoying favourite pastimes and rituals, imaginative play with a responsive adult and beginning to demonstrate a sense of humour. Her language will have progressed to a vocabulary of several words but she will understand much more. All play and toys should aim to respond to this rapidly changing development.

- Good playthings are often simple in design, but with a variety of uses.
- A baby needs toys that are easily manipulated so choose toys with large parts.
- Remember to include toys that have tactile properties – warm and pleasant to touch.

Activity

A baby who is learning to crawl is keen to practise her skills. How can you help? Look at her main play area – how might the layout promote her mobility?

1 Devise a plan of the play area and draw it to scale.
2 Check the furniture is solid enough for her to pull up on and that floors are non-slip with no loose mats.
3 What exciting, safe, things can you place within range – is there anything dangerous she could reach?
4 What toys are available to promote her gross motor skills– try to find equipment to support her and help her to learn to climb, push, pull, rock and ride.
5 Justify, in writing, the layout, the equipment and the play materials you have chosen.
6 What special safety equipment might you need to have in place in the play areas? See page 195.

REMEMBER!

- Keep her feet bare to encourage grip and balance.
- Make sure her clothes do not trip or make her movement difficult.
- Your role is to help the baby move to her next developmental stage, when she is ready, by providing appropriate stimulation and encouragement.

SAFE PRACTICE

Baby walkers are not recommended, as they are prone to topple and often enable a baby to reach dangerous areas, especially stairs, in seconds. They also provide a false sense of balance and so may actually delay walking.

Activity

1 What do these safety warning signs mean?

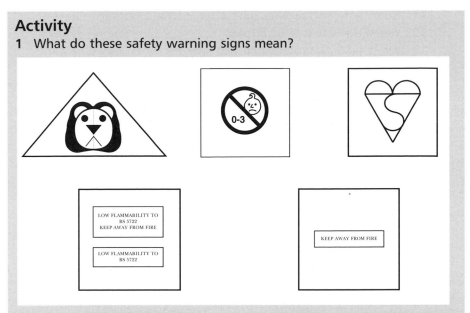

2 How many of the toys and pieces of child-care equipment you have researched have had safety marks on them?

3 Do all toys, by law, have to have a recognisable safety standard?

4 How would you ensure that second-hand toys and equipment are safe?

You will need to research in the library and through safety officers at your local town hall and through voluntary bodies.

QUICK CHECK

1 Which bed covering is no longer recommended for babies and why?

2 Describe **three** safety features you would look for when buying a cot.

3 Where is the safest place to fit a car seat?

4 Should car safety seats be bought by age or weight recommendation?

5 Describe **three** safety features you would look for when buying a pram or pushchair.

6 How close should a mobile be placed to a baby of three months for her to see it best?

7 Describe the most important sensory experience a new baby will have.

8 At what age would a baby gain most from a rattle? Why?

9 What special precautions are needed to ensure a baby learns safely 'by discovery'?

10 A baby, to gain maximum benefit from a treasure basket, needs to have obtained certain gross motor skills – what are they and why are they necessary?

11 How can a baby's bath time offer learning opportunities?
12 When do babies need shoes?
13 What safety factors would you look for when buying toys?
14 Why are baby walkers not recommended?
15 Describe the main duties of a carer when providing play activities for a mobile baby.

9 CARE OUTSIDE THE HOME

> **This chapter covers:**
> - **National Standards**
> - **Childminders**
> - **Day care**
> - **Child protection**

National Standards

In 1998 in England the Government launched the National Childcare Strategy to improve and standardise care for children, outside the home. The strategy comprises 14 written standards, with desired quality outcomes. These are coupled with associated supporting criteria to help practitioners reach these outcomes. The strategy was introduced to ensure that all children cared for away from home were provided with safe and secure environments. An additional criterion (Annex A) was included for people providing full day care for babies.

A further aim of the standards was to achieve a continuous improvement in the quality of child care. With this in mind, in 1999 the regulation of day care providers moved to a new Early Years Directorate within the Office for Standards in Education (OFSTED). All providers of full and sessional day care, childminding, crèches and out of school care now have to comply with the standards.

These developments should mean national improvement in the care given to babies when away from home. It is hoped they will lead to parents having increased confidence and reassurance when leaving their babies in others' hands.

Table 9.1 Annex A National Standards full day care babies/children under 2

These are additional criteria to be met by a registered person providing full day care who wishes to care for babies.

ORGANISATION
A.1 The registered person ensures that:
- children aged under two years are cared for in groups of no more than 12;
- staff caring for babies are competent to do so;
- at least 50% of staff caring for babies have received training in this specific area;
- the person in charge of the babies room has suitable experience of working with children under two years;
- arrangement for staffing minimise the number of carers for the individual child.

PHYSICAL ENVIRONMENT
A.2 The registered person ensures that:
- there is a separate base room for children under two. However, they should be able to have contact with older children and can be transferred to an older group after they reach the age of 18 months if that is appropriate for their individual development;
- nappy changing facilities are provided which meet environmental health standards;
- quiet areas are provided to enable individual sleep patterns to be facilitated.

EQUIPMENT
A.3 The registered person ensures that:
- activities, toys and equipment are appropriate for the child's age and provide varied sensory opportunities and experiences both indoors and outdoors;
- some domestic style furniture is provided to assist children in developing mobility and to continue normal life experiences;
- cots or other appropriate furniture are provided for children to rest or sleep.

SAFETY
A.4 The registered person ensures that:
- when in high or low chairs, children are restrained in safety harnesses;
- sleeping babies are frequently checked.

FOOD AND DRINK
A.5 The registered person ensures that:
- feeding and nappy changing takes place in accordance with the child's individual needs and not as part of a nursery routine;
- normally, babies are held whilst bottle feeding, preferably by the same carer;
- an area is provided with access to drinking water and facilities for the hygienic preparation of babies; feeds;
- suitable sterilisation equipment is used for babies' feeding equipment and dummies;
- records are kept of babies' food intake for parents.

PARTNERSHIP WITH PARENTS
A.6 The registered person ensures that there is a daily system of exchange of information between the parent and key person. This includes information about the child's changing development and care needs and routines.

CARE AND LEARNING
A.7 The registered person ensures that:
- children have the opportunity to interact with a consistent adult at frequent intervals throughout the day;
- there is clear planning of babies' activities.

Childminders

Childminders work in their own homes, providing care, play and learning opportunities for young children within a home setting. They are essential providers of day care for young children, currently offering more than 200,000 full-time places nationwide. Parents often prefer their baby to be cared for in a domestic setting within a small group of children.

Anyone caring for one or more children under eight years, for more than two hours a day and receiving payment, must be registered for their work. Childminders are registered and inspected by OFSTED Early Years Directorate and must comply with the National Standards for Childminding.

Registration is dependent on:

- the suitability of the applicant to care for babies and young children and provide a warm, stimulating and happy environment for them
- assessment of safety and hygiene within the home
- a satisfactory medical check
- a satisfactory police check for themselves, other helpers and anyone else over the age of 16 living in the home where the children are minded.

Activity

1 Read the Department for Education and Skills National Standards 'Under Eights Day Care and Childminding – Childminding' Standards 1 and 2 – 'Suitable person' and 'Organisation'.
2 What qualifications do the supporting criteria suggest for someone working as a Childminder?
3 How many babies under one year can be cared for at one time?

Day care

With the expansion in the number of working mothers, increasing numbers of babies are being cared for in day care settings, either full time, or on sessional basis.

Day care may be delivered through local authorities, by private company nurseries or though workplace crèches. The premises, whether purpose built or converted, must be safe and secure, with all necessary safety equipment fitted and meeting the relevant Health and Safety regulations. Separate facilities are required for preparing babies' feeds and food, heating bottles and nappy changing. Sleeping areas must be quiet and away from other noisy or boisterous older children. Equipment and furnishings should be child centred.

Table 9.2 The role of the Early Years worker with babies in day care

Professional skills and knowledge needed	Essential personal qualities
Skills to:	■ genuine interest in working with babies
■ implement effective, safe, care routines	■ patience and sensitivity
■ plan and implement stimulating and appropriate play activities	■ ability to take and act upon constructive criticism/self awareness
■ undertake regular, accurate, non-judgemental observations	
■ implement anti-bias practice	■ empathy understand and respect confidentiality
■ show initiative, when appropriate	■ confident and assertive, but not arrogant
■ work with parents as partners	■ punctual and reliable
■ communicate effectively	■ a current and satisfactory Disclosure of Criminal Record
■ work effectively in a team	
■ respond proactively to a baby's development	*Appearance:*
	■ short, unvarnished nails – no bulky rings
Knowledge of:	■ safe, sensible shoes
■ child development child care	■ clean clothing and/or clean uniform
■ the importance of the parents' role others' roles in the setting	*Health:*
■ setting's policies	■ protected by immunisation
■ current child-care issues and practice initiatives	■ energetic
■ first aid	■ good personal hygiene

Key point
An Early Years worker must be able to understand each baby is an individual with individual needs.

Outdoor nursery areas, used by babies for play and sleeping, must be secure and inaccessible to dogs and the general public. Regular checking of the condition of the garden, boundary fencing and potential hazards from poisonous plants, litter, water and animal excreta should be part of good practice.

All settings should aim to offer continuity of care for babies to make a seamless link between the home and nursery. As far as possible routines and rituals should reflect the babies' current experiences, particularly in areas such as sleeping and feeding.

Babies need space and opportunity to crawl, explore, experiment and learn through their developing senses. Their physical skills are emerging, and they are making and learning new sounds. All day care planning should be directed to meeting their emerging development.

How to work effectively with parents

Understand how difficult it is for the parents to pass their baby's care onto strangers. Do not be judgemental or rival parents for their baby's affections.

Always give parents honest explanations if you are genuinely unable, or unwilling, to follow their wishes regarding their baby.

Remember that a professional relationship is based on mutual respect – it is not necessary, or appropriate, to become personal friends with parents.

Extend your understanding of differences in culture and religious practices and how these might apply to the care of young babies. Ensure, as far as possible, that care is consistent with particular wishes.

For parents who have communication difficulties be creative in solutions – for example use tapes and Braille, dual written language information, interpreters, gestures, eye contact, photographs, toys and books. Use phone calls or letters for maintaining contacting with parents frequently delayed or working shift patterns.

Fully explain the daily routines their baby will experience in day care – be open to questions and be honest in answers and explanations. Ask parent's permission before making changes to routines, for example outings.

Always behave with courtesy and respect towards parents.

Give full attention when talking to parents, remembering the importance of open body language. Make time for them and listen attentively.

Update your own knowledge and skills.

Understand that your role is to support parents and provide continuity between the home and the setting. This is particularly important when working with babies who are unable to verbalise their needs.

Respect parents' privacy.

Be honest and open in all communication and assure parents of confidentiality. However, check they understand that any concerns about a baby's safety or well being will be passed on to senior staff.

Remember any negativity from parents towards staff may stem from lack of confidence, low self-esteem, or previous bad experiences. So present a positive attitude by being encouraging and check all explanations are understood.

REMEMBER: parents know their baby best.

A baby who is cared for away from the home for considerable periods of time requires skilled and sensitive care. Effective liaison and strong links between day care staff and parents ensures the baby has the best environment in which to develop.

Caring for a baby away from her home requires a full understanding of her particular needs and interpreting the signs she gives to express her needs.

As an Early Years worker you will also need the maturity and confidence to work closely with parents and create an environment where both parents' and workers' roles are known and valued.

KEY POINT

Babies need consistent care for healthy emotional development. Organisation of staffing must reflect this.

DAY CARE ADMISSION

Before a baby's admission to day care, parents need to visit the setting and meet the staff. They also require written information about the nursery, its procedures and policies to take away and read at leisure. Many nurseries also offer a home visit, which can act as a valuable bridge between the home and day care setting. It is most useful if the worker who will be responsible for the baby makes the visit. The meeting allows for the Early Years' worker to meet the baby in a known, relaxed and familiar environment, and gives parents the opportunity to ask questions and share any anxieties. It is a valuable opportunity to explain the role and importance of the key worker in the baby's emotional development – see below.

Information required from parents

As well as basic information such as name and address, more facts are necessary to gain a full picture of a baby and her individual needs.

Information required from parents should include the following.

■ Baby's feeding, sleeping, comfort objects and settling routines.
■ Any special medical requirements, including known allergies, and immunisation status.
■ Any cultural and religious requirements – skin and hair care, diet, clothing.
■ Dietary requirements.
■ Addresses and telephone numbers of: GP, parents' home and work and emergency contact numbers for back-up adult contact.
■ The names of the adults permitted to collect the baby at the end of a session. Some settings require parents to provide a photograph of those authorised to collect their baby.

- In addition, signed forms for permission to take the baby out of the nursery on outings and for emergency medical treatment are often obtained at this time.

KEY POINTS

- This information is personal and must be treated confidentially.
- The information must always be current and relevant, and updated as necessary.

Information to be given to the parents

Information to be given to the parents should include the following.

- Background information about the nursery and its ethos, including its Equal Opportunity Policy and any religious or special cultural affiliation.
- How the nursery is organised – including staff ratio, whether the key worker system operates, if so the name and contact number of the baby's worker.
- How children of specific ages are cared for – whether into 'age rooms' or family units – and the qualifications of the staff.
- How the baby's progress will be monitored and how parents will be kept informed.
- What parents are required to provide. This may include all the baby's formula milk, and weaning foods, nappies and clothing changes (these must be labelled).
- If the nursery provides milk and weaning foods, the parents needs to tell the nursery about any dietary, medical or cultural wishes they have.
- The policy of personal possessions for the baby – what happens if anything is mislaid?
- How a baby's day is structured, the learning opportunities provided, and how parents are kept informed about progress.
- What happens if a baby is ill.
- How parental involvement is encouraged.
- The length of the nursery day, the fees and when they must be paid. What happens during holidays and how much notice must be given if a baby leaves.
- The complaints procedures.

REMEMBER!

- Effective communication is a two-way process – always find time to listen to questions and worries, as well as asking for information. Nurseries are busy, sometimes noisy places, so find a quiet, private place for information exchange.
- How you communicate is important, so think about the tone and volume of your voice, your facial expression when listening and how you use eye

contact and gestures. Think, too, about actual words you use – technical terms may be unfamiliar to some parents and others may not have English as a first language.

SETTLING IN

Day care is usually organised so that babies are kept together and separate from the older children, for at least part of the day. This allows the environment to be specific for this younger age range, and for a higher staff ratio to exist of one adult to three babies.

Unlike preparing an older child it is difficult to get a baby ready for separation from her mother, so the settling-in period is especially important. The time needed for each baby may vary, but a likely timetable for full-time day care is suggested below.

The age at which babies are admitted to day care will vary, sometimes as young as six weeks but more often at six months. The younger the baby the easier the separation will appear, as such a young child will not have learnt to discriminate between known and unknown adults. However, she will be distressed by being flooded by a variety of different carers handling her and attempting to understand her needs. She needs a limited number of carers attending to her so she can begin to make new, secure attachments.

REMEMBER!

A baby of six to nine months will show separation anxiety – this is part of normal social and emotional development. Consistency of care will help reduce her stress, see below.

KEY WORKER

Most nurseries now use the key worker system when organising care for babies. A key worker is a designated staff member who cares fully for one or more specific babies during every session that the babies attend and for the length of their stay in the nursery.

Key worker responsibilities include:

- planning the baby's day to include her learning programme;
- monitoring and recording the baby's development;
- liaising with the baby's parents
- meeting all her needs during her time in the nursery. This means undertaking all personal physical care – nappy changing, greeting and settling the baby on arrival in the morning, comforting any distress, bottle-feeding and other meals. The worker is responsible for returning

the baby to the care of her parents at the end of the day, with either a written or oral report.

A key worker makes separation for a baby, from her prime carer, easier. It helps promotes healthy emotional development, at a possibly vulnerable time for a baby. The success of a key worker system will, to some extent, depend on all staff appreciating its theory in the promotion of healthy emotional development. See Attachment, page 158.

All staff need to understand the value of a key worker to an individual baby and why her needs should be met by her particular worker as far as possible. In a busy environment it may appear easier for any member of staff to change an uncomfortable baby immediately, rather than wait a few minutes for her designated worker to be available, but this undermines the system and may confuse and unsettle the baby.

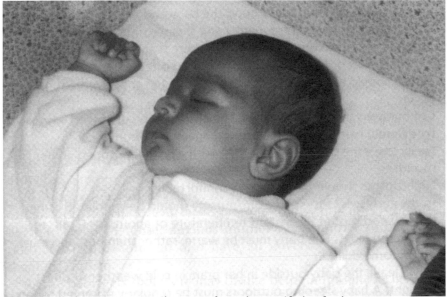

A baby will sleep more easily away from home if she feels secure

Even when the key worker system is not in practice a nominated member of staff should take special responsibility for individual babies admitted. Continuity is important for the baby to settle and for her needs to be met. It helps the parents to have a familiar worker with whom they have confidence to talk about their baby and her day. Often this will be an informal discussion, but increasingly nurseries are using diaries to record the baby's day. These usually include information on feeding, sleeping, play, any minor skin problems or ailments, comments on developmental milestones achieved and records of any distress the baby has had and how it was resolved. This sharing of information promotes a partnership between parents and nursery, helping not only during the crucial early weeks of separation, but also in setting positive patterns for continuing liaison for parent, baby and nursery staff.

KEY POINTS

■ Remember, however close you may come, as a worker, to a baby in your care, her stay with you will inevitably be temporary and her parents are her prime carers.

■ Nursery policy will need to address issues such as procedures to cover absence of a key worker during illness and holidays.

■ Parents must always feel confident their baby will have her physical, social, emotional and intellectual needs met, and their cultural and religious wishes respected when she is cared for by substitute carers.

■ Allow sufficient time for sharing information with parents – if you seem rushed they may not feel confident to ask questions or share any worries they may have.

Table 9.3 Likely timetable for settling a baby into full-time day care

Day	First week – mornings only	Second week
1	Two-hour morning. Baby attends with her parent who works	Four-hour morning. Parent settles baby then leaves. Key worker gives baby her bottles and changes her nappies
2	Two-hour morning. As above	Five-hour day. Parent settles baby then leaves. Key worker feeds, changes and settles baby for rest
3	Two-hour morning. As above	Full six-hour day. Parent settles baby in morning, leaves and returns to collect baby before other children leave
4	Three-hour morning. Parent leaves baby in nursery for an hour then returns to feed her. Key worker changes her nappies	Full six-hour day. As above
5	Four-hour morning. Parent leaves baby for two hours. Baby is fed and changed by key worker	Full day, as above, but baby is collected with the other babies

Note: This suggested plan is for a baby who is being bottle-fed; additional adjustments would be needed for a baby who is being breast-fed.

Activity

Visit three day care settings in your area (if available) that provide places for babies and answer the following questions.

1 Are these centres provided by the local authority, privately, or a mixture of both?

2 What are the charges for full day care?

3 If possible, discuss with the nursery managers the qualifications of the staff working with the young babies. Is a standard qualification required? If so, what is it? What is the NVQ level equivalent? Have staff taken additional training to work with babies?

4 Do all settings operate a key worker system?

5 How is the baby's day recorded and how is this information given to the parents?

6 What is the youngest age that babies are admitted to the nursery?

7 Is there a written care and education routine for the babies?

8 What facilities are provided for parents in the nurseries?

9 Compare and contrast the different schemes for settling new babies in the three nurseries.

10 Write up your findings and evaluate how well you consider the babies' needs are met in these three settings.

REST AND SLEEP ROUTINES IN DAY CARE

In day care settings, babies will need periods of rest and sleep each day. Some babies may have a well-established sleep pattern, while others may vary from day to day in their requirements. A flexible approach will enable you to match a baby's rest and sleep routine with her home routine and parent's wishes, ensuring continuity of care, which will make the baby feel secure.

You will need to find out from the baby's parent or carer:

- the routine that best suits the baby's needs
- if the baby has a comfort object
- the baby's preferred sleep position
- whether the baby enjoys a routine of music, singing, rocking, patting or stroking before settling to sleep
- if the baby likes to be cuddled on waking.

KEY POINT

Before settling a baby to rest or sleep make sure she is wearing comfortable clothes and has a dry nappy – never put her down in a wet or soiled nappy. Her hands and face may need wiping or washing following a feed, a meal, floor or messy play. In day care each baby must have her own cot in a well-ventilated (not draughty), warm and safe 'sleep' room or quiet area. The cots should be spaced not less than 1 m (3 ft) apart to allow for air to circulate and lessen the risk of cross-infection. It also lets adults move freely between the cots. A quiet, relaxed atmosphere with at least one adult remaining in attendance to supervise the sleep period helps the babies to settle and provides reassurance that a familiar carer is near.

Bean bags, large cushions and sofas can be used for rest periods for older babies. However, to prevent a fall or accidental suffocation the babies must be supervised at all times and never left unattended, even if they are not yet able to roll over on their own.

SAFE PRACTICE

■ Make sure every baby has her own clean cot and bedding. Wash the sheets and blankets weekly, and every time they are wet or soiled. Air mattresses regularly. Check the automatic safety catches on cots are working properly.

■ Monitor babies sleeping outdoors every 10 minutes for signs of chilling or becoming unwell. A signed record should be made of all checks.

■ Use cat and insect nets on prams for babies who are sleeping outdoors to prevent harm.

■ Check daily that pram brakes, harnesses and anchor points are in good order.

■ See also Chapter 8 for care of nursery equipment.

Activity

Ask the parents of a baby you know well, if you may keep a 24-hour sleep diary for her. You will be recording her sleeping patterns for a month. Chose a baby who attends full time, is crawling, and is well settled into day care. Record the following.

1 The times and length the baby sleeps each day.

2 How much sleep she has at home, what time she settles for the night and if she wakes during the night.

3 Calculate how much sleep she has, on average, in 24 hours.

(Note: This information could be recorded in graph form.)

Expand your findings with additional written information on the following.

1 Whether you consider she has settled, regular sleeping times and patterns.

2 If any events (for example, change in routine, illness and absence of key worker) appear to change or disrupt her usual pattern.

3 Does she need a comforter to settle?

4 What rituals and physical comfort the baby needs before settling to sleep – and if there are differences between home and day care.

5 Ask her parents if her pattern alters at weekends.

6 Have you noticed if there have been changes during the month that you have been keeping the diary?

COMMUNICATING WITH BABIES

Particular skills are needed when communicating effectively with babies

Language
- Be aware of what you say to a baby and use your voice expressively.
- Speak regularly to her during her routine care.
- Be close so she can focus on your face and see, hear and touch you.
- Use expressions to indicate a range of emotions.

How you appear to babies
- Try and be on her level.
- Use her name and touch her gently to gain attention.
- Use gestures and signs.
- Be aware of other cultures, their signs and gestures etc.

Be aware of noise
- Keep noise levels low; high levels and sudden unexpected noises may increase her insecurity.
- Never have background music on in the baby room; use music only for active listening.
- Never shout or talk in loud voices to colleagues across babies.

Too many adults
- Babies need to attach to regular faces and carers, so avoid too many adults caring for her. Effective use of the key worker system will help reduce her anxiety.

BREAST-FEEDING IN DAY CARE

Many mothers now wish to continue breast-feeding even though they plan to return to work. Being able to breast-feed means a mother can remain close to her baby even when separated for comparatively long periods of time. To allow this to happen may mean one of the following:

- the mother working close to her baby's carer or nursery so she can come and feed when needed
- expressing breast milk to be given during her absence
- partial breast-feeding – breast-feeding at the beginning and end of the day, with bottles of expressed breast or formula milk being given while the mother is at work.

This last approach is only possible when lactation is well established. The breasts need regular stimulation to produce adequate supplies of milk, especially in the early days of feeding. See Table 5.1 on page 127 for common breast-feeding difficulties.

Expressing breast milk

Necessary equipment and facilities will include:

- a pump – this works by producing a vacuum and a squeezing action over the areola, in a similar manner to the baby's jaws. Pumps can be hand-, battery- or mains electricity-operated. The breasts must be stimulated in this way regularly during the day and night to maintain the milk supply. Milk can be expressed manually but it will take much longer to produce the necessary amounts for several hours of separation from the baby
- sterile storage containers – sterile bottles, teats and sterilising equipment
- a vacuum cool bag to carry the expressed milk
- a room, with a lock, that is warm, private, clean with a comfortable chair
- hand-washing facilities and equipment nearby
- storage facility for expressed milks, e.g. refrigerator or freezer, nearby.

Wherever a mother feeds her baby or expresses breast milk she needs to feel private, relaxed, comfortable and welcome.

Expressed breast milk must be stored in sterile, covered containers, labelled and dated.

Expressed breast milk must be used within 24 hours if stored in a refrigerator and within 3 months if frozen. It should be thoroughly defrosted before use and transported in an insulated carrier bag. Never keep it warm for bacteria to breed.

Cleanliness and sterility of all equipment are as necessary for expressed breast milk as for formula milk – see Preparation of feeds, page 130, and Procedure for giving a bottle, page 133.

Making a mother feel welcome and giving her privacy and time either to express her milk or feed her baby will make the experience satisfying. Try not to rush her, nor make her feel she is in the way or taking up valuable time or space. If she feels under pressure, this may make expressing more difficult, and make both her and the baby anxious if she is breastfeeding.

BOTTLE-FEEDING IN DAY CARE

Many parents and carers are asked to bring to the nursery or childminder the reconstituted formula milks for their own baby. If this is the practice in your nursery check that the bottles are:
- labelled clearly with the child's name, to avoid any possible confusion
- transported safely by an insulated carrier bag
- stored at the correct temperature in a clean, regularly defrosted refrigerator.

Ensure that:
- babies are always held close when being bottle-fed – do not feed a baby in her chair
- charts are kept of how much milk a baby takes at each feed and that this information is given to the parents, by the key worker, at the end of each day
- babies are always fed according to medical advice and the wishes and cultural preferences of parents are fully respected
- procedures for emergency milk supplies are arranged and known by all staff.

Weaning
For more on weaning, see page 136.

Activity
Devise a chart for daily use to inform a parent of a baby's feeding routine in your nursery. What information would you need to include for effective parent/carer liaison?

SAFE PRACTICE

When handling milk feeds for babies in group care, hygiene procedures must be especially rigorous. Infection is easily transmitted from baby to baby and from carer to baby. Babies with special medical needs, low birth-weight and pre-term babies may be particularly vulnerable.

CLOTHING

Parents may be asked to bring in changes of clothing for their baby. Check these are suitable and discuss any queries with the parents. For example, a dress may inhibit a baby about to attempt to crawl or clothing may be too warm – often the temperature in a day care setting is higher than the home environment and so clothing may need to be lighter. Special warmer, outdoor clothing may be needed for any outing. Remember to respect cultural and personal wishes over specific clothing items. Clothing will need to be labelled with the name of the baby.

Nappies

Day care settings may supply, or ask parents to provide, their own disposable nappies, while other settings will prefer to use reusable nappies. These are often laundered on the premises.

See page 82 for more on the management of nappy changing.

Skin and dental care

Although not routine, there may be occasions when you will bath a baby in day care (see Bathing a baby, page 72). For routine care some parents may wish to bring in particular toiletries and creams for their baby's use. They may prefer you to use wet wipes to clean the baby's bottom – check they do not make the baby sore.

Babies in day care should have their own toothbrushes that are kept clean and in separate holders.

For specific cultural issues for skin care, see page 73.

AN UNWELL BABY IN DAY CARE

If a baby attending day care is unwell, her parents may be asked to keep her at home until she is recovered. This is both to reduce the risk of infection to other children, but also a baby will feel more comfortable in her own environment.

Giving medicines

On some occasions, day care staff may need to administer medicines. The setting must have a clear policy regarding giving baby's medicines, which should be well known by all staff and agreed by the parents.

The National Standards for Day Care state as follows.

- Medicines must be stored in their original containers, clearly labelled and inaccessible to children.
- Medicines should not usually be administered unless they have been prescribed for that child by a doctor

- The parent must gives prior written permission for the administration of any medication.
- Written records must be kept of all medicines administered to children and parents must sign the record book to acknowledge the entry.
- If the administration of prescription medicines requires technical/medical knowledge then individual training should be provided for staff from a qualified health professional. Training must be specific to the individual child concerned.

MEASURES NECESSARY TO PREVENT CROSS-INFECTION IN DAY CARE SETTINGS

Dealing with body fluids

It is standard procedure in most day care settings to use latex disposable gloves when changing babies' nappies – at bath time, nappy changes and when 'topping and tailing'. Not only does this protect against infection, it prevents discrimination against a baby who has a disclosed blood-borne infection. A new pair of gloves should be worn for each individual baby at every nappy change and disposed of, safely, immediately after use. Gloves should be removed as soon as nappy changing is complete and hands washed. Wearing gloves should not diminish the opportunity for interaction between the carer and the baby during these routines.

Dealing with spillage and soiled articles

Put on disposable gloves (and a protective disposable apron) when cleaning up body fluids (blood, urine, faeces or vomit) or dealing with soiled articles. Then:

- cover the body fluid, and wipe up, with paper towels
- clean the soiled area with hot water and household detergent using a disposable cloth
- wash the area with a bleach solution made up of 1 part bleach to 10 parts cold water – or a disinfectant of correct strength can be used (check manufacturer's dilution instructions)
- wash cleaning mops with a bleach solution and allow to dry
- soak blood-stained reusable nappies or clothing in cold water, to remove the stain, before laundering. Articles soiled with vomit or faeces must be sluiced in cold water in a lavatory (or in a sink used only for this purpose) and disinfected before laundering in the usual way
- always follow the guidelines of your day care setting and local authority when dealing with body fluids.

Keep bleach and disinfectants out of the reach of babies.

Routine hygiene measures for all babies

■ Dispose of used swabs, paper towels, cloths, gloves and aprons in a sealed tie-bag according to the setting practice.
■ Disinfect and wash changing mats after each nappy change.
■ Launder towels and face cloths daily – soiled, damp towels that are left lying around or hanging close together on individual hooks are a source for bacterial growth.

Personal hygiene measures

■ Cover any cut or wound you may have with a maximum protection waterproof dressing (unless you are allergic to them).
■ Wash your hands thoroughly after handling soiled articles or cleaning up body fluids.
■ A carer with diarrhoea or vomiting should not be working with babies until they have recovered.

PLAY EXPERIENCES

Babies need stimulating play and freedom to explore and discover. You must provide appropriate toys and activities, equipment and opportunities for them to learn and experiment. Play materials, in good condition, should be readily available, including figures, dolls, puppets and picture books representing different cultures, with features of different skin types and ethnicity. Introduce clapping and action rhymes, songs and tapes, and lullabies in different language and dialects. Ask staff to sing the songs they grew up with and use a variety of musical instruments to reflect different traditions and rhythms.

Toys and materials should not be stereotyped by gender and should positively reflect a multicultural environment. Posters and pictures around the room should display positive images – black people, women and people with disabilities.

KEY POINT

■ Play experiences must be reviewed regularly to ensure they are meeting the babies' needs.
■ Changes of toys, activities and outings are an integral part of routine planning.
■ Designated meetings should take place within the baby room team to plan and evaluate the learning opportunities being offered to the babies.

Play materials, equipment and toys will be used more heavily than in the home and by more babies. To prevent accidents and cross-infection:

■ equipment needs regular monitoring for condition and safety
■ toys must be washed regularly and checked for wear and tear.

OBSERVATION AND RECORD KEEPING

Every baby attending day care should be regularly observed and the results recorded and filed with the baby's records. These should provide a total picture of a baby's development and ensure her needs are met most effectively. Observations must be systematic and objective, and scheduled into the routine of the setting. The observations should be discussed with supervisors and shared with the parents.

Activity

When working in a day care setting, part of your professional duty is to plan and deliver routines for the babies in your care. Plan a day's routine for:
(a) a baby of six months, who is not yet mobile; and
(b) a baby of nine months who is competent in crawling and is keen to practise this skill.
Describe, implement and evaluate your routines. You must include:
■ all physical care given – skin care, nutrition and sleep management – and incorporate the rationale for this care;
■ learning experiences, which should reflect and complement the developmental stage and needs of both babies;
■ the play equipment and materials needed for the routines, and how to use and present them imaginatively, creatively and safely;
■ how each baby's development can be safely stimulated;
■ your own personal learning, when evaluating your plans. Consider how effective your routines were and state any changes you would make in future plans.
Use the chapters of this book as a resource in your planning and implementation.

REMEMBER!

■ Play is an integral part of a baby's day.
■ Routine care and daily activities should be fun. All have potential for promoting aspects of development and learning.
■ Stimulate the baby's all-round development.

Always take care to promote and encourage emerging skills – the next developmental stage. This is especially important in a baby who may be delayed in one developmental area (see Chapter 10).

> The information in this chapter addresses issues specific to caring for babies in day care. For essential, supportive material, on care and the promotion of development you should cross-refer to the following chapters:
> - Chapters 3 and 4 for information on basic care issues
> - Chapter 5 for nutrition, sterilisation of equipment and preparation of feeds
> - Chapter 6 for the promotion of physical, intellectual language emotional and social development
> - Chapter 7 for caring for the ill baby
> - Chapter 8 for equipment, toys, activities and play
> - Chapter 10 for information about babies with special needs
> - Appendix for First Aid.

Child protection

It is hard for Early Years workers to imagine why anyone would wish to harm a baby. The reality is, however, that babies are particularly at risk. The NSPCC report babies are five times more likely to be killed, through abuse, than any other age group and that this number has been rising over recent years. The perpetrators are usually the prime carers.

CHILD ABUSE

Child abuse is action or deliberate inaction that results in harm to a baby. While there is often overlap between the categories, abuse is usually divided into three areas, namely physical abuse, emotional abuse and sexual abuse.

Physical abuse
The intentional use of physical force, which results in harm, either death or injury.

Emotional abuse
A baby's basic needs for love and protection are not met resulting in her failure to develop healthy emotions.

Sexual abuse

A baby is used for an adult's sexual gratification.

Although all these types of abuse can happen to babies, physical abuse is potentially the most life threatening.

Why is a baby vulnerable?

A baby is totally dependant upon her parents and carers. She is not able to call out for help, or run away, and she often stays at home where her injuries remain unseen. A baby is delicate and minimal force may cause irreparable damage, for example, shaking a baby can cause brain injury or death.

Stresses on families

Many parents, particularly in today's society, have little knowledge of how demanding a normal baby will be, particularly in the first few weeks of life. A baby may cry and behave in an unpredictable manner and appear unresponsive, for example, not smiling or proving difficult to settle or pacify. All this may increase parental worry and existing feelings of inadequacy. Having a new baby, however wanted, planned for and eagerly anticipated, inevitably places stress on families through:

- loss of sleep
- financial pressures – babies are expensive and family income often drops when a mother stops work
- relationships between men and women altering when a third human – the baby – enters the home. Men may feel rejected, jealous, or inadequate if, for example, they have difficulty in mollifying a crying baby
- having a baby is a major life event after which the family's life will change permanently – nothing will be the same again
- mothers often feel they have lost control of their lives
- difficulties in finding and funding day care for working parents.

Additional pressures are placed on:

- young, unsupported or isolated parents
- adults who have difficulty in controlling strong emotions
- families under stress through poverty, chronic illness and poor housing
- families with a step-parent or cohabitee who is not the father of the baby
- parents who themselves suffered abuse as a child
- parents separated from their baby after birth – the baby may be pre-term, ill or in a special care unit

- a mother recovering from a traumatic and difficult labour and birth;
- drink or drug-dependent members.

The pressures listed above indicate that a family may require additional support. However, they do not necessarily mean a family will abuse their baby.

ROLE OF THE EARLY YEARS WORKER

Professional workers require good knowledge of any baby in their care, which should be supported by ongoing, objective written observations of a baby's development. This makes you well suited to identify early worrying signs. Below you will find listed what to look for.

Physical abuse
- Adult bite marks.
- Cigarette or other burns
- Scalds, sometimes associated with 'dunking' in hot water.
- Finger tip bruising.
- Hand slap marks on the face and body.
- Finger grip marks around the chest.
- Bruising and/or bleeding around the mouth and lips, and damage to the tissue under the tongue (often the result of forced bottle-feeding).
- Bleeding in the sclera – the whites of the eye – associated with a baby being shaken. Bleeding in the brain and associated damage also can occur.
- A baby who does not move a limb or where movement is asymmetrical.
- Where injuries are inconsistent with the story given. For example, a six-week-old baby could not 'roll off a bed', pull a cup of boiling water over herself etc.
- Twisting fractures of the long bones, for example, thighs or arms.
- Any unexplained injuries where the parents have delayed in seeking medical help.
- Injuries for which no explanations are given.

REMEMBER!

Bruising is more noticeable in white skin; it may be less apparent on babies with dark skin.

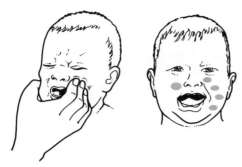

a) Thumb and finger marks on cheeks

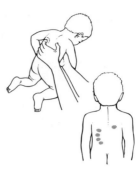

b) Finger marks around chest

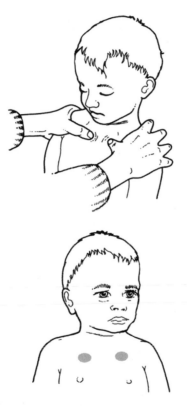

c) Thumb marks below the
collar bone

Emotional abuse

Usually emotional abuse becomes apparent over a period of months and
is often associated with dclay in reaching social and emotional milestones.
See Chapter 6, especially the chart on page 157.
Signs might include:

Handle with care. Babies are fragile and precious, never shake a baby

- delayed smiling
- lack of responsiveness
- unhappy baby/exceptionally passive 'frozen' baby
- failure to bond or attach with prime carer
- poor sleep habits.

Sexual abuse
- Bruising and damage around the genitalia.

KEY POINTS

Categories of abuse usually overlap, for example, physical or sexual abuse will mean, inevitably, that a baby's emotional needs are unmet.

Other signs of abuse
Other signs are often present in a baby who is abused, whatever category. These may include:

- faltering growth
- general delay in meeting developmental milestones.

Worrying family behaviour, or attitudes, may include:

- physical and emotional neglect, which can include dirty clothing, poor skin condition, for example, extreme nappy rash and cradle cap, prop feeding
- parents who 'discipline' their babies by shouting or smacking
- parents who have unrealistic expectations of their baby, for example, expecting a new baby to sleep through the night, an older baby to understand and remember the word 'no'
- parents or carers who have erratic attendance patterns for their baby in day care and/or fail to attend meetings to discuss progress, or attend child health clinics.

REMEMBER!

A pre-mobile baby cannot be bruised from 'rolling from a bed'; however an active crawling baby can.

ACTION

Working effectively with a baby means that you will inevitably develop close, professional relationships with her family. Occasionally this can lead to child-care workers finding difficulty in objective consideration of possible signs of abuse. This can include the care worker having problems in accepting that a parent might cause harm to their child. However difficult it may be, remember your first priority must be for the baby. If you have concerns about injuries, do not make unfounded accusations. Discuss your concerns, at the first opportunity, with the senior member of staff in the baby room. Always record, in writing at the time, any physical signs of injury about which you are worried and ask a senior staff member to countersign the observation. All settings must have agreed child protection procedures, so ensure you know, understand and follow them. See Activity.

KEY POINTS

- Always follow your settings' agreed procedures.
- Seek support and guidance from experienced staff.
- Do not forget that an abused baby is at greater risk than an older child.

Activity

Discuss with your supervisor or senior in the baby room the local child-care protection policy in your placement and ask to read it.
1 Where is it kept?
2 At what stage is it discussed with new staff and students?
3 Is it clearly written with your role explained?
4 What is National Standard 13 Full Day Care and its associated Supporting Criteria?
5 Does your local procedure fulfil these criteria?

REMEMBER!

Emotions can run high if there are anxieties that a baby has been intentionally harmed but however distressing the situation:

■ always remain professional;
■ do not jump to conclusions or be judgemental;
■ do not make assumptions or unfounded allegations;
■ never gossip, or talk about any concerns, outside the nursery.

QUICK CHECK

1 What are the 'National Standards'?
2 Describe the checks undertaken before someone becomes a childminder?
3 Summarise the role of the key worker. Why is it important?
4 What information should be exchanged between parents and staff when preparing for the admission of a baby to day care?
5 Outline **five** ways of working effectively work with parents.
6 What do you understand by the term 'separation anxiety' and at what age does it appear in a baby?
7 How can you ensure a baby has safe, secure sleep in day care?
8 What is the best way for expressed breast milk and artificial feeds to be transported to day care. What precautions are required to ensure safe milk storage in the setting?
9 Give the **five** criteria, from the National Standards, regarding the administration of medicine in day care settings.
10 Why is it good practice to wear latex gloves when changing babies' nappies in day care?
11 How would you manage the situation if a baby's soiled nappy was inadvertently dropped on the floor and the contents spilled?
12 'Written observations of babies are an integral part of good practice in day care.' Justify this statement.

13 Why are babies particularly vulnerable to child abuse?
14 List the pressures on families, which might increase the chance of a baby being abused.
15 Describe the **three** categories of child abuse and say why they often overlap.

10 BABIES WITH SPECIAL NEEDS

> **This chapter covers:**
> - **Introduction to special needs**
> - **Possible causes of special needs**
> - **Types of special needs**
> - **The family – parents and siblings**
> - **Meeting the baby's needs**

Introduction to special needs

The term 'special needs' is used by child-care professionals in relation to babies whose development is not following the recognised pattern seen in most babies. Not all babies of similar ages are at the same stage of development. Babies with special needs are simply at different points in the developmental continuum.

All parents wish for, and expect, a healthy baby. Preconceptual and antenatal care reduce many of the risks to the unborn child. The special tests and investigations offered during pregnancy (see Chapter 1, pages 22–7) may identify certain conditions.

KEY POINTS

- While special tests of pregnancy may identify particular conditions, they cannot alter them. Parents must be supported both in their decision whether to have the test and in their decision whether or not to terminate a pregnancy.
- Genetic counselling is available for parents seeking information about an inherited condition and the risk of passing it on to children or grandchildren (see Chapter 1, page 11).

Possible causes of special needs

Special needs may be due to:
- hereditary (inherited) factors;
- antenatal, birth and postnatal developments;
- child-care and parenting factors.

Table 10.1 Some possible causes of special needs

Hereditary factors
Genetic inheritance — Cystic fibrosis, sickle cell and thalassaemia conditions, phenylketonuria, Tay-Sachs disease and others
Chromosomal inheritance — Down's syndrome, fragile X syndrome
Sex-linked inheritance — Haemophilia, Duchenne muscular dystrophy

Key points
- Hereditary disorders are passed on from parents to their children and are always present at birth even if not immediately identifiable.
- One or more special needs may be present but one may predominate.

Prenatal factors
Substances: drugs, tobacco, alcohol
Maternal infections including: rubella, toxoplasmosis, cytomegalovirus, listeriosis, HIV, some sexually transmitted infections (STIs)
Threatened miscarriage

At birth
Anoxia (lack of oxygen), prematurity, post-maturity, low birth-weight, difficult delivery

Postnatal developments
Infections including: bacterial meningitis, measles, mumps, diphtheria, poliomyelitis
Accidents/injuries: particularly those damaging the brain and spinal cord
Childhood cancers: leukaemia, sarcomas, retinoblastoma, Wilm's tumour
Child abuse of any kind
Allergic reactions including: asthma and eczema

Child-care and parenting factors
Frequent changes in prime carers during Early Years
Emotional deprivation
Family stress
Difficulties with parenting

Unknown factors
Sometimes it is not possible to identify a clear cause for a special need

Key points
- Conditions present at birth are said to be congenital.
- Congenital conditions are not necessarily hereditary, for example, congenital heart disease, cleft lip and/or palate.
- Special needs may not become obvious until a baby grows and develops; hence the importance of health promotion and developmental review programmes.

Sometimes it is not possible to identify a clear cause. Table 10.1 on page 237 sets out some of the possible causes of special needs.

IDENTIFYING SPECIAL NEEDS

Special needs may be identified:
- antenatally
- at birth
- through child health promotion and screening programmes
- through local Sure Start programmes
- by follow-up to a parent's observations and concerns
- by professional observation in the home and day care settings
- following an accident or serious illness.

While a baby's special need may be very obvious and clear at, or just after, birth – for example, cleft lip or palate, spina bifida and Down's syndrome – others such as cerebral palsy, various heart conditions, and vision and hearing impairment may be 'hidden', only becoming apparent in later months when developmental delay is observed in the baby.

KEY POINT

A baby who is profoundly deaf from birth may initially coo, gurgle and babble as a hearing baby.

The list below, 'Towards prevention and early identification of special needs', sets out measures that may prevent, or identify, special needs at an early stage.

Towards prevention and early identification of special needs

- Genetic counselling
- Preconceptual care
- High standards of antenatal, perinatal and neonatal care
- Immunisation programmes
- Comprehensive child health promotion programmes and efficient referral systems
- Loving and secure emotional environments in which babies can thrive and be happy
- Healthy and safe environments, which lessen the risk of illnesses, infections and accidents

---

- Throughout infancy, child health promotion and screening programmes are offered (see Chapter 4, pages 113–16). Observation of babies by family doctors, health visitors, Early Years workers and parents can identify, at an early age, those who may have special needs. Appropriate help can often limit or reverse the difficulties or delay.
- Immunisation is an effective form of preventive health care for babies. It is offered routinely from the age of two months (see Chapter 7, pages 169–71). Occasionally there are contra-indications to immunisation.

Types of special need

There are many types of special need. You will be able to find out from the baby's parents, and other professionals, the difficulties a baby is experiencing. The development tables in Chapter 6 on pages 162–6 will help you understand the stages of normal development.

Remember that the word 'type' refers to the special need and not to the baby.

You may care for babies with any of the following.

- **Physical conditions** Cerebral palsy, cleft lip or palate, spina bifida, cystic fibrosis, sickle cell condition, limb deficiencies and others. These result from damage or injury to the brain, spinal cord or control of movement, or malfunction of the body and its systems.
- **Sensory impairment** Vision and hearing difficulties.
- **Learning delay** Down's syndrome, fragile X syndrome and sensory impairment.
- **Emotional difficulties** While the foundation for emotional difficulties may be partly laid down in the first year of life, the effects may not be evident until later in childhood. The most likely reasons will be separation from, and frequent changes of, primary carers, lack of affection and physical care, and child abuse.

Sometimes it is not possible to clearly identify the particular cause.

- Possible developmental delay may be identified in the first year. More commonly, however, difficulties become more apparent as childhood progresses.

- A baby's special need may affect only a minor part of her life or it may be a major and challenging factor.
- Long-term implications for babies with special needs include physical, intellectual and emotional developmental delay.

The family – parents and siblings

No parents expect their baby to have developmental delay, require extra help, perhaps undergo intrusive medical procedures or even to die. The whole sudden experience of having a baby with special needs can be deeply upsetting and isolating.

PARENT'S REACTIONS

When a special need is recognised, parents need time to understand, adapt and accept; and time to adjust and learn about their baby as an individual with her own personality. Often, the only information parents have about certain conditions is affected by the prejudice of society. Their own experiences may be very limited.

KEY POINT

The birth of a baby with special needs may be seen as a tragedy, and friends may offer condolences rather than congratulations because they do not know what to say.

Whether a special need is known at birth, or in later months, many parents will go through the different emotional stages associated with bereavement – grieving for their apparently 'lost' baby – before they are able to accept and adjust. Such reactions are seen across all cultures and social classes. Typically parents experience the following:
- shock, grief, numbness, confusion and an inability to come to terms with or fully comprehend what has happened
- denial of any long-term disabling condition
- feelings of guilt and apportioning of blame, particularly if the baby has an inherited condition, or the mother smoked or drank heavily in pregnancy. Anger and blame may be directed at the doctor for not recognising or preventing the special need antenatally or at birth. Parents may blame themselves, or each other, if their baby's special need is the result of an accident or serious illness
- gradual orientation, acceptance and adjustment. The parents are now able to relate to their baby and take pleasure in her.

There is no time limit to this process of acceptance and adjustment. It may take several years. Parents work through the stages in their own time.

Parents' adjustment

In spite of the sadness and stress they feel, most parents learn to love their baby and are aware of the greater degree of dependency and responsibility there is always going to be. Their protective instincts are usually heightened, sometimes to the point of over-protection. Adjusting to the implication that their baby will not 'get better' and striving to provide the care, opportunity and stimulation required (often despite the attitudes of society) can be a challenging process.

KEY POINT

Some parents find it difficult to cope and may never reach the stage of adjustment. They may be reluctant to share their anxieties with family, friends or professional carers. Some babies with special needs are fostered or adopted.

Questions parents ask

Initially, many questions are asked – 'Why did it happen?', 'What's wrong with her?', 'Why us?', 'Will she die?', 'Will she learn to walk and talk?' There may be no ready answers. When the cause cannot be determined it often makes the situation harder for the parents to accept, although knowing the cause does not automatically make life easier.

AREAS OF DIFFICULTY

The following areas of difficulty may be experienced.

- Mother–baby bonding may be difficult. For medical reasons, a mother and her new baby may be separated from each other, or a mother may be reluctant to hold, cuddle and feed her baby, fearful of yet more powerful emotions should her baby die. Parents may find their baby's physical appearance upsetting. The baby may be rejected.
- Babies with complex and multiple special needs require constant care. Feeding difficulties, crying and failing to settle to sleep, and into a pattern consistent with the family routine, cause parents distress and anxiety. This may lead to lack of confidence in their ability to care effectively for their baby's needs.
- Relationships may be strained. Stress and anxiety can lead to irritability and arguments. Separation and divorce are not uncommon,

although in some families the relationship grows stronger as they find the energy and determination to access the support and provision their baby needs.

- Social isolation from family, friends and local community (and perhaps in the child health clinic) may be experienced because their baby is 'different' and does not fit in to the normal pattern – many people still have little understanding of special needs.
- There may be financial pressures, perhaps because of a loss of earnings due to caring responsibilities.

Activity
You are employed as a nanny caring for a baby, now 10 days old, with special needs. The baby's mother is distressed and reluctant to hold, cuddle and care for her baby although she will offer her the bottle. Think of ways in which you could help and support the mother to get close to and relate to her baby.

MEETING THE NEEDS OF PARENTS AND FAMILY

Recognising and supporting the parents' needs can reduce the length of the grieving process. Support must aim to lessen stress and anxiety and give the parents confidence in their ability to care for the baby.

In particular, parents need the following.

- Easy access to information about their baby's condition and the help available. Parents have a right to know where to go for help – not knowing, or travelling around from place to place trying to find help, is confusing and stressful.
- Support for their own emotional needs. As their baby reaches the age at which she would have achieved skills such as sitting up, crawling and walking, the sense of loss and sadness frequently re-emerges. Unsupported needs have damaging effects on the whole family. Professional counselling is available, but the support of a loving, caring extended family is often the most positive means of help.
- Practical help in the home from relatives, friends or the social services department.
- Contact and friendship with other parents of babies with special needs through special need support groups or self-help groups. These offer the opportunity to share feelings and concerns, which, perhaps, could not be comfortably shared with the professionals.
- Time to be with other members of the family and meet their needs.

- Parents need reassurance that their emotions are normal reactions. Pretending they do not exist does not make them go away.
- Help and counselling are available. A 'special needs' health visitor, or the family's regular health visitor, can be a point of professional contact. A health visitor is outside the family circle, so is someone in whom parents may find it easier to trust and confide.

Link workers

Link workers from black and ethnic minorities should be available from both statutory and voluntary agencies, enabling families to obtain the support, information and resources they need. Similarly, parents for whom English is neither their home nor community language, or who have communication difficulties, need interpreters who are skilled in special needs issues, as well as information presented on tapes, in large print and in Braille.

THE SIBLINGS

The effects on brothers and sisters vary according to their age, birth order and the number of children in the family.

Siblings may experience the following.
- Over protection or, possibly, neglect.
- Jealousy and resentment at the attention given to their baby brother or sister (over and above what might be considered 'normal' when a new baby arrives).
- A shift in the family balance, which means they may have to take on a domestic role.
- Worry that they will 'catch' their sibling's condition.
- Teasing and social isolation.
- Emotional swings, from being loving and protective to disturbed behaviour such as regression, attention-seeking, moodiness, anxiety, low self-esteem, embarrassment or guilt.

KEY POINTS

- Not all siblings experience such emotional and social disadvantage. Much depends on individual personality and the bond between them and their brother or sister with special needs. Many remain happy and well adjusted.
- You may care for siblings in a day care, school or home setting. Observation of their play and behaviour (perhaps in the home corner), or of their drawings, painting and general demeanour, may indicate they are experiencing

difficulties. They may exhibit regressive behaviour, resorting to temper tantrums and thumb-sucking, or become withdrawn and clinging.

Siblings may feel anxious and concerned

Meeting the siblings' needs
- Individual attention and reassurance they are loved and valued.
- One-to-one key worker provision for a child in a nursery or education setting.
- Time on their own with their parents.
- Opportunity for older children to express their feelings and be listened to uncritically by parents, carers or professionals.
- Correct information about their brother or sister's needs appropriate to their level of understanding.

REMEMBER!

Always encourage a sibling to care for their brother or sister in small, everyday ways, just as an older child would normally care for a younger member of the family. This includes cuddling, talking, playing and fetching clothes and nappies during bathing and changing routines.

Siblings need individual quality time with parents

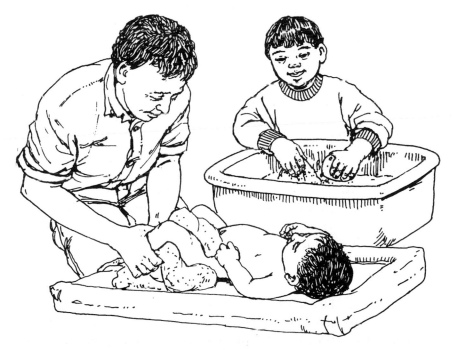

Sibling participation in a caring routine

Meeting the baby's needs

Most babies with special needs are loved and accepted within their family, but some experience loss of love and approval from the important people in their life. They have a right to be part of the wider community and society, but often the negative attitudes of society lead to discrimination and isolation.

Babies with special needs have a right to:

- love, security, respect and stability of care
- appropriate specialist care and therapy
- play opportunities, stimulation and social interaction
- day care facilities with key worker support and flexible provision.

EQUAL OPPORTUNITIES

All children are equal and must be accepted and valued for who they are. Babies with special needs are first and foremost babies with ordinary needs and their own individual likes and dislikes. While they may require special learning programmes or different forms of therapy, they also need plenty of opportunity to play and interact with their carers and peers. Always look beyond the special need and make sure the baby's ordinary needs are not being overlooked.

The use of inappropriate words and terminology when talking about special needs is insulting, and devalues, labels and categorises babies. Such language focuses on the special need rather than the baby. Always remember to use a baby's name; terms such 'the Down's baby' or 'the deaf/blind baby' are offensive and must not be used.

KEY POINTS

- Babies with special needs have the same requirements for love, security and protection as the other babies you care for.
- Positive images of babies, children and adults with special needs from a variety of cultures should be represented in care settings through pictures, posters, books and displays. Dolls and puppets can reflect both boys and girls with different kinds of special needs.

SUPPORT SYSTEMS

Parents as partners

The key to successful assessment, review procedures and provision of services is an effective partnership between all those providing a service.

Parents are crucial members of the service team. Every effort should be made to keep babies with special needs at home with their family. This can only be achieved if sustained, flexible and child-centred services are available that allow families choice and make it possible for the baby to be cared for at home. Each family is unique. Considerable extra help may be needed at particular times and at others a small input of help can make all the difference in keeping the family together. Accessible help and support should be available when needed. This gives parents the confidence and control they need to shape their own lives.

Statutory services

The two main statutory service providers for babies with special needs are:

■ the health service
■ social services.

Health service systems and support

Usually, the first professionals a baby and her family see are from the health service. The most likely causes of special needs identified through the health service are physical conditions, sensory impairment and developmental delay. Health service care is likely to be a combination of hospital specialist care, and community care from the primary health care team. The family doctor will care for day-to-day health problems and concerns, and give immunisations. Home nursing care and loans of medical equipment such as suction apparatus, feeding support equipment and oxygen are provided by the community paediatric nursing service (not available in all areas). The family health visitor, or a 'special needs health visitor', visits the family at home offering support, advice and information. Health care provision is set out on page 248.

KEY POINT

If you have information about a baby's medical condition it must remain confidential and should not be shared with others without permission from the parents.

Social services systems and support

Under the Children Act 1989, local authority social services departments have a duty to provide a range of support services enabling a baby with special needs to be cared for at home. Social workers may make arrangements for day care (nurseries, childminders), respite care and family aide provision. They also offer counselling to parents or carers and have statutory duties towards children being looked after by social services or who

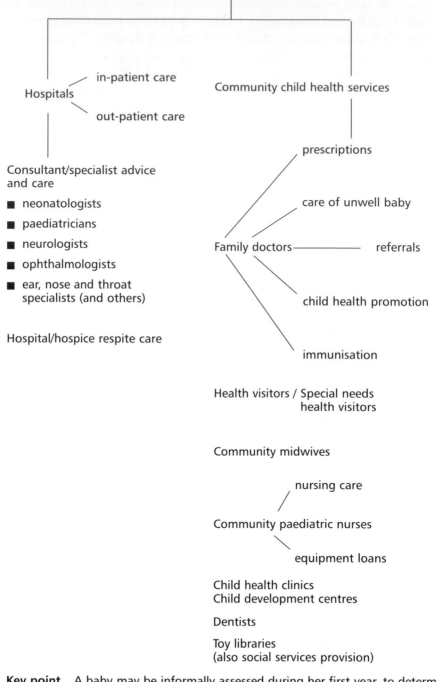

HEALTH SERVICE PROVISION

Hospitals — in-patient care
Hospitals — out-patient care

Consultant/specialist advice and care
- neonatologists
- paediatricians
- neurologists
- ophthalmologists
- ear, nose and throat specialists (and others)

Hospital/hospice respite care

Community child health services

prescriptions

care of unwell baby

Family doctors —————— referrals

child health promotion

immunisation

Health visitors / Special needs health visitors

Community midwives

nursing care

Community paediatric nurses

equipment loans

Child health clinics
Child development centres

Dentists

Toy libraries
(also social services provision)

Key point   A baby may be informally assessed during her first year, to determine her need and how best to provide for that need. Formal assessment may be carried out after the age of 2 years (or under 2 years with parental permission).

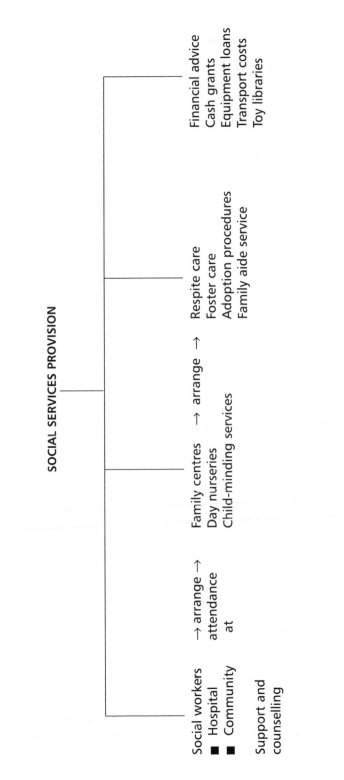

SOCIAL SERVICES PROVISION

Social workers
■ Hospital
■ Community

Support and
counselling

→ arrange →
attendance
at

Family centres
Day nurseries
Child-minding services

→ arrange →

Respite care
Foster care
Adoption procedures
Family aide service

Financial advice
Cash grants
Equipment loans
Transport costs
Toy libraries

are being adopted. Cash grants for specific aids and adaptations to the home can also be arranged.

Family centres

Family centres offer a support service to a wide range of families, including those with children with special needs. They may provide:
- day care and playgroup sessions
- child health clinics
- counselling and help with parenting skills
- toy libraries.

A family centre may operate an 'open door' policy or a family can be referred from health or social services.

Respite care

Respite care is a period of relief for parents from caring for a baby with profound or complex special needs. The baby may be cared for on a paediatric ward, in a children's hospice, or in a home setting with a specialist carer, for a short or longer period of time. Respite care allows the parents time to be together (and with their other children), to rest and recover for a while from their role as full-time carers. An effective system of respite care can mean the difference between a baby remaining in her family, or being looked after by social services. It should be part of the total 'care package' for the baby and her family.

Toy library provision

Toy library provision may be organised by social services, health services or voluntary organisations. Toys made of sturdy materials, and suitable for different ages and stages of development, are available for babies and children to play with in a safe setting. Many toys are specifically for use as learning aids for those with special needs. A toy library can be set up in a day nursery, child development centre, health centre or other suitable accommodation. Toy libraries offer a loan service for a small fee.

DAY CARE PROVISION

A baby with special needs may attend a specialist or inclusive day care setting on a full-time or sessional basis, or may be cared for by a childminder. Inclusive settings, in which babies and young children with and without special needs are cared for together, are becoming increasingly more common. An inclusive day care setting must be the choice of the family; it may not be appropriate for all babies. A specialist setting may more readily meet the baby's needs. A childminder may positively choose to care for a baby with special needs.

Day care settings and registered childminders must comply with the National Standards (see Chapter 9, page 210) for their specific type of care, taking particular note of Standard 10, 'Special Needs (including special educational needs and disabilities)'. All babies require a high quality of care – one-to-one key workers are necessary for babies with special needs as they are likely to need a great deal of extra help and supervision with physical care routines and mobility.

KEY POINT

- A child-care worker is part of a professional multidisciplinary team whose members may include the primary health care team, paediatrician, physiotherapist and speech therapist. Parents are always considered as valuable members of the team.
- When caring for a baby with special needs it is important to be aware of your own role and the roles of the other team members, and to liaise effectively with them.

VOLUNTARY PROVISION

Voluntary organisations are a beneficial additional source of help for babies with special needs and their families, supporting the work of health and social services. The care and support they offer is flexible and positive.

The Portage home teaching service

The Portage home teaching service, an early intervention programme, was developed in the town of Portage, Wisconsin, USA, in the 1960s. It is a valuable early learning resource for young children with special needs, providing a home-based daily teaching and learning programme for babies and pre-school children with learning disabilities and physical conditions. For example, a baby with Down's syndrome or cerebral palsy could be helped by Portage, including learning Makaton sign language.

Portage visitors come from a variety of backgrounds such as teaching, nursing, child-care and playgroup work or they may be parents whose own children have grown up. They receive special training and focus on what the baby can rather than cannot do, believing in the principle of 'one step at a time'.

KEY POINT

Portage home visitors work closely with parents who are actively encouraged to implement the programme themselves and, in effect, become their child's

Makaton is used to help speech development

teachers with the visitor assuming the role of consultant and supporter. Progress and achievement can be enjoyed by parents, siblings and extended members of the family.

Weekly visits are made to the baby's home. Both the Portage visitor and parents assess the baby's development through a planned programme of constructive activities and play (tasks). The programme particularly concentrates on gross motor and fine manipulative skills, language, cognitive development, self-help skills, stimulation and socialisation. Each task is broken down into stages so that a baby achieves new skills in small steps. Toys and books to develop particular skills are provided through a loan scheme operated by Portage.

Activity

Invite a Portage visitor to talk about his or her work with babies, at a staff development session at your workplace. In particular, ask about the importance of parental participation in the programme and the evaluation process.

Befriending schemes

Volunteer befrienders are well-informed, experienced parents who have been through their own personal experience of having a child with special

Steven with his Portage visitor, learning to sign

needs and have faced their own feelings before reaching the stage of acceptance and adjustment. Many families value the support they receive from parent befrienders and eventually become befrienders themselves. Examples of befriending schemes are Face to Face and Homestart.

KEY POINT

Part of the initial important bonding process between a mother and her baby is built upon their emerging communications. Eye-to-eye contact may be absent with a baby whose sight is impaired, and smiling may be delayed. Apparent lack of response can cause a parent frustration and undermine confidence. Early involvement for parents with a support agency or group, who have personal experience of such feelings is often helpful.

STIMULATION, PLAY AND LEARNING

Through her senses, and movement, a baby gathers information to make sense of the world around her. Always encourage a baby with special needs to use all parts of her body to explore what she touches, smells, tastes, sees and hears. Encourage vocalisation and babbling as you would for any baby and always respond when she attempts to communicate with you.

The principles of good practice in providing sensory stimulation and an interesting and interactive environment apply to all babies, with or without special needs, and whether they are cared for at home or in a day care setting (see Chapter 9, pages 226).

Safe, uncluttered, well-lit spaces, with appropriate equipment, provide the opportunity for babies to develop their motor skills, balance and movement. Positive adult interaction encourages the development of self-confidence and social skills.

PHYSICAL CARE

Physical care routines provide carers with the opportunity for close personal contact with a baby. Do not rush these times – sensitivity to the baby's feelings is important.

Feeding and meal times

A baby with a cleft lip or palate usually has difficulty in feeding. Specially designed teats or spoon- feeding may help. Sometimes, a small prosthesis (similar to a dental mould), is fitted over the palate during feeds, and removed and cleaned at the end of the feed. Pre-term babies, and those with congenital heart disorders may tire easily when sucking, and alternating breast-feeding or bottle-feeding with tube feeding may be necessary.

KEY POINTS

- Initially, some babies with cerebral palsy may need to be tube fed. This may lead to difficulty in the baby learning to suck. A mother requires understanding and support at this time. Tensions developing from such a situation are easily passed on to the baby.
- A baby who is 'floppy' needs to be well supported under the ribs to help her keep an upright position and extend her chest.

Meal times for babies with special needs may take a long time. Encourage a baby to explore her food and take finger foods when she is able to do so, depending on her ability to chew and swallow. Prompt weaning for babies with cerebral palsy helps to develop chewing and tongue control (important in promoting speech, and for healthy teeth and gums). However, crumbly foods should be avoided because babies with cerebral palsy often have a poor cough reflex. For safety and stability always use a suction feeding bowl and check it is firmly fixed at each meal time.

KEY POINTS

- Introduce new foods very slowly for babies who have chewing or swallowing difficulties.
- Check that your First Aid skills are up to date, especially the procedure to use if a baby is choking (see Appendix: First Aid, page 261–2).

Personal hygiene routines

Carry out personal hygiene routines as you would for babies without special needs. Most babies enjoy water and water play, and find these times of close adult contact pleasurable. They feel reassured by a cuddle or hug from their carer. Special bath seats that support and protect an older baby are available. Always make sure your practice is safe for both young and older babies (see Chapter 3, page 73). Change a baby's nappy as often as necessary to keep her clean and comfortable.

Dental care should start as soon as the first tooth appears.

KEY POINTS

- In any condition where there is loss of movement and sensation it is important to be aware of the danger of pressure sores. A baby with paralysis will feel no pressure or pain and is especially vulnerable to sores. She will not indicate distress even if sores are present.
- Good skin care practice is essential for babies with congenital dislocation of the hip who are wearing a splint or plaster cast.

Dressing and undressing

Clothes should be comfortable, enjoyable to wear and easy to put on and take off, allowing the baby as much independence as possible. Like all babies, those with special needs will enjoy clothes in a variety of colours and fabrics. Wide or stretchable neck openings, large armholes and front fastenings are sensible.

Sleep routines

Aim to develop a settling sleep routine for babies with special needs. A baby with cerebral palsy may need moving and making more comfortable in the night to prevent spasms. A special sleeping position may be recommended for her by the physiotherapist.

Movement and positioning

A baby's muscles and limbs that do not move of their own accord must be exercised by the carer. A physiotherapist will arrange passive exercises for you to undertake for the baby. You will also be advised on how to lift carefully to ensure the baby's comfort and safety. When caring for a baby with a disorder of movement, handle her limbs with care, avoid jerking and never hurry a movement.

The usual baby pushchairs, car seats and body slings will, initially, be suitable for getting around.

REMEMBER!

- A special need may be present at birth or arise at any time in later months.

- Support for the parents and siblings is essential.
- A baby's special needs should not override her 'ordinary' needs.
- Always use appropriate language; never label a baby by her special need.
- Health and social services are the main statutory care and management providers for a baby with special needs
- Offer a baby appropriate stimulation, play and learning opportunities.
- Care sensitively for a baby's physical needs.
- Child care workers are part of the multidisciplinary team.

QUICK CHECK

1 What do you understand by the term 'special needs'?
2 What postnatal developments can cause a baby to have special needs?
3 Name **four** ways in which special needs in babies may be prevented or identified at an early age.
4 Describe the different emotional stages parents may go through when they learn their baby has special needs.
5 Describe the difficulties with 'mother–baby bonding' that may occur.
6 For which families would a 'link worker' be particularly beneficial?
7 In a day care setting how might you recognise the difficulties a child may be experiencing whose baby sister has special needs?
8 What are the basic needs of a baby with special needs?
9 Which **two** statutory services are the main service providers for babies with special needs?
10 What do you understand by the term 'inclusive setting'?
11 Briefly, describe the Portage home teaching service.
12 What feeding aids might help a baby with cleft lip or palate?
13 Why should you avoid offering crumbly foods to a baby with cerebral palsy?
14 Why is skin care so important for a baby with paralysis?
15 Name the professional who would advise you on handling, lifting and positioning techniques for a baby with a disorder of movement.

APPENDIX: FIRST AID

The carer is responsible for the safety of babies in her care. Accidents that happen to immobile babies are the result of failure on the part of the carer to protect them, either through carelessness or by a lack of anticipation. A baby who is crawling is inquisitive and increasingly able to reach potential hazards but she will not understand danger or how to keep herself safe. You need to link your developmental knowledge to provide a stimulating, but safe, environment for the baby. However, if accidents do happen a skilled and reasoned response is essential.

WHAT IS FIRST AID?

First Aid is temporary treatment given before the arrival of more skilled personnel. It should be quick and simple and aimed at preventing the baby's condition from worsening.

KEY POINTS

- In day care, all staff should have good current knowledge of First Aid. At least one member of staff should be trained and identified as the setting's designated First Aider.
- Telephone numbers, for parents, hospitals and doctors, should be prominently displayed.

Emergencies

THE UNCONSCIOUS INFANT

If a baby is not breathing and her heart has stopped beating, for example, due to possible Sudden Infant Death, immediate action must be taken.

1 Remove the baby from any immediate danger

2 Quickly assess the baby's responsiveness
Gently tap or flick the bottom of the infant's foot, call her name. If no response send immediately for help.

Never shake a baby to check for consciousness.

3 Check if she is breathing

Open the airway

- Place one hand on the baby's forehead and tilt the head gently back – do not overextend the neck.
- Clear any obvious obstruction from the front of the mouth only.
- Put your fingertips under the point of her chin and lift to open the airway – do not push on the soft tissue under the chin as this may obstruct the airway.

Then:

(a) *look*   is the abdomen or chest, rising and falling?
(b) *listen*   can you hear breathing sounds?
(c) *feel*   put your cheek in front of her face, can you feel breaths?

- You must continue to keep her airway open while checking.
- If breathing is taking place cradle the baby in your arms with her head tilted downwards to drain any vomit. Await help, or take her to help, whichever is quicker or easier.

4 Rescue breathing

If she is not breathing or is only making occasional gasps commence rescue breathing:

- keep her airway open, as above
- take a deep breath
- cover her mouth and nose with yours, ensuring you have good seal to prevent air escaping
- blow gently and steadily into her mouth and nose over 1 to 1½ seconds to make her chest rise. Remove your mouth to see her chest fall as the air comes out
- give two effective rescue breaths and then check for signs of circulation.

Nose only rescue breathing

If the baby is big you may find it difficult to obtain a good seal with your lips around her mouth and nose. If so, use your mouth around her nose alone, closing her mouth to stop air escaping. Continue rescue breathing as above.

- Only count effective breaths – those where you can see her chest, or abdomen, rise and fall.
- If at any time you cannot see this, check:
  - her airway is still open
  - you have a firm seal around her mouth and/or nose
  - that the baby's mouth is closed, if you are attempting nose only breathing.

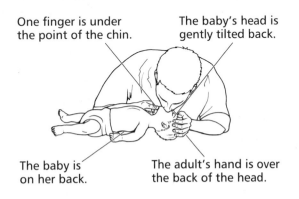

One finger is under the point of the chin.

The baby's head is gently tilted back.

The baby is on her back.

The adult's hand is over the back of the head.

Rescue breathing

5 Assess for signs of circulation

If circulation has ceased it means the infant's heart has stopped. It must be stimulated to encourage it to beat and if this cannot be achieved the baby will die. If resuscitation is delayed then brain damage may occur. Heart massage may be dangerous if a regular beat is present, but it is difficult for staff in the stress of an emergency to find a pulse. Speed is important so check instead by seeing if there is movement, swallowing, coughing or regular breathing.

If none, or if you are unsure, then commence chest compression.

CHEST COMPRESSION

- Place two finger *tips* at the bottom of the sternum (the breast bone) one finger's breadth below an imaginary line joining the infant's nipples.
- With the *tips* of two fingers press down to depress the sternum to approximately one-third to one-half the depth of the infant's chest.
- Release and repeat at a rate of about 100 times a minute.

After five compressions:
- ■ open the airway and give one effective rescue breath;
- ■ then immediately recommence chest compressions as above.

Continue compressions and rescue breaths in a ratio of 5 compressions to 1 breath, until the baby is breathing and moving spontaneously, or until medical help arrives.

THE RECOVERY POSITION

The recovery position for use when the baby is spontaneously breathing regularly and unaided

For the recovery position, place the baby on her side, ensuring her airway is open and any vomit can drain out freely. Keep her in this position by placing a rolled towel down the length of her back.

KEY POINT

While awaiting the arrival of medical help monitor her condition carefully.

BLEEDING

Minor external bleeding usually clots and heals itself. If the bleeding is severe, treat with direct pressure (a firm bandage, for example), raise the affected part and seek medical help.

BURNS AND SCALDS

The prime aim of treatment is to cool the affected part quickly. Do not try to remove clothing as this may pull off delicate skin. Burnt fabric is sterile and will help prevent infection entering

Immerse the affected area in tepid water, preferably in a bath, or under a running tap, for a minimum of 10 minutes. Seek medical help – even small burns and scalds can cause shock in a baby.

Do not apply any ointments, oils or burst any blisters.

CHOKING AND INHALING

Babies who are being weaned and unused to lumps in their food may choke. Occasionally small toys, left around by older siblings, can be inhaled (breathed into the windpipes or lungs) and restrict breathing.

If an obvious obstruction is present at the front of the mouth remove it. Do not sweep the mouth with your fingers as this may force objects down the throat, or embed them in the soft tissues.

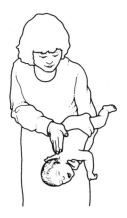

Aim to get the head lower than the chest to help gravity move the blockage. Lay the baby's head face downwards with your forearm supporting her head and chest.

Give up to five smart blows to the middle of the back between the shoulder blades.

If this fails to dislodge the obstruction, and the baby continues to have difficulty breathing, then perform up to five chest thrusts.

Chest thrusts

Turn the baby on to her back, with her head low. Support her back and head with your forearm.

CHEST THRUSTS

Chest thrusts are similar to chest compression but they should be:
■ more vigorous
■ at the rate of 20 per minute
■ given in batches of up to five thrusts with three-second intervals – check her mouth to see if the obstruction has been dislodged.

If this is successful and she is breathing, place her in the recovery position.

If unsuccessful, repeat in cycles of five back blows and five chest thrusts for three cycles and then seek urgent medical help.

KEY POINT

Do not attempt the abdominal thrusts that are used for adults who choke. They are too vigorous for a baby and may damage her organs.

Conclusion

Accidents happen often when we are least prepared. Skills and knowledge need constant updating. The St John Ambulance and the British Red Cross Society both run excellent short courses that are ideal for professional child-care workers.

SUGGESTED FURTHER READING

(Most recent editions have been quoted wherever possible.)

Beaver, Marion, Brewster, Jo, Jones, Pauline, Keene, Anne, Neaum, Sally & Tallack, Jill *Babies and Young Children (Book 1 (2nd edn) and Book 2 (2nd edn))*, Nelson Thornes, 1999

Bee, Helen *The Developing Child (with interactive CD Rom)*, Pearson, 1999

Bowlby, J. *The Making and Breaking of Affectional Bonds*, Routledge and imprint of Taylor & Francis Books Ltd, 1979

—— *Attachment. Vol. 1 of the Attachment and Loss Trilogy*, Pimlico, 1997

Dare, Angela & O'Donovan, Margaret *Good Practice in Caring for Young Children with Special Needs* (2nd edn), Nelson Thornes, 2002

Goldschmied, Elinor & Jackson, Sonia, *People Under Three*, Routledge, 1995

Hall, David, Hill, Peter & Elliman, David *The Child Surveillance Handbook* (2nd edn), Radcliffe Medical Press, 1994 (reprint 1996)

Heath, Dr Alan and Bainbridge, Nicki *Baby Massage*, Dorling Kindersley, 2000

Hilton, Tessa, Messenger, Maire & Graham, Philip (ed.) *The Great Ormond Street New Baby and Child Care Book: The Essential Guide for Parents of Children aged 0–5*, Vermilion, 1997

Hobart, Christine & Frankel, Jill *A Practical Guide to Working with Young Children*, Nelson Thornes, 1992

—— *A Practical Guide to Child Observation and Assessment*, Nelson Thornes, 1999

—— *A Practical Guide to Activities for Young Children (2nd edn)*, Nelson Thornes, 1999

—— *Good Practice in Child Protection*, Nelson Thornes, 1998

—— *Childminding, A Guide to Good Practice (2nd edn)*, Nelson Thornes, 2003

Matheson, Elizabeth (ed.), *This Little Puffin*, Puffin, 1991 (useful nursery rhymes and songs)

Mukherji, P. & O'Dea, T. *Understanding Children's Language and Literacy*, Nelson Thornes, 2000

Sadek, Elizabeth & Sadek, Jacqueline *Good Practice in Nursery Management*, Nelson Thornes, 1996

Sheridan, Mary D. *From Birth to Five Years – Children's Developmental Progress* (revised and updated by Frost, M. and Sharma, A.), Routledge, 1997

Silberg, J. *Games to Play with Babies* Brilliant Publications, 1999

St John Ambulance, St Andrew's Ambulance Association and the British Red Cross, *First Aid Manual* (8th edn), Dorling Kindersley Ltd, 2002

Winnicott, D. *The Child, the Family and the Outside World*, Penguin, 1991

USEFUL ADDRESSES AND WEBSITES

Anna Freud Centre, 21 Maresfield Gardens, London NW3 5SD Tel 020 7794 2313 *www.annafreudcentre.org* – Helps mothers recover from post-natal depression and restore the relationship with their baby.

Action for Sick Children c/o National Children's Bureau, 8 Wakely Street, London EC1V 7QE Tel 020 7843 6444 *www.actionforsickchildren.org* – Lobbies for good practice in caring for sick children in hospital.

Association of Breastfeeding Mothers, PO Box 207 Bridgwater, Somerset TA6 Helpline 020 7813 1481 *http://home.clara.net/abm* – Advice on breastfeeding and local support groups.

Association for Postnatal Illness, 145 Dawes Road, London SW6 7EB Helpline 020 7386 0868 *www.apni.org* – Advice on postnatal illness.

Baby Milk Action (BMAC), 23 St Andrew's Street, Cambridge CB2 3AX Tel 01223 464420 *www.babymilkaction.org* – Aims to save lives and to end the avoidable suffering caused by inappropriate infant feeding throughout the world.

British Red Cross Society, 9 Grosvenor Crescent, London SW1X 7EJ *www.redcross.org.uk*

Cry-sis, BM Crysis, London WCIN 3XY Helpline 020 7404 5011 *www.our-space.co.uk/serene.htm* – Help and support to parents of babies who cry excessively.

Kidsactive, Pryor's Bank, Bishop's Park. London SW6 3LA Tel 020 7731 1435 *www.Kidsactive.org.uk* – Promotes inclusive play opportunities for disabled children.

La Leche League of Great Britain, PO Box 29 West Bridgford, Nottingham N62 7NP Helpline 020 7242 1278 *www.lalecheleague.org.uk* – Advice and support on breast-feeding.

Meet-a-Mum Association (MAMA), 58 Malden Avenue, South Norwood, London SE25 6HS Helpline 020 8768 0123 *www.mama.org.uk* – Telephone help and local support groups for lonely and/or isolated mothers.

Multiple Birth Foundation, Queen Charlotte's and Chelsea Hospital, Level 4 Du Cane Road, London W12 0HS Tel 020 8383 3519 *www.multiplebirths.org.uk* – Information for parents and professionals on multiple births.

National Association of Toy and Leisure Libraries, 68 Churchway, London NW1 1LT

Tel 020 7387 9592 *www.natl.org.uk* – Loans a wide variety of play equipment and materials and provides friendly meeting places for parents and carers.

National Childbirth Trust (NCT), Alexandra House, Oldham Terrace, Acton London W3 6NH Tel 0870 444 8798 *www.nct-online.org* – Advice on breast-feeding and child care – organises local antenatal and post-natal support groups.

National Children's Bureau, 8 Wakely Street, London EC1V 7QE Tel 020 7843 6000 *www.ncb.org.uk* – Promotes the interest and well-being of all children.

National Childminding Association (NCMA), 8 Mason's Hill, Bromley, Kent BR2 9EY Tel 020 8290 8973 *www.ncma.org.uk* – Provides information on all aspects of childminding.

NSPCC, Weston House, 42 Curtain Road, London EC2A 3NH Tel 0808 800 5000 *www.nspcc.org* – Advice, information and support on all areas of child protection.

NHS Direct Online government health information website. Helpline 0845 4647 *www.nhs.direct.uk*

Resuscitation Council (UK), 5th Floor Tavistock House, North Tavistock Square, London WC1H 9HR *www.resus.org.uk* – Produces protocols for resuscitation practice for health and other personnel.

SANDS – Stillbirth and Neonatal Death Society, 28 Portland Place, London W1B 1LY Helpline: 020 7436 5881 *www.uk-sands.org* – Support for parents and families whose baby is stillborn or dies soon after birth.

SCOPE, 6 Market Road, London N7 9PW Tel 020 7619 7100 *www.scope.org.uk* – Disability organisation whose focus group is people with cerebral palsy.

'Sure Start' Government programme to support children and families in the early years. Tel 0870 001 2345 *www.surestart.gov.uk*

The British Association for Early Childhood Education, 136 Cavell Street, London E1 2JA Tel 020 7539 5400 *www.early-education.org.uk* Promotes the right of all children to have access to high quality early education and gives advice on best practice from birth to eight years. (In conjunction with the DfES.)

The Child Bereavement Trust, Aston House, West Wycombe, High Wycombe, Bucks HP14 3AG Tel 01494 446648 *www.childbereavement. org.uk* – Specialises in training for professionals to help bereaved families.

The Foundation for the Study of Infant Deaths (Cot Death Research and Support), 11–19 Artillery Row, London SW1P 1RT Helpline 0870 787 0554 *www.sids.org.uk/fsid* – Support and information for bereaved parents.

The Maternity Alliance, Third Floor West, 2–6 Northburgh Street, London EC1V 0AY Information line 020 7588 8582 *www.maternityal-*

liance.org.uk – Information and advice to families on all aspects of pregnancy and new parenthood.

The National Society for Phenylketonuria (NSPKU) PO Box 26642, London N14 4ZF

Tel 0845 603 9136 *www.ukonline.co.uk/nspku* – Management of PKU and dietary information.

Twins and Multiple Births Association (TAMBA), 2 The Willows, Gardner Road, Guildford, Surrey 9U1 4PG Tel information 0870 770 3305, Helpline 01732 868 3000 *www.tamba.org.uk* – Advice and support for parents who have multiple births – organises local Twins Clubs.

INDEX

Page references in italics indicate illustrations and diagrams, those in **bold** indicate tables